To my daughter Isabella
and my son Conrad

Florian Homm

ROGUE FINANCIER

The Adventures of an Estranged Capitalist

FBV

The Deutsche Nationalbibliothek
lists this publication in the Deutsche Nationalbibliografie; detailed bibliographic information is available online at http://dnb.d-nb.de

1st edition 2013

Nymphenburger Straße 86
D-80636 München
Tel.: 089 651285-0
Fax: 089 652096

Editing: Shelley Steinhorst, Dive in Languages
Proofreading: Rainer Weber
Image on the Cover: Eva Feilkas
Printing house: Books on Demand GmbH, Norderstedt
Printed in Germany

Picture section, p 12: Steffen Kugler, picture-alliance/dpa
Picture section, p 13: Christof Koepsel, Bongarts/Getty Images
Picture section, p 14: Lars Baron, Bongarts/Getty Images
Picture section, p 16: www.our-school-liberia.com

ISBN Print 978-3-89879-849-5
ISBN E-Book (PDF) 978-3-86248-424-9

Further informations are available at

www.finanzbuchverlag.de

Please visit our other publishing houses at
www.muenchner-verlagsgruppe.de

Florian Homm is donating 100 percent of his share of the proceeds of this book to the Liberia Renaissance Foundation to benefit Liberian school children.

Acknowledgements

First and foremost I want to thank my ex-wife, for not only putting up with my craziness and instability for two decades, but also for raising both of our children almost completely alone. Her goodness and wisdom were an inspiration to me to lead a more positive and honest life. I forgive her for the year of divorce hell, in which she terrorized me far more than my worst enemies in the corporate world. I also want to thank my son Conrad and my daughter Isabella for the most wonderful weekend I had experienced in over a decade. It is fantastic how the two have been able to forgive me. I am proud of you, children! I give thanks to my mother who is truly one-of-a-kind, and who raised me in the most liberal and independent way that one can imagine, and who stimulated and nurtured my ambition and desire for success. You have all inspired me to face my past and put things right and to write this book. Special thanks go to my deceased sister Barbara. Her maxim "No Risk—No Fun" and her thirst for life always had a profound influence on me. Barbara and Necko would have recommended that I do one thing and one thing only in this situation: confront your enemies, do good and do it right.

My gratitude goes to Christian Jund, as well, my bold and visionary publisher, who had the courage to take on such an infamous, excessively controversial character such as myself. I thank Georg Hodolitsch, for managing to get the best out of me. Dear Almuth, many thanks for your beautiful words. I thank the entire "K" family for their support in getting this book on the market. Howard Marks, alias Mr. Nice, you showed me how one gets back on their feet when lying on the ground. You understood my crazy mission. You smiled and shared your wisdom with me. I thank DM for the help in formulating the "second dimension," which improved this book immensely, and I thank GM for bringing us together.

I want to thank, in particular, Mr. Rentrop and Mr. Schwoerer for their excellent ideas.

Special thanks go to my transatlantic legal team, for their know-how, patience and therapeutic support.

The president of Liberia, the Nobel peace prize winner Ellen Johnson Sirleaf, one of the greatest women of our time, has provided me with a lasting positive influence. She imparts a feeling of decisiveness to help the disadvantaged and unfortunate. Ambassador Thomas McKinley motivated and pushed me non -stop for 10 years to help in places where it was the most needed. They are the "brain parents" of the Liberia Renaissance Educational Complex. They also made me into a better person. Marcel and Olivia have achieved amazing things to keep the Liberian dream alive. They all have my gratitude.

Giorgio showed me, what's important in friendship, him being such a faithless bastard and deceiving me heartlessly even after I had saved his miserable life. Through you I have found two incredible friends. And so I pray for Giorgio and wish him all the best. DR, you're the biggest traitor among mediocre people. I made you a millionaire. You were a part of my family, and I took in your parents as my honored guests in my home. You thanked me with hate and wickedness. I even kept you from enduring a legal process in Germany and forgave you for your deception. Thank you for showing me what I don't want to be. Did you know that the virgin Maria in the Koran was more often mentioned in the Koran than in the New Testament? In accordance with the teachings of Maria and my personal faith, I pray for you and bless you. Forgiving you is not easy.

I shouldn't forget to thank two journalists. Their one-sided and malicious reports, based on idiotic assumptions, poor research and cheap sensation grabbing, stood out conspicuously, beyond all measure. Mr. T from *Bloomberg* wrote an inaccurate article in a shocking way, in which he threw doubt on both my place of birth and my degrees from Harvard College and the Harvard Business School, alleging that I had never played basketball for Germany. The second disreputable mention goes to the *Financial Times Deutschland*, although I was quite impressed after a long and open discussion with Mr. B. The most excellent and amusing article ever written about me, also appeared in the *Financial Times Deutschland* and was penned by two first-class investigative reporters: Sven Clausen and Christian Höller. A monstrously one-dimensional picture of me was created in a series of articles, which helped in starting a global man hunt, violating every kind of human right and preventing an official legal process in America and Europe. Dear Journalists, your shoddy work has encouraged me to set things straight, which will then, hopefully, inspire others among your colleagues to carry out their investigative work a bit more professionally in the future. I have prayed for you. I sincerely hope that your malicious energy can be channeled in a more Christian way in the future.

I thank my friend Uhlemann, who was the only person from my personal database of 10,000 contacts who offered me a safe place to wait out the storm.

Kevin, thanks for your prayers. JD and Marco, thanks for trying to get in contact with me for half a decade. Please understand that my situation is very challenging.

Christian, I look forward to the day that we can play chess in Morocco again. Stay strong and stay a winner in your heroic fight against M.S. Dear Jacob, former Mossad agent, lawyer and mini-tycoon. You have always proven yourself to be one of the few true friends, even after I was no longer useful to you. Hakki, one could always trust your word, and that is your strength. Thanks.

Sascha and Guillermo. You are among the few at ACMH who were authentic, grateful and competent. What more could one want?

I thank Ciaran and Donna for advancing the charitable project Maximum Impact Medicine (MIM) with the greatest determination. Keep setting yourselves high goals! You will save and improve the life of thousands, maybe millions. As long as there are people like you, who are fighting for a better world, there is hope for all of us.

I thank my "revolutionary" friends for protecting and guiding me during many tense moments. I thank my Celtic friend for opening up my heart to Maria, mother of God, and for God and Christ's wonderful message. God has given my soul a second chance. He had at least half a dozen opportunities to call me to him easily, and still left me alive. God, I regret and am immensely grateful. Finally, to my guardian angels: you have put in a lot of overtime and received too little appreciation. I love you. Stay with me and keep watching my back.

Contents

Author's Note

This story is based on fact, but for the sake of mitigating potential litigation and protecting others, certain details have been changed.

This book's author is an alleged notorious financier. Therefore, his life story becomes an easy feast for conventional critics. What could be easier than to discredit someone in trouble with governmental and private plaintiffs, someone with a bounty for capture? A baboon could criticize it—and I ask them to do so. The stereotyping of hedge fund managers, for example, is designed to invite reactions. But as Andy Warhol rightly said, "Do not pay any attention to what they write about you. Just measure it in inches." The greatest failure would be to write a book that arouses no reactions, opinions or controversy. Numerous threats and condemnations are consequently inevitable. Such is the nature of men.

Unlike many life stories, this is not a lame attempt at self-justification or a small-minded venture to squeeze a few bucks from the readership. While I am without doubt self-obsessed, I try to avoid self-righteous masturbation. Overall, no doubt I come across as a villainous and greedy operator. That's OK, because a good reputation is a great burden and mine is already hopelessly tarnished. I can afford to be honest; and as for posterity, I take Groucho Marx's view, "Why should I care about posterity? What's posterity ever done for me?"

This book is principally about transformation, our ability to learn from our history and the ability to view our follies with perspective and a sense of self-irony.

The author's royalties from the sale of the book are donated to the Liberia Renaissance Foundation in Switzerland, which funds the Liberia Renaissance

Educational Complex (www.our-school-liberia.com/en), set up to improve the education and future prospects of over 200 gifted Liberian children every year. Although I have been a major supporter, I exert zero influence. The foundation is properly audited by a major accounting firm and deploys its funds with maximum transparency, efficiency and effectiveness.

It is strongly recommended that no one imitate the actions described in this book.

Two things are infinite: the universe and human stupidity; and I'm not sure about the universe.

Albert Einstein

Preface

Is not life a hundred times too short for us to bore ourselves?
Friedrich Nietzsche

18 September 2007

I was feeling bone-headed and trashed as I headed towards my Pilatus PC12 at Palma de Mallorca's private airport, passing the planes of several other tycoons who either live or vacation on the island. The night before, I had given my loyal personal assistant Daniela 50,000 euros in cash as a farewell gift, 20,000 euros to my Ecuadorian caretaker Giovanni, and a tenner to my maid. I had not slept for 48 hours, preparing my departure with Prussian precision. The dawn sky was a lucid aquamarine, and a fresh Balearic breeze blew into my face.

The security at the airport had been very light that morning, as usual. Nobody checked my identification or my baggage. The security people knew me very well. They also knew I was a fully accredited diplomat and that searching me was a political faux pas.

I put on a face of respectability as the sleepy airport security guard escorted me to the plane. I had $500,000 stashed in my underwear, my briefcase and my cigar box. My mule and friend Giorgio, who was accompanying me, was carrying even more—roughly $700,000; but that is his job. He was getting paid $30,000 for less than an hour's work. Giorgio is a former entrepreneur who got too greedy and turned his respectable business into a money Laundromat for some very nasty people. After an involuntary period of reflection, Giorgio decided he no longer wanted to be a mobster and became my advisor. He specializes in sensitive personal and business challenges and in solving problems, mostly when I am threatened or when I need an information edge before buying major assets or entering a jumbo short position. Giorgio also makes sure my Italian does not get too rusty.

What we were doing was entirely legal—we were simply moving my cash within Spain. I had the cash withdrawal slips from my Swiss bank on me just in case the Guardia Civil and their drug-sniffing dogs showed up for a random check, completely ignoring diplomatic protocol. We were heading to Valencia where everybody would lose our trail. Thereafter, moving the cash into Colombia would get a bit sketchier.

As we boarded the plane and slinked into the custom-made white leather armchairs, a thought occurred to me. "Wolfi," I said to the pilot, "hold the plane. I need to talk to my lawyer." Wolfi has black curly hair, an imposing, very muscular physique and extensive combat experience. He would easily munch little red riding hood if he had to. He would augment his pay package by listening in on sensitive information and using it to advance his personal portfolio. He has worked for me for several years, during the last two of which I had spent more time with him in the air than with my children on the ground. The man flies like Baron von Richthofen. He has taken me through Icelandic blizzards and Sahara sandstorms. He has landed on cornfields in France and gravel roads in Mali. He is a womanizer and a cocky son of a bitch, but reliable, competent and trustworthy.

I dialed Adam Kravitz in Miami. Adam is my friend and has been my lawyer for over a decade. He is bright, argumentative and well versed in history. He is also loyal and capable, two critical traits of those who work closely with me. "Adam, is my resignation on PR Newswire? Has it gone out?" I could tell he was fully alert at 1.30 a.m. Miami time when I heard his voice. As usual, he told me to relax and asked, "Florian, have you ever been dissatisfied with my work?" I refused to give him the gratification of my satisfaction and just said thanks, then told Wolfi to get us out of there immediately.

The press release Adam had issued detailed my resignation as chief investment officer and largest shareholder of my hedge fund, Absolute Capital Management Holding PLC, due to irreconcilable differences with senior management. The London-Stock-Exchange-listed group was managing over $3 billion for several thousand ultra-loaded individuals, family offices and institutions, with about a dozen offices on four continents.

The story of my departure would be the most-read business report that day on *Bloomberg* worldwide. It would hit ACMH like a bombshell—on that same day the share price dropped by 88 percent. I had chucked my company mobile phone into Palma harbor at dawn, saying farewell to this Mediterranean paradise. From now on, I would be impossible to reach for everyone, except Giorgio. Even Adam would never know my whereabouts. I was going private, very private, far from the maddening crowd. My final destination was Cartagena de Indias, Colombia, where I would commence my well-deserved second retirement.

*

Manager Magazin, one of Germany's most influential business publications, had shortly before ranked me among the country's 300 richest with an estimated net worth of about half a billion dollars. They were not far off. I owned castles, palaces, country estates, luxury apartments and moved around in my private jets, a four-bedroom yacht, a speedboat, a Rolls-Royce convertible and a customized, pimped-out Mercedes S-Class Cabriolet. My grand master art collection was exquisite. Cash and securities numbered in the hundreds of millions. I even had my own 10,000-square-foot nightclub on Palma's Paseo Maritimo. I was a baby tycoon.

Since 2004, I was also a fully accredited diplomat for Liberia at UNESCO in Paris. I had contact with major political figures like Shimon Peres and the German foreign minister Guido Westerwelle, international tycoons like Señor Rico, and celebrities such as Michael Douglas and Boris Becker. I was also Germany's most public financier, appearing on prime time national television and in major newspapers and magazines.

I was called a maverick based on my track record, and a share-price killer for my short selling raids. A German industrialist, whose company I was trying to discredit, called me the "antichrist of finance," and a chairman of a Swiss manufacturer of baby food called me the "Nazi from the north, working for the Jews in New York." Conversely, one English journalist called me Robin Hood after I donated 2 million euros to retain key ACMH employees. I had granted a whopping 33 million euros worth of securities to the funds a few months earlier to assure their stability during a market correction. I had given seven-figure sums to benevolent causes. Capital market professionals described me as a cross between Mike Tyson and Einstein, Jekyll and Hyde, the Klaus Kinski of hedge fund management, an amoral functional psychopath, Frank Copperwood, the Godfather of Mallorca and even Robin Hood. In 2006, ACMH received the Best Hedge Fund Group and Best Fund accolades at the Hedge Fund Review European awards. True to form, I had not bothered to go to the dinner—only wimps would waste precious time on celebrations. Companies feared me. I had even overcome multiple sclerosis. I was a wolf among sheep.

However, prior to my resignation things had not been quite as well as they appeared on the surface. In 2005 I had paid material fines of 40,000 euros to the German Stock Exchange Commission (a misdemeanor) and received an 18-month criminal probation for market manipulation. In November 2006, I had been shot and barely survived a brutal robbery in Caracas, Venezuela. My dad and I had not talked in twenty-five years. My sister had died of multiple sclerosis a year earlier. My brother had avoided all contact since my parent's divorce. My children did not know me. I had failed to attend any of my son's twelve birthdays. The divorce between myself and my wife Susan, citing neglect and irreconcilable differences, was granted in early 2007.

Any neutral observer would immediately realize my complete failure in the friends and family category—but I am not a neutral observer when it comes to me. Quite frankly, given my disturbing background and Germanic warrior genetics, family contentment had ranked very low on my agenda, if at all. I shared Charles de Gaulle's view: "The better I get to know men, the more I find myself loving dogs." I had four.

Despite the divorce, Susan and I had not completely given up on our relationship and were attempting reconciliation although one of several problems was that she was trying much harder than I was. During this phase, I had moved my Russian paramour, a former table dancer, model, and bar owner, into a landmark villa in downtown Palma, a short walk from my Palma office. The woman was living proof of how low I had sunk. She was a fake blonde with hair extensions, fake tits, fake fingernails and no brains, just an astute instinctual commercial sense of how best to sell herself to the highest bidder. At least we had something in common. She treated the staff like indentured servants in medieval Russia, painted her fingernails with lurid designs and had moved her mother and five-year-old half-sister in with her. Age- and character-wise, the mother would have been a more suitable partner for me, but she simply did not possess the lithe, curvaceous body of a 27-year old lingerie model. My tastes, like my gestalt, had become rather primitive by this point.

I had swapped families and had made a mindless pair trade. A pair trade is a financial transaction where the investor is expecting the position he owns to outperform the position he is short, thereby generating a profit. I was *long* Miss Table Dance, Moscow's tackiest, her mom and her mom's four-year old daughter; I was *short* Susan Devine, class, devotion, true love, an 18-year marriage, and my children. Even I had to laugh at my obvious fatuity. This was clearly a losing proposition. Even the 5-million-euro villa was lame compared to my former premises. The pool was tiny and there wasn't even a tennis court, a zoo, an 8,000-square-feet guesthouse or an orange grove. The only place from which I could see the port properly was the spacious but abandoned roof terrace. I was heading downhill fast.

I knew the trade sucked when I entered it but was too brain-damaged and horny to bail out right away. It seemed like I was on autopilot towards self-destruction. Nonetheless, I was still rational enough to exit this relationship as the novelty factor wore off. The relationship lasted for about three months, and I timed it perfectly, just before my September departure I gave her the pink slip but not without a severance payment. After I dinged Miss Moscow, she kept asking me to buy her an apartment. She also told me she would be with me even if I were a poor man. The logic of this paradox both perplexed and amused me. She equated her pain of separation to the loss of her favorite childhood doll. To top it off, a friend from the high-level nobility had helped me rent the villa from a very elusive and private heiress to one of Europe's most important industrial fortunes. Both would never forgive me for bringing my rubble there, but I could live with that. Sorry girls, shit happens. One episode exemplifies my profoundly confused mental and moral state at the time.

I had begun dating Carmen, a 27-year-old Russian, a younger, fresher and taller version of Pamela Anderson. One morning at dawn, I returned to my Palma estate from a night of club hopping with her. The sun was rising and the crisp spring air flowing gently from the hills above Palma was gently breezing over my face. There was no alcohol in my blood. I had been dancing and frolicking all night but had stopped drinking around midnight. Nor was I tired. I had organized a breakfast meeting and a trip to London and would have just enough time to go for a swim and shave. I cannot fully remember what happened next. I lost my awareness and crashed head on into a wall doing 100 kilometers an hour on a narrow country road I had driven on hundreds of times before.

This accident was not a coincidence. I knew I was disgracing two decades of love and profound friendship. I had completely debased our union. I was erasing my soul mate's memory with a pinup model, a former stripper and table dancer. Carmen had always deployed all her natural and artificial attributes to maximum advantage. She had certainly been skillful enough to own her own bar about a mile from my nightclub on the Paseo Maritimo. Can I blame her? Of course not! She was just doing her thing and I was into it. At least I thought so for a while.

Susan, on the other hand, has always been a devout and caring soul. She is a giver not a taker. Sometime in her teens she decided to develop her mind and grow her soul—rather than inject silicon into her breasts—and build the world's largest personal care collection. The woman speaks five languages well and goes into shops to buy sausages for abandoned street dogs. What more do I need to say about her?

God despised me for wronging his mini-Mary, his light bearer and my pathfinder, some of several names I had given Susan during our relationship. That morning God's wrath was as unmistakable as was my own death wish. I had let my soul deteriorate to a mere pity by that point in my life. I had let Mammon rule me. I was primitive and liked vulgar. I was blinded by riches, power and self-seeking pleasures. I felt god's disdain. I knew my actions were dead wrong and was subconsciously moving towards self-destruction. I was on autopilot to Hades. I was weak and drifting. Nothing could stop my downward spiral. My fate was sealed.

The car was totaled. My legs were crunched. I should have been dead or at least crippled. It took the welders an hour to free me up. The meniscus of my left knee was busted. The windshield was shattered but miraculously I only had a few broken ribs and minor facial cuts. Like many times before, this was a miracle. I was alive. My time had not yet come. Why? I had no idea. I certainly had tried hard enough to end my pathetic existence right then and there.

Once my ex-wife discovered I was hoeing around, and miles away from reconciliation, all remaining love was lost. And then the accountants and lawyers came out to play. She was not very amused, and who could blame her? By mid summer I had fully recovered from my temporary confusion both morally and physically. I was as sleazy and corrupt as ever.

After Susan had left Mallorca and returned to the States, I organized a heist of "our" remarkable art and antiques collection at "our" villa in Palma. I had brought Italian and Dutch master paintings and drawings into the marriage. Of course, the collection grew significantly during our marriage, so Susan was morally entitled to something. I was both attached to the art and knew what these masterpieces were worth. In sunnier days, we had placed all the art and antiques into a foundation that was owned 100 percent by Susan in case my multiple sclerosis got the better of me. At the time of the heist I was already living with my Russian paramour but still had a valid rental contract and keys for the estate in Palma. The magnificent mansion and three guesthouses, with over 24,000 square feet of living space and eleven acres of land, were also in

Susan's name. My logic was that it would be far more beneficial to hold any future discussions about her collection if the most valuable pieces were stored in a safe Zurich facility under my control.

The heist was organized for early September, and I arranged a moving team from Switzerland and a day off for the domestic staff. This would be smooth sailing. My toy girl was sitting in my S-Class mindlessly preening her hair and checking her make-up as I entered the house. As soon as I was inside, I saw the arresting and wholly unexpected sight of my ex walking down the monumental staircase into the reception hall. What I didn't see were the Rembrandts, Vernets, Dalis, Impressionists or Expressionists. The ferocious battleship scenes, Boucher imitations and neoclassical portraits were still on the 30-foot-high walls of the antechamber, but they were far too big to take down and transport easily by non-specialists. Everything worth north of six figures that could be moved had vanished. Susan had obviously beaten me to the punch. She, better than anyone else, had me figured out. And to make things worse, she was perfectly in her right to do whatever she wanted with her property.

Attack is usually my best defense, so I laid into her for moving all "my" stuff. "How can you steal art that was mine long before we even existed as a couple? Have you no conscience?" After the first tirade, I was threatening her with a flood of lawyers, which would contest the actual ownership in international courts of law. As I berated her for stealing my mother's gifts as well, adding that I would never do such a lowly thing, the doorbell went. The Swiss moving van was parked right in front of the mansion. The driver's face was on the security video screen and he was asking for Dr Homm, seeking admission to the estate. "I am now truly fucked," was my immediate thought as I let them through the gates. I could not have looked more ridiculous. Susan and her older brother Kevin, who was with her, were sprinting to the entrance to see what was going on. They saw not only the moving van and the crew but also my toy Russian in her tight miniskirt.

The moving crew was totally confused. They had an order to move approximately thirty museum-quality paintings. I was acting like the owner, but the shipping order was made out in Susan's name—that way I could always argue in court that we had agreed jointly to move the art to Switzerland. It would be her word against mine. I could deal with that.

Unfortunately, my ex grabbed the shipment slip from the mover like an attacking cobra, checked out at all the details and gave me a look so dirty that even an amoral creature like me blushed with shame. If she wanted to get extra bitchy, I was thinking to myself, she could charge me with attempted art theft, a serious crime with a whopping ten-year statute of limitations. I had been skunked like a novice facing a grand master. This woman knew me too well. She had perfectly anticipated my moves. After all, she had learned from one of the finest mercantile creatures in the western hemisphere.

She was racing back into the house. I chased her down the corridor and tried to grab the slip from her. Meanwhile Kevin was flipping out, jumping up and down like a Zulu warrior screaming "*Policia, policia*" at full volume. I had always liked Kevin but found this response hilarious and completely nutty. I may have appeared threatening and disheveled, but I was hardly going to bite their heads off like some berserk werewolf. At least, I wasn't thinking along those lines.

I had made a lot of my money by raiding and short-selling companies. You need to be fairly insensitive and aggressive to do that job well. This scene was docile by comparison. Although popularity was never my concern, my analysis of the situation—and I am nothing if not highly analytical—told me that I was certainly not going to pummel Susan and her brother to score the loading slip. The ugly facts dawned on me. The most valuable antiques were gone forever and I was now no better than a common thief to my ex. I decided to let bygones be bygones—the most important rule of investing—and move on.

While Kevin was perfecting his tribal dance, I observed that my ex had lost at least fifteen pounds since I had last seen her. Our separation had clearly benefited her. She was probably tuning herself up for the singles market. Notwithstanding, Susan looked like some sensual, aloof supermodel in her mid-thirties, very appetizing with a touch of wisdom and maturity. Her movements and anger had made her prominent cheekbones flush with a tinge of natural rouge. She had not looked that hot in years. But nonetheless, at that moment it was an appealing, erotic thought.

When she had left, I organized my 24/7 support crew of lawyers, accountants and assistants. It took us less than thirty minutes to cancel all the share options that had not yet been fully executed and endorsed by Susan's other brother Philip, her legal representative, for our children. I saved millions of euros. The day's losses did not seem so dramatic after all. I could always buy a few more paintings.

After the debacle, my mother suddenly decided that the artwork she had given to me decades ago had only been on temporary loan and was subject to recall on 24-hour notice. This, of course, was ridiculous. Uschi simply did not want Susan to have a chunk of the Homm art collection. Unwilling to contemplate this pathetic episode any further or engage my ex in a tedious lawsuit, which I would probably lose anyway, I wrote Uschi a large check to compensate her for the emotional distress. She was happy—she had enjoyed a feeling of generosity by giving her son some valuable family art, and then got paid for doing so. And I ended up getting screwed by both my ex and my mother.

Susan Elaine Devine. It was her fault that the last eighteen years had been the happiest and most balanced of my life. She had forced me to have some great kids (given my own childhood, I had never wanted kids) and was a superb and loving mother. She was instrumental in building VMR, my first public company. Shame on her for trying to make me a better, happier, richer man! The extra shares she had wiggled away from me in the third divorce renegotiation would be pretty much worthless when I resigned from ACMH. That little thought made me feel better. Such is the nature of moral bankruptcy.

That moral knot had for some time become increasingly mixed up with a mounting sense of professional frustration that was fast mutating into total and abject disillusionment. In addition to the nerve-wracking and time-consuming war with my ex, I was spending the rest of my time fighting off a number of backstabbing ACMH colleagues, especially JR and his handyman D. My abrupt exit from the world of high finance and high society would certainly cause ripples. Some people who had money in ACMH were capable of unpredictable and unpleasant responses to seeing the value of their investments plummet due to my imminent departure. Strictly one-sided media assaults based on blunt lies and distorted truths were inevitable, but that was essentially a side issue.

The fundamental problem was that I was sick of my universe. As the whole Western financial world was gearing up to go boom, I was experiencing a big bang of my own. I had planned to turn ACMH into a show that would last beyond my own day-to-day involvement, but as with the wider financial voodoo, the performance was over. There was nothing left in the hat, and rather than being the phenomenal rush that it used to be, the show was now eating me. I was a witness to my own disintegration, which had got to the point where I couldn't even physically smile any more, like some obscene mirror image of the clown who can't take off his grinning mask. Surely anything was better than consorting with sketchy night creatures and spending all my waking hours with viciously disloyal parasites. Well, nearly anything—suicide was strictly out of the question. I have flirted with death on half a dozen occasions and didn't buy the after-life propaganda at the time. Hell and heaven are right here on earth and I already knew both places well.

I had reached most of the goals I ever set out to accomplish in the areas of education, sports, sex, wealth, power, adventure and fame. I had represented my country as an athlete. I had graduated from Harvard College and Harvard Business School. I had been a major capital markets player for more than two decades, made a few hundreds of millions of dollars, and was famous and infamous within my chosen profession. I was a ruthless, well-educated, upper class, somewhat psychopathic financier, a fully accredited diplomat conversant in seven languages, with a hard-core ghetto survival mentality coupled with a jet-set playboy demeanor. My life was highly intense and, technically speaking, successful. I felt emptier than a deflated sex doll.

Even if I was truly morally bankrupt, and even if the wall of frustration was now falling down on top of me, could I at least still pass muster as a likeable rogue? "Admit it, you're a jerk," I concluded after brief reflection.

*

The night before resigning, it had taken Giorgio and me several hours to stash the $1.2 million in Swiss francs, euros and dollars in my underwear, magazines, suit pockets, my wallet, briefcase and cigar boxes. I was literally overflowing with money. A little spending cash would come in handy where I was going. As long as you are moving 1,000-Swiss-franc and 500-euro notes, things are cool. You can easily stash 100,000 euros in a burly wallet—that's only 200 tightly compacted 500-euro bills; but try stashing $200,000. That requires a shoebox of bills. I was wearing tight Calvin Klein underwear with very strong elastic straps so I could stash the cash around my waist, alongside my genitals and even between my buttocks. The end result easily added two inches to my waist and crotch area. I am inordinately vain, and thought that not only did I look like I was on the bad side of fifty, I had morphed into the Michelin man.

As the jet climbed I was profoundly unsettled, my mind in a dense fog. All I knew is that I had to change simply in order to survive, but the collateral damage I was leaving behind was severe. I was breaking all connections to my former existence: colleagues, clients, acquaintances, friends, bimbos, dogs, family and children, and annihilating my vast fortune in the process.

André Gide summed it up well: "One does not discover new lands without consenting to lose sight of the shore for a very long time." I had no idea whether I would ever see the shore again.

Part I
Takeoff

1. Homm, Sweet Homm

No price is too high to pay for the privilege of owning yourself.
Friedrich Nietzsche

Your home is regarded as a model home, your life as a model life. But all this splendor, and you along with it . . . it's just as though it were built upon a shifting quagmire. A moment may come, a word can be spoken, and both you and all this splendor will collapse.
Henrik Ibsen

My home was never a model home. It was already broken.

On my mother's side the family roots can be traced back to the sixteenth century, and include Peter Josef Valckenberg, mayor of the Holy Roman Imperial City of Worms in the early nineteenth century. As well as being mayor, Peter Josef was a sharp entrepreneur and was the man who globalized *liebfraumilch*, having bought the monastery and surrounding vineyards where it was made.

There are a few bluebloods down the line of this powerful and influential family originating from the Rhineland-Palatinate and Franconia. A family emblem depicts a fire-spewing dragon holding a shield embellished, oddly, configured with the Star of David. When I had an emblem ring made for my then wife in Boston, the Armenian jeweler asked me whether I wanted to keep the Jewish star or whether I might not prefer the more Christian pentagram as a more suitable alternative for a non-Jewish couple. We looked at each other for a moment, laughed simultaneously and went for the David star. We were not going to distort history for the sake of appearances.

Was it possible that Mayor Valckenberg had Jewish origins? Necko would scream in his grave if he heard me right now. Valckenberg would certainly not be the first German with Jewish ancestry who bought into the industrial nobility and forgot his Semitic origins in the process. We have some strange family portraits, which surfaced from our neighbor's attic after World War II, depicting my mother Uschi's wonderful Mexican grandmother with the name Maria Eva Peres, not great, who had been unceremoniously obliterated from the original family tree shortly after World War I. My ex-wife was convinced my mother and I are partially Jewish.

In addition to moneyed patriarchs with hidden Semitic roots are generations of commodity traders; textile and coal barons; a member of a parliament; a former resistance fighter who conducted espionage for the Allied Forces; and a central figure in Hitler's Nazi Germany, the Olympic gold medalist and retailing tycoon, my great-uncle Dr Josef Neckermann. Necko, as we called him, became my role model and also my de facto grandpa.

I never got to know my maternal grandparents, nor my uncle Mockel, because they were either killed in a car accident or murdered by American soldiers in 1948. Nobody knows for sure. My grandmother, the sister of Necko, according to various accounts was an elegant and attractive woman. She enjoyed a privileged upbringing with maids, drivers, cooks and private tutors. She was outgoing and emotional and more grounded than my grandfather was. Both loved the good life. My grandparents led an open marriage, almost an inconceivable notion at the time. Yet their diaries and personal letters reveal an intense and happy relationship. My mother has nothing but fond memories of her parents in spite of the obvious philandering. They were liberal, extremely tolerant and forgiving. The children enjoyed all privileges and few restrictions. Without a doubt, their parents showered them with love.

My grandfather, Dr Hans Lang, had been the top graduate among thousands of German university students, held a PhD in law and moved weapons for the opposition in the 1930s. He wrote two articles sharply criticizing the Nazis and as a consequence lost his license to practice law. In his early thirties he moved from Bavaria to Berlin to pursue a successful career as a textile manufacturer and wholesaler. After the *Anschluss* in 1938, he had been seconded to the Reichswehr's Logistics Headquarters in Berlin, where he stayed until 1945. According to relatives, it is highly likely he provided the Allies with highly sensitive information throughout the war from a clandestine communication base in Hofheim, Germany. He was never drafted. His language capabilities (Russian, Hungarian, Polish, Italian, Spanish, English, Greek and Serbo-Croatian), organizational skills and extensive international contacts were simply too critical for the Nazis to waste on the battlefield. As a senior technocrat in the war effort, he was never drafted nor did he see any military action. I would like to have known this enigmatic opportunistic agent provocateur, surely an interesting man.

He was de-Nazified the same day the Allies arrived in his hometown. Normally such a process involving a major technocrat would take months, if not years. Necko, for example, was found guilty of war crimes. Even after his incarceration, Necko was subject to severe travel and work restrictions for several years. Yet immediately after the war, my grandfather became Senior Liaison between Allied Forces Procurement and the German southern and central municipalities. In the autobiography of my aunt (Kristin Feireiss, *Wie ein Haus aus Karten*, Ullstein Verlag), I read that he was supposed to be one the largest German black-market dealers of his time.

My mother and relatives suggest he was also a spy for the Allied Forces for most of the war, in particular for the Americans, explaining his immediate clearance and remarkable privileges once the Allied Forces arrived. His "official" enterprises showed millions in sales and profits. It is likely his clandestine operations were even more profitable. His mother said, "He lived a very dangerous life," and his daughter Tini concluded, "My father had numerous powerful enemies." Just like me he tried to hedge his personal risks. While I hooked up with the dark side, powerful Kurdish operators and later on Irish Republicans, my grandfather counted Frankfurt's Police President among his "preferred" business partners to secure protection. One associate was offered a fortune and spent three years in prison in order to keep my grandfather out.

Germany's black market activity was organized according to zones. The French had their operations in the west; the British in the north and the Americans were active in central and southern Germany. The Russians had very little to offer in terms of merchandise, so the eastern zone saw action from all groups.

Few Germans got in on the game at a senior level, and even fewer were independent operators. However, given his profound grasp of logistics and senior contacts within the US procurement system, Hans was a natural to hawk US goods to his fellow countrymen. This would also explain his ascent from a man whose empire was destroyed by the war to a nabob in only three years. He wore Russian sable coats, drove the most expensive cars and lived in a palatial residence. Without the slightest doubt Hans Lang was a tycoon and he lived on the edge or on the other side of legality, just like me.

Only a few years after the War, the black market easily constituted a third of all economic activity in monetary terms. According to primary sources his chief competition was no other German operator but black market organizations run by mid-level American military and Special Operations personnel in Munich, Heidelberg, Wurzburg, Nuremberg, Stuttgart and Frankfurt. The American organizations only employed Germans for menial tasks such as packaging and retail distribution. Hans had his own organization with sizable warehouses and other smaller distribution facilities throughout the American occupation zone. Both groups were sourcing much of their merchandise from similar outlets. This would result in regular conflicts, and violent disputes were frequent. While not defenseless, Hans lost consignments to his more powerful and more connected American adversaries in organized raids on his warehouses. Was Hans Lang and most of his family the victim of an unfortunate accident? This is highly unlikely. A very large US army track literally ran over Hans' Opel. It is likely all the passengers died immediately being crushed to death. Then the truck backed up, pushed the car about thirty yards along the autobahn and shoved it down a cliff on the side of the road. This assured the hit and run accident or the deliberate murder of Hans Lang and most of his family would go unnoticed for a while, leaving the perpetrators ample time to escape the scene without detection. The German police investigation was handed over to the US military police because the tire tracks and paint residues conclusively showed the crash resulted from impact with a very large and heavily motorized US army truck. The American truck would have had considerable damage.

A simple inventory review would have revealed which US army vehicle was involved in the "accident" and who drove the truck at the time. Yet nothing happened. The Americans never even bothered to respond to the German police's requests for clarification. The Americans had won the war and like all victors were acting with impunity. End of story!

My mother tells me how much I remind her of her father. According to her, my language skills, physical attributes, facial expressions, attitude in the face of extreme adversity and gestures are remarkably similar. She does not see her father as an unscrupulous profiteer but as a brilliant man and caring father, a free market advocate, a rebel and at worst a risk taker who did his utmost to assure the wellbeing of his family and friends in desperate times.

The funeral in Wurzburg was attended by thousands of people. Being orphaned, my mother and her two sisters were taken in by her uncle, Necko, and his wife Annemie. Necko assumed control of the Lange fortune. The trustee chosen for my mother and her aunts was a senior employee in Necko's organization.

As I learn more about our family history, I realize my mother and aunts were raised like second-class children within the Neckermann clan. They were not really loved. Their money was. My mother was not allowed to attend university in spite of multiple pleas by the school's principal. Instead, she was forced to become master tailor, a vocation she never practiced for a day of her life.

My aunt Jula, a helpless soul and failure and degenerate according to the hypocritical Neckermann standards, was banned from the family. My aunt Tini was not allowed to invite her own sister to her wedding, unless she was prepared to face total banishment herself. Who were Necko and Annemie to banish and threaten their stepdaughters? True parents love unconditionally. They do not blackmail or exclude their children. Their doors and hearts are always open. Not surprisingly, Necko's inheritance was not divided in seven equal parts among his children upon his death. Predictably, Necko's and Annemie's own children, Evi, Johannes and Peter, received 99 percent of the assets.

Emotional needs were routinely ignored and potential scandals swept under the carpet. Any hint of a trouble was ignored, covered up and never talked about again. The Neckermann's obsession with their public image left no room for weakness and human imperfections. Likewise, my single-minded quest for wealth also left little time and energy for the emotional needs of my wife and children.

On my father's side, the origins are far more pedestrian and about a thousand years old. Allegedly, weapon bearers and goons for the local robber baron in the Dark Ages, the family ultimately eked out a decent existence as local handymen, plumbers and electricians. Typically, Christmas gifts from our grandparents were two pairs of socks for each grandchild. Their use, however, was severely restricted, as they were to remain perpetual captives at my grandparents' home and could only be worn when we visited them. Once we'd gone home, the socks would be returned to their gatekeepers until the next visit. I loved those socks.

I remember the burial of my grandfather Willi distinctly, because it got me a bloody lip. There were hundreds of people at the ceremony, many of them old Nazis. Umpteen older women were crying as if they had just lost their firstborn to Charles Manson. My elder sister Barbara and I were part of the condolence line, which included my parents, his much younger widow (my stepgrandmother Sophie), the grandchildren and some lesser relatives. The grief and pain didn't register with my sister and me. We were glad the old schmuck was out of our lives. In fact, we knew the man too well to mourn him. He had tried to embezzle my father's inheritance, was the cheapest of little men and never had a kind word for anyone socially inferior to him. He'd sold new washing machines in which he'd put used motors, keeping the original motors for himself. When the machines broke down soon after he'd off-loaded them, he'd charge his customers for the new motor plus a hefty installation fee. The man was a small-time swindler, unlike me.

I viewed the whole scene as a gigantic comedy of misperceptions. The local hyenas had all showed up to honor the passing of their leader. What got to me more than anything were the expressions of sorrow and heartfelt handshakes we received. It was hard for me to keep a straight face. As I stared at the crowd in disbelief, my sister turned to me, pinched my arm and whispered in my ear, "Get your act together and stop being so irreverent, Florian. Show the pain you feel inside of you and let your tears run freely." Meanwhile the priest is telling us how Willi's limitless generosity and energy enriched all of our lives. Barbara moved within inches of my face and said, "Cry for Willi's lost love. He stood for what is best about us Germans: discipline, organization, and obeisance, muscles like Krupp steel, quick as a flash and tough as leather." She was quoting verbatim from Hitler's speech to the Hitler Youth in Nuremberg in 1935. Her jibe was on the money. Willi spent years in French POW camps before returning after the war, and his second wife's father was the Nazi mayor of our hometown, Oberursel.

Then Barbara clicked her feet together like an SS sergeant and acted as if she was about to salute the crowd. I lost it right then and there and began to cry with suppressed laughter, convulsing visibly. The onlookers were concerned that my grandfather's passing was too much for me to bear. A very concerned couple in their nineties stepped forward and squeezed my arm and hand earnestly trying to calm me down. I was either going to laugh out loud hysterically, piss in my pants, or both.

In order to avoid any of these outcomes I bit my lower lip hard enough to draw blood, and plenty of it. The taste had an instant sobering effect on me. As I swallowed the first drops I managed to collect myself, avoiding all eye contact with my sister, the mourners and the nice old couple. I stared stupidly at my cheap polished black shoes, ordering my mind and emotions. Minutes later,

I excused myself saying I was unwell, found a park bench and read the local newspaper, which I had brought with me in case I got bored at the funeral.

Upon further reflection, and given that I was disinherited by them, it is obvious that Sophie and Willi Homm were small-minded, miserable, hypocritical, petit bourgeois ex-Nazis. As a consequence, they merit no further attention.

When my mother married my father Jochen, the contrast could not have been more striking. Jochen was the prototypical Arian: six feet five, blue-eyed, blond, athletic, a champion skier, tennis player and fencer. He came from a small-time entrepreneurial background. She was a member of the upper class. As a Hitler Jugend standout he had been asked to join Hitler's personal bodyguard in 1944 but declined the offer. In the spring of 1945, my father and his squadron of 14-16-year-old boys were asked to march on Berlin to help the Fuhrer secure the Endsieg, the final victory. My father bailed out with another friend in the early morning. His classmates died either in the final battle or in Russian lead mines after the war. He had made the right move in deserting.

My father's demeanor was outwardly charming. He was street smart, calculating and cold-blooded. His sense of humor and flirtation was epic, certainly when measured by German standards. Women would flock to him. He also had a fatherly caring side, which diminished with time. I remember him staying up all night at my bedside after an excruciatingly painful ankle injury. He also worked day and night to pay for my private school and college education. I frequently accompanied him on business trips where he shared his view of the world with me. He advised me how I could reach the top of the pyramid. He was caring, even attentive, as I was growing up, but our priorities shifted dramatically when I enrolled at Harvard University. Jochen, very much like Necko, was increasingly interested in climbing the social ladder, while I was increasingly developing a skill set and curriculum vitae that would maximize my future wealth. Unlike them, I was utterly disinterested in my reputation and role in society as long as it did not interfere with my plans to become a billionaire. Three generations of foolish men had sold their souls and families for money and social status.

Jochen did not attend my 1989 wedding ceremony in Gruyeres, Switzerland—my mistake had been that, unlike my siblings, I had not completely abandoned my mother during the divorce process—but observed the celebrations from the castle walls with his lover. During the divorce wars, I strived to treat my parents fairly and maintain contact with each of them. As the favored child my father never forgave me for not siding with him. He perceived my actions as disloyal and felt betrayed. I ended up losing my father twenty years ago. I could sell my soul to the devil but refused to abandon my mother. I have always maintained an innate sense of fairness. Moreover, I don't respond to blackmail, emotional or financial.

Our wedding gifts were a fake $25 Rolex for me, and an imitation Gucci bag made in Thailand for Susan, delivered by one of his underlings. I was genuinely distraught and upset. For most of my life, I had looked up to my father. My ex-wife, always a wise woman, believed my extensive bouts with juvenile crime, my anger and my high-profile media and frequently hostile business practices later in life were all desperate attempts to communicate with my father and get his attention and love. For fifteen years I reached out to him but he refused all contact. I sent letters, photos of our family and called. Jochen never responded. He has yet to meet his grandchildren. Susan told our children Jochen died years ago. Figuratively speaking she was right. Ten years ago I abandoned the effort to connect with him. I reconciled myself to the fact that after the death of my sister, and a brother without the faintest interest in me, I had little family to speak of except for my mother. Regardless, my door is always open for my father and brother.

My mother looked like Sophia Loren, quite tall with well-formed curves, high cheekbones, noticeably darker skin and wavy auburn hair. She is highly intelligent, serious, suspicious, introverted and reserved. It takes her about twelve years to warm up to anybody. She would always complain that she had so few friends but her efforts to make friends were at best spurious. I tried to help her by buying Dale Carnegie's *How to Make Friends and Influence People.* She read it and told me, "Sucking up to people is fake and obsequious. Carnegie is insincere and a flake. Plus it takes too much of a character transformation for me to play that brownnosing game. I would rather be miserable than be everybody's darling." Without doubt my mother is authentic. She attended our wedding, gave generous gifts and antagonized and intimidated my father's best friends. She made quite a few terrifying scenes but that was OK with me. "She's my mum, she can do what she wants," I laughed, watching her zero in and terrorize her favorite targets.

Her style, money, intellect and tradition married my father's pure commercial energy and naked social ambition. What a zany, symbiotic combination. And to be fair to my father, he used my mum's inheritance wisely to build a regional, medium-sized and highly profitable construction company which helped pay for our expensive education.

Their children were of course gigantic. My sister was over six feet tall, my brother Hajo is six feet ten and I am six feet seven. My brother, with his steel blue-grey eyes, blond hair, light skin, round head and massive frame resembles a Nazi's wet dream, whereas my sister and I were more oversized Latin/Arian hybrids. Hajo is a graduate of the London School of Economics and an engineer. He worked with my father for several years before becoming an antiques dealer. His mathematical skills are extraordinary, and he was a gifted painter in his youth. He never liked me, possibly because my father paid more attention to me than to him. He was delighted when my father abandoned me during the divorce wars. He once told me that one could choose one's friends but not one's brother.

My parents, neither of whom attended university, placed significant emphasis on education, cultural refinement, and extensive travel. In that way, our parents opened our eyes to a broader world. On my twelfth birthday my father gave me a copy of Egon Corti's *The Rise of the House of Rothschild*, which I devoured in two days and which would remain with me. Necko's stoutly Catholic family felt it was strange that a non-Jew would be interested in that world to the extent of wanting to work in it, as for them it was solely for the Jews. And so my contrarian personality meant that naturally I was intrigued: what do the Jews do, what do they know, how do I learn it? Of course, this issue was literally close by, given that the Frankfurt Jewish area is where the Rothschilds came from. I told myself if I decided to have children, preferably boys, I would send them all over the world to create a bombastic financial empire just like the moneychanger Meyer Amschel Rothschild from down the road.

My father also told me, "The closer you get to the money, the easier it is to grab." That basic lesson made perfect sense to me. The first seed for a career in finance had been planted successfully. Until then, I had fed deer chestnuts during the harsh winters and stocked rivers and ponds around Oberursel with brook trout in the spring, with the idea of becoming a forest ranger. That career choice was fading quickly.

In terms of status we were part of the upper middle-class by the seventies, whereas the Neckermann side was part of the economic and social elite. As part of Necko's family entourage, we were invited to numerous high society events and I met tons of celebrities. My moral education was, however, lowly and deficient if not entirely Machiavellian. My mother was a notorious philanderer. One of her boyfriends was only two years older than me. She once spent a nerve-wracking week with me in my London house, awaiting his arrival. He never showed and I got to play psychiatrist for several days.

My mother wasn't the model of a perfect wife in every respect. Uschi's very liberal attitude to her own sexual fulfillment is explained by her upbringing. Her parents had led an open marriage as she was growing up. After I got married, Uschi would openly encourage me to have love affairs in the presence of my wife. She firmly believed that a few amorous diversions would do wonders for our marriage and sex life.

My father was not that interested in sex and friendship, being much keener on wealth and status. He was absolutely unscrupulous in business, just like my grandfather, Necko and me. He would not blink an eye when he fired an employee who had been with the firm for twenty years if it served his economic objectives at that moment. He did not se any benefit in being liked by his workforce.

He was feared. That seemed to work better. He could be brutally rational and astoundingly controlled, calculating and almost completely devoid of any emotion.

It has occurred to me that my success in proprietary trading and hedge fund management over 90 percent of my career is correlated to an inherent ability to shut out unproductive emotions and focus exclusively on rational, frequently counterintuitive, fact-based analysis and solutions. However, I never shared his cynical views. I firmly believe well treated and well-compensated employees are more productive. Moreover, outstanding employees are almost impossible to replace. The cost of retraining and the search process for new talent is usually very frustrating, time-consuming and expensive. You want to hold on to your stars as long as possible and keep them happy.

Typically, my father would pace the company grounds at 6.30 a.m., harshly reprimanding anyone who showed up less than fifteen minutes before work began officially at 7.00. Most employees showed up by 6.30. An extra half-hour of free work from 100 employees could easily result in an additional annual profit of 100,000 Deutschmark, which over a decade is 1 million Deutschmark, ignoring the compounding effect. A million bucks was a considerable fortune thirty years ago. Nobody at Harvard Business School taught you how to become a millionaire by sweating your staff a few extra minutes each day. If it meant bawling at the employees a little more than usual, it was clearly worth the effort. If a supplier or subcontractor did not have the means to engage lawyers he might not get paid, or if he did it could be substantially less than expected. My dad knew how to play hardball. So would I.

Two things were of utmost importance to Jochen. One, if you did some shady things to get ahead that was all right, but you needed to cover your tracks at all times and never get caught. The second was to maintain a perfect front of respectability. This focus on unscrupulous advancement without regard for others definitely polluted my psyche. It probably explains why I never let drugs or irregularities interfere with my advancement. Image and social standing meant everything to him. On that point we would differ tremendously later.

The man was vain, highly disciplined and emotionally detached. My mother was emotional and volatile. After about a decade of fairly civil, mutually beneficial co-existence, they began to clash on at least a weekly basis. However, both parents continued to support our advancement vigorously as long as we performed in areas to their liking.

Besides a profound education in amorality, the other mainstay of my youth was this constant and vicious fighting between my mother and father. These fights were not conducted behind closed doors but in front of us children, and later also in front of other relatives and friends.

Given the violent nature of home life, brutality became a form of self-expression. My brother and I would get into gargantuan fights using everything from fist-sized rocks, spades, air guns, knives, shovels and even axes to inflict maximum damage on each other. My body, especially my head, bears numerous scars from these encounters. We last faced off when we were both at university. I won that battle convincingly.

Hajo's and my bad and well-deserved reputation as violence prone thugs lasted into our early twenties. In addition, all the Homm children were chronic shoplifters. I started experimenting with breaking and entering at the tender age of 11, scoring enough cash to buy several fishing rods and enough chocolate to last my friends and me for several months.

All of this is not to say that I did not have a sense of right and wrong, because I did. I was the most loyal friend anyone could wish for and a fierce in your face enemy. But when my sense of right and wrong was combined with a lack of supervision within a generally amoral context, it led to the adoption of a rather idiosyncratic moral compass. Ideas of morality and justice are seldom straightforward.

I went to the Frankfurt International School because the public school in Oberursel was incredibly leftist and my parents didn't want my brother and me to become raging communists like Barbara, who was a member of the Maoist Communist League of West Germany, the KBW. The head of the Dresdner Bank, Jürgen Ponto, would be killed in Oberursel, and Ulrike Meinhof came from there. They were essentially affluent middle- and upper-middle-class kids. It led to some lively family discussions. When my father took my sister to school in his Mercedes she insisted on being dropped off 500 yards from the gates so that she wasn't seen to be from a family of capitalist pigs. Everybody ran around in their military parkas thinking they were Castro or Che Guevara on a mission in Bolivia.

I failed to become engaged by any of it, and found it more humorous than anything else. I distrusted the ruthless and single-minded stalwarts of the German *Wirtschaftswunder*. But at least these money and status hungry opportunists were consistent and authentic. Most of the upper-class kids wearing Mao t-shirts and extremely expensive and fashionable military boots and parkas were living off supra-sized allowances from their parents. Their revolutionary attempts were hollow and insincere. They were as false as the Rolex watch my father gave me on my wedding day. "If they were not so pathetic they would almost be funny" was my irrevocable conclusion. I was a pretty detached kid—intellectually, spiritually—and as a teenager I thought "What is this senseless dialogue about? Why is everybody always so frigging serious all the time?" The parents obviously need to work in a factory for a month and the kids needed to visit Eastern Germany or live in Russia to grasp reality. I had done both.

Barbara had lived and worked with rebel groups in Central America. I respected that. Perhaps some of the leftist thinking rubbed off in ways of which I was then unaware. When working in London later, rather than live in Belgravia, South Kensington or Mayfair, which is where all my colleagues resided, I chose to be in Hackney—a very rough neighborhood where several of my friends and basketball teammates were borderline characters: used-car salesmen (i.e. car thieves), cigarette vendors (i.e. smugglers) and spivs (i.e. stolen goods merchants).

However, this strange character, the ghetto-dwelling investment banker, was a logical outgrowth of my irreverent nature and my kinship with my sister Barbara. It was my way of hanging with the *Lumpenproletariat* and rebelling against what was expected of me by my peers. I was not prepared to conform and adapt the hollow airs of the upwardly mobile without a struggle. I had seen real wealth growing up. We lived in a seventeen-room mansion with an indoor swimming pool, sauna, a library, a respectable art collection and indoor and outdoor fireplaces; Necko lived in this mammoth compound on twenty acres of prime real estate, almost a village onto itself, with a world-class indoor and outdoor horse-riding center, a helicopter landing pad and a nuclear bunker designed to accommodate twenty people comfortably. Therefore, folks flaunting material goods did not easily impress me. Most yuppies would talk about their most recent economic or lifestyle conquests: their favorite cars, five-star resorts, Lord what's-his-name's party and their latest apartment purchase on Eaton Square. Had they talked about Lear jets, 200-foot yachts, grand master collections or Lake Como lakefront palaces with their own marina, I may have listened. My hard-core Hackney friends were vastly more amusing. It was much funnier listening to Paul and Billy telling me how they stole Tiny Rowland's Rolls-Royce from outside Annabel's nightclub, or chatting up hot East End birds in steamy after-hour clubs.

As a kid I was interested in fishing, collecting chestnuts to feed the deer in the winter, breaking into garden sheds and robbing isolated houses in the woods, shoplifting with my brother and sister—typical teenage rebellions, especially given the very little supervision we enjoyed from the age of about 5 or 6. Living in Hackney or in a shoddy part of Brooklyn with my Cajun girlfriend Collette was also the result of our wild and whacky, unorthodox upbringing and the left wing, anti-materialistic vibes we had been exposed to in the late sixties and early seventies.

At middle school, my entourage was composed exclusively of the most unpopular children. I was the ringleader of the disenfranchised reject society, a rather motley crew. Zack had more zits than hair and was always in trouble for grabbing the tits of the cook in the cafeteria. He clearly had problems reconciling his nascent sexuality with commonly accepted codes of behavior. Scotty was a plump dwarf, albeit an intelligent one, who was constantly abused by the older jocks. Ursula was this six-foot cross-eyed anorexic, a pitiful sight, who spoke with an incomprehensible lisp. There was a black kid, Raymond, who could not jump, play the hoops or dance to save his life. I was probably the most popular among the least popular students. These kids were my best friends and I was their loyal protector and avenger.

Obviously some of my more notorious, derelict actions did not go unpunished. Given our consistently poor conduct until the age of fourteen, my brother and I were the unofficial janitors at FIS. My parents also got to know the local shopkeepers quite intimately, given the number of times they had to bail us out for shoplifting.

School photos were a regular disaster. Between the age of six and fourteen, every picture shows us either with facial wounds or at least scratches and bruises. It got so bad our parents gave us boxing gloves for Christmas to avoid permanent disfigurement or disability. That turned out to be a great idea because it allowed us to refine our raw physical skills into more structured and effective combat techniques without premature technical knockouts, debilitating injuries or permanent mental damage. Fortunately for us, we started to do well in sports: track and field, soccer, skiing, basketball and tennis. This mellowed our smoldering aggressive impulses noticeably.

I vastly improved my combat skills when I played basketball with the American GIs at the nearby Camp King army barracks. At the time, many young US criminals had the choice to go to prison or join the army. The smarter ones joined the army instead of doing jail time at home, but of course that did not make them angels or saints. Approximately half of the GIs in Germany had criminal records in the US and many knew only one way to resolve conflicts: non-verbally. In some ways it was a family rite of passage to go there, my father also knew the place well because after the war he sourced American goods there, which he sold to his fellow countrymen. He was also engaged as an occasional translator there. It was perfectly logical that I would spend part of my youth hanging out at the base with the brothers fighting ghetto-style, playing the hoops with an inner-city attitude and chasing army twang. Vitally, given that also Necko had a relationship with the place also made me feel closer to my great-uncle.

*

While I was studying Ebonics and basketball with the GIs at Camp King, my older sister was going through a very tough phase at university. She had changed course from law to psychology and my parents withdrew all financial support. According to their thinking, Barbara was supposed to study law or business, not some flaky subject like mind shrinking. To make up for the financial shortfall, she worked as a bartender in some seedy joints and as a consequence engaged in a few too many amorous encounters that would negatively impact her already frail emotional constitution and fragile self-esteem.

Her membership in dubious connections suggested a profound political neurosis. Self-doubt, resulting from too much ethereal introspection, was compounded by a leftist trust-fund boyfriend diagnosed with schizophrenia and manic depression. After several months of too much sex, too little money and excessive head shrinking, my dear sister voluntarily committed herself to the local institution, a mental hospital, for extensive in-depth analysis. Many years later when I discussed this dark episode with her, she simply responded, "No risk, no fun."

Astonishingly, even my parents had finally woken up to her obvious pain and desperate call for attention and cash flow. In their own strange way, they loved us, albeit within their possibilities. They obviously struggled with expressing their most heartfelt emotions, and were also terrified that people might think their daughter was a complete nutcase. What would that say about them?

Be that as it may, we planned to kidnap Barbara from the cuckoo's nest. When we arrived my sister made flesh-eating zombies look like reverent Mennonites at an agricultural fair. Heavily sedated and with a blown-up face, Barbara told us how she was doped up three times a day and how she hated the place but did not have the courage to ask for release. She had tried a few times, the only result being her antidepressant dosage was upped significantly. They convinced her she would need years of analysis to resolve her Oedipus complex and any interruption of the treatment at this stage would be suicidal. Well, three days before our visit she had indeed tried to fly like an eagle from the third floor balcony after puking out an abominable pharmacological concoction.

My father had convinced the senior orderly with a 100-Deutschmark note that Barbara wanted to take a walk in the adjoining park to watch the sunset, and that I would stay at the "nerve sanatorium" as some sort of guarantee to assure her return.

Just before nightfall on this cold December Sunday, Barbara was successfully hijacked from the hospital and I got to stay with the "inmates." It took the head psychiatrist about three hours to realize Barbara might not be coming back. Just to buy time, I told him that they probably went to get dinner at a nice restaurant to get a break from the drug-infested food at his joint.

Meanwhile I used my spare time to acquaint myself with my new best friends. At least every third person there was certainly much saner than I was. They had been committed by their children, parents, husbands or wives, mostly for reasons relating to inheritance issues, maintenance, care costs and so on. For once I was genuinely appalled. Given the vast amount of drugs these folks were taking with their dinner, I was getting a little worried that this was Germany's version of the Roach Motel. You can always enter but you can never leave.

At 8 p.m. sharp the head of the camp took me into a soundproof padded cell to tell me Barbara had not signed her release papers and therefore constituted a serious risk not only to herself but also to the ethical standards, procedural legitimacy and reputation of his institution. Until she came back to sign the papers, they would have to hold me there as a hostage. I was shocked, borderline terrified. These guys wanted to trade me in for Barbara like some FARC prisoner desperately hoping for a swap on the Panamanian/Colombian border. "When would they start force feeding me those Quaaludes?" I thought to myself.

As he retired to his office, probably to shoot up a mother lode of morphine or to torture some Alzheimer patients, I enacted my first Ardennes counteroffensive. I called a meeting of about fifteen of my new best friends—at least those who were not completely doped out of their mind—and explained what had happened. I was surprised how sympathetic and outraged these alleged nutcases were, especially those who had been committed based on some bogus judicial process initiated by greedy relatives.

Within a few minutes, I had managed to incite sufficient outrage. Some inmates demanded to see the head shrink on my behalf. Another very alert group, which claimed to know my sister particularly well, was banging their dinner plates on the plastic tabletops screaming "*Freiheit, Freiheit, last den Jungen frei.*" ("Freedom, freedom, let the boy go.") This protest chant did not last very long as it was awkward and had no rhyme. I came up with my own vastly superior slogan: "*Scheißfaschisten, Psychoterroristen! Scheißfaschisten, Psychoterroristen!*" ("Shit-fascists, psycho-terrorists!") We quickly gained momentum and soon the place was rocking. Everyone seemed to be enjoying our little singsong. Some zombies had woken up and were joining in. Unfortunately, by this point the head psychiatrist had left the building, and the night psycho-warden had not yet arrived. The Filipino head nurse was non-plussed, while the orderlies probably thought "business as usual." Since we had not yet set out to destroy the place, no physical intervention or verbal response was deemed necessary. "Way too passive," I concluded. This was more like a Gandhi sit-down than a beer-hall putsch. We might as well have been screaming into a level-nine hurricane. Nobody listened; nobody cared.

Clearly, I could not lose momentum now, so I drew up a petition, which outlined that I was being held against my free will, that I was a minor and that all those who signed this form supported my immediate release and protested my unlawful detainment. I threatened legal action, having no clue what that meant at that time. It sounded important. I would learn a lot more about legal action in future years. I gave this sophomoric legal document to the Filipino head nurse who barely spoke German. In some bizarre Tagalog/German gibberish, she informed me she could not do anything until the night-shift shrink arrived.

Anyhow, the petition was worthless. Everyone who signed it had already been declared incapable of managing their own affairs, let alone mine.

Dr Jaspers finally arrived as I was taking down the third fire extinguisher to enable my more proactive friends to engage the infrastructure and staff non-verbally. Comprehending instantly what I was up to, he isolated me from my fellow combatants and yanked me into his ramshackle office to ask me who I was and when I had been committed to this fine institution. I told him what had happened. He stared at me in disbelief for about thirty seconds, and then asked me to produce some identity. I showed him my passport, and he checked the patient register to verify my story. He was truly appalled when he realized I had been kidnapped by his boss and was a minor. He told me he did not know my sister very well because she was usually in a pharmacologically induced coma by the time he arrived. He apologized for his boss, who had the tendency to take his job a bit too seriously at times, realized I was truly the victim of a rather bizarre chain of events and escorted me past the security gate to freedom.

Given that the hijacking had been a total success, my parents had forgotten all about me. There was no one waiting for me outside, not even a lousy taxi, and I hadn't been given any money to get home. I had to lock myself into a train toilet for the better part of an hour to avoid the conductor, thereafter hitchhiking from the Oberursel station. I made it home at about 3 a.m. Everyone was sound asleep. Typical.

My sister recovered rather well. My parents funded her. She completed her studies and became a practicing psychologist. She ended up marrying a top commercial banker and joined the Christian Democratic Union, Germany's right-wing conservative party. The Mao posters and Che Guevara t-shirts disappeared and there was no more hanging out with dubious anarchists. She had finally come to her senses.

It helped that Necko had arranged someone with strong arguments to convince her manic depressive, schizo trust-fund boyfriend to terminate their relationship with immediate effect. It was sweet of Necko to do that. I realized at the time that Necko was obviously well connected, which impressed me profoundly. Pillars of society could have extensive connections doing their "work." "Interesting," I thought, and stored the data in one of the more accessible drawers in my brain, to bring to bear in certain problems later in my life.

The war between my parents was now becoming ferocious. Someone tried to clear out the joint Swiss bank accounts, while some of the more valuable paintings of my mother's jewelry miraculously disappeared. The low point was when my mother attempted to destroy my father's company by selling the ground it stood on, while on the other hand someone attempted to cancel her health insurance and organized a break-in of her apartment to steal a lesser Italian master. Little did I know at the time, I would repeat the same pattern twenty years later. My parents would finally divorce after thirty-three grueling years.

With the divorce finalized both their private lives improved dramatically. However, their relationship with their children did not. My father refused any contact with me as I had sided with the enemy, my mother. I had tried to maintain a dialogue with both of them, which of course was a total failure, given my father's self-righteousness and my mother's vindictiveness. Barbara and Hajo refused to have anything to do with Uschi and me for almost a decade since Jochen would squash them emotionally and financially if they contacted me. Barbara and Hajo were sucking up to Sophie, my maternal step grandmother, who had undermined Uschi at every twist and turn for three decades. They obviously made the right strategic moves—while each of them received a substantial inheritance from Sophie, I was disinherited and received nothing, not even my cherished childhood socks.

My mother did show her human side as Hajo and Barbara eventually realized how little they mattered to my father and his prospective "Mrs. Homm no 2." When they returned to the motherly fold, Uschi welcomed them with open arms. She is a *mensch*. She always cared for us. She will not forget but readily forgives.

Barbara was two years older than I was. Her mind was alive with a wicked sense of humor, and she had the uncanny ability to size up people in seconds. My daughter has the same skills. She never studied, even less than me if that was possible, but still received high marks and graduated from university. We had the best times together and she would introduce me to her hot older girlfriends, who helped me discover my sexuality.

We would rave together about our deranged parents and got on famously. Her best imitation was my father goose-stepping like an SS officer on the company grounds, making the Hitler greeting to an imaginary crowd while handing out death penalties and threatening severe torture to late arrivals. I laughed so hard I cried, especially because since the age of twelve I had witnessed him do this over many summers while the morning roll call when I was working at the company.

Barbara was a big-time adventurer, living with her much older boyfriend in Crete when she was only fifteen. She spent half a year in Nicaragua during the civil war supporting Sandinista rebels, and another three months living with MR-13 insurgents in Guatemala. "No risk, no fun" really was her life motto. Besides being insanely egotistical and self-involved, I can fault her for nothing.

She died of severe pneumonia caused by multiple sclerosis in 2006. I cried at her burial and have missed by big sister ever since. She had an iron will to live. She had been an outrageous rebel and an awkward conformist. She died much too early. A regret that will never leave me is that I did not visit her more during her illness.

*

Throughout my childhood I spent as much time as possible away from the glasshouse called home, fishing, hiking and playing sports. I had two close childhood friends (Klaus and Ulli) who kept me from losing faith in mankind all together. I was bored to death in school and my grades epitomized mediocrity and possibly stupidity. I thought fighting, bitching and screwing around was what adults do best and all of the time. My ex-wife was convinced that I was always seeking the love and hugs I was obviously not getting. Although our parents loved us to the best of their ability—they were certainly supportive financially and exposed us to a broader universe, placing significant emphasis on education, travel and languages—the problem was that their ability to love was impaired, due to emotional fracture, tragic historical circumstances and the consequences of the quest for wealth, status and social prominence.

A key element was this bizarre mix of great wealth and great commitment to rebellion as embodied in the extreme leftist thinking adhered to by my sister, who certainly adopted that stance due to being a natural contrarian. To some extent, I stood in the middle and absorbed the value both of wealth and of rebellious irreverence. While you don't have to agree or take up the positions of those around you, there is no question that we are a product of our time and our surroundings, and the role of self-determination in creating who you are can easily be given too much emphasis. Often one is not aware of these influences at the time, but where you are and where you have come from will of course impact on you, whether you think so or not. There is a great delusion of individuality and choice, but your choices are possibly somewhat pre-defined—and certainly the scope of the choice is limited.

At the age of fourteen I was thoroughly clueless and lost. I was the product of a hundred years of solitude where each generation mindlessly repeated and compounded the customs and errors of the one preceding it. I also had too many zits, greasy shoulder-length hair and could not even score a date. I was still awkward at basketball, having grown way too fast. I had no *Leitmotiv*, I had nothing to aim for—at least nothing I could see at the time. I was in a deep funk, a phoenix deeply buried in the ashes with little or no prospect of ever emerging into the light. It occurred to me that if I was truly the product of my parents and my environment, then God help me and those around me. I was doomed. Thankfully, it was around this time that the influence of an *Übermensch*, my great-uncle, really began to grip me, to focus my mind and shape my future.

Dr Josef Neckermann (1912—1992) was the all-powerful patriarch of the Neckermann dynasty. His empire included Germany's second largest mail-order business as well as major insurance, retailing and tourism assets. About 30,000 people worked for Necko around the globe, mostly in Europe. At its peak, Neckermann AG was one of the thirty largest companies on the Frankfurt Stock Exchange. He won several individual Olympic medals, including two golds as a member of the German dressage team. He also sponsored and financed countless amateur athletes who became Olympic champions.

He was an incredibly disciplined opportunistic entrepreneur. He was extremely demanding of himself and those around him. I would be no less demanding and even despotic later in my career. Anything but total victory—which also had to include the subsequent complete destruction of opponents—constituted failure. Imperfection was unacceptable. Unless you were willing to sacrifice every ounce of your blood to achieve your objectives, Necko considered you a lightweight. Necko once told me, "Mediocrity is like having sex with an ugly, aged, rotund woman with a moustache." He was on speaking terms and had access to all the German and many international heavyweights of his era. He was the king of bargain-basement shopping, the mail-order pioneer. Over 90 percent of Germans knew who he was and could recite his catchy advertising slogan (*Neckermann macht's möglich*).

Almost everyone in the enlarged Neckermann clan sucked up to him. In his commercial prime, however, putting up an act got you nowhere with him. He simply did not care and had no time in his busy schedule to consider family circus acrobatics. Yet these clowns continued posing or putting up absurd fronts to flatter or impress. They were looking for love and recognition from the patriarch, which could never succeed given Necko's time management challenges. Necko's view of life was epitomized by two sayings, "Defeat begins with second place" and "Life is War." He was not interested in "petty" emotional sensitivities during his ascent. To me Necko was God. No, actually God worked for Necko. But Necko was far simpler than most realized. First and foremost, he absolutely loved aspiring and dedicated athletes and would do anything to support them. Athleticism was and remained his age of innocence. Second, he respected power and success and he detested bullshit and small talk.

Although he would religiously observe Christmas festivities, and even played Santa Claus on several occasions, Necko's classic family gathering appearance included sitting with the family for a maximum of two courses before being pulled away from the table by some urgent matter and retiring to his office where he would call his business contacts while watching sports programs. Later on in life, I unconsciously adopted many of the same mannerisms when it came to family obligations even for breakfast, lunch and dinner: grab a drink, stuff your face and get out in less than 300 seconds. However, when you were in a deep jam, Necko would do anything to find a solution for you right then and there. When my friends asked for help, I never turned them down either.

Like many successful individuals, Necko had a very dark side to him. He joined the Nazi Party in 1937, and was one of the major clothing suppliers to the German army during World War II. One of his maxims was "connections are everything, only morons do not exploit them." He definitely nourished his bond with the Nazi top-brass. He employed forced labor, Jews and war prisoners in his gargantuan textile factories. He visited concentration camps. In 1934 he bought his first Jewish enterprise. Immediately prior to the war, in 1938, he had "purchased" Germany's third largest mail-order and textile conglomerates from Karl Amson Joel, the grandfather of Billy Joel (yes, the singer). Only years after the war and following a lengthy and intense trial, which he lost 19 years after the end of the war, was Necko forced to pay Billy Joel senior two million Deutschmark in reparations. The trial exposed several of Necko's blatant lies. His selective and very limited memory of the holocaust and his role in the German war effort as expressed in his autobiography constitutes the low point of his career. But did he have a choice? Unlike me, Necko was first and foremost interested in his social standing, grand achievements and his legacy. Any admission of collusion and guilt would have equated to reputational suicide. I was far less concerned about my reputation and far more interested in the size of my bank account.

Necko was a big-time profiteer of Hitler's anti-Jewish expropriation policies. The Joel acquisition propelled him from a well-to-do regional entrepreneur to an international textile and retailing magnate. Given his intense ambition and single-minded drive to succeed, he did not think twice about moving into Joel's Berlin Villa. He was also entrusted with Germany's diamond reserves to purchase strategic weapon systems towards the end of the war. He almost died in an American internment camp after the war from abuse and medical neglect. Thereafter, according to his autobiography, he re-launched his industrial empire with vengeance from a very modest and poorly capitalized base to become a prime example of the German economic miracle, the *Wirtschaftswunder*, by the mid-1960s, which was itself set up by the intense industrial revolution that had resulted from instilling Prussian military discipline into economics in the late nineteenth century.

When I was twelve years old, I would watch the share price displays in the windows of the banks. The Neckermann AG shares were prominently featured with global blue chips like Mercedes Benz, BASF and Bayer. I watched the daily changes and was amazed how much Necko's fortune could change in just a few days. I asked my dad about dividends. It was obvious to me that when Necko wanted to spend a fortune on dinner, a motorized go-cart for the kids or a new horse all he had to do was sell a few share certificates or collect some dividends. The higher the price, the more he would get for selling. This was very interesting stuff to me at the time.

The *Wirtschaftswunder* started wobbling for him in the mid-1970s as he didn't quite make it smoothly through the first oil crisis, the inflationary period and the increasingly tight credit situation. He was always a slave to debt, and financing that debt, and in the end he was on the brink of insolvency and had to sell precisely because he had disproportionate loans rather than equity. While I knew next to nothing about finance in my mid-teens, I resolved to stay away from bank debt. Before his empire was sold to a despised competitor in a fire sale, I heard Necko bitch a lot about his dependence on his "wimpy bankers" on several occasions. I reckoned whatever business I would build one day could not depend on bank loans to succeed.

My future activities would be cash based. And this points to a crucial facet of his story, and by extension mine—he wanted to be the best, the *wunder* in *Wirtschaftswunder*, and strived for the status, but unlike the later generation (myself included), he did not operate according to the demands of raw, hard-core, pure financial capitalism as practiced by the Jews. Of course, he wanted to be wealthy and enjoyed being so, but the status of being pre-eminent drove him much more than chasing some figure to have in the bank. This was the time when I think the focus of people's ambitions shifted away from status and achievement much more towards wealth for its own sake. The idea of 30,000 people working for me struck me as bizarre and utterly unnecessary. It made a lot more sense to build a large fortune with the absolute minimum amount of people. The concept of the billionaire financier or the modern-day Rothschild, rather than the industrial tycoon or captain of industry, was evolving in my untainted analytical mind.

I adored Necko and was fascinated by the controversies and the multiple lives he had lived. It all seemed very exciting. I was impressed by his discipline, endless energy, perseverance, general irreverence and survival instincts. He was also generous. When he went to a restaurant he always imagined that there was an extra person at the table on whom he would spend the same as everybody else, and that sum would be the tip. At Christmas he paid Hajo and me each fifty Deutschmarks, an inconceivable amount of money for a kid, to wade into the lake in his grounds to pluck him a water-rose. Mother would hold me back, screaming, as I was already knee-high in the freezing water, but I would go deeper to get Necko his rose.

When I was 16 and qualified for the German junior national basketball team, he became more interested in me and my future. His foundation, the Deutsche Sporthilfe, was also providing very useful pocket money for me, although Necko had no clue I was among the sponsored athletes. It allowed me to retire in style to the famous Kronberg Castle Hotel when bitch-outs with my parents reached epic dimensions. This maverick had experienced all the peaks and troughs of life. He had seen heaven and hell on earth. He has been an important member of the NSDAP, a big time industrialist, a flagrant opportunist, a historical figure, a top athlete, an important philanthropist and a bona fide celebrity. He was incredibly rich, and when his conglomerate overextended itself lost most of his money in a distress sale to a larger competitor. He had bounced back from the brink of death, bankruptcy and disaster several times. In short, Necko became my idol and my *leitmotiv* (minus the Nazi stuff).

The only thing that really bothered me about him besides the Nazi stuff was his lame, self-congratulatory autobiography. He claimed that he was completely unaware of the holocaust (this was not possible for someone in his position unless they were deaf, mute, dumb and brain amputated) and the sordid practices of the Nazis, while spinning a long bogus tale defending his forthright treatment of Joel senior. He was a victim of circumstance, and unforeseen historical events prevented his payment from reaching Joel; in short, the usual sound vibes to justify one's roguish behavior. While Necko was enlarging his textile empire with orders and full support from the Nazi government, Joel senior was a destitute immigrant arrival in New York with no chance for legal recourse and a grim future. I somehow don't believe the payment transfer failed for reasons beyond his control. He stiffed Joel and had to pay up after the war. Any other explanation strikes me as a fairy tale.

But I had finally picked up on a thread for my future. I was going to be the best in all aspects of life that were important to Necko, whether they be sports, business, power, wealth, controversy, even notoriety. Some aspects did not register, however, and striving for friendship and a fulfilling family life never occurred to me. Necko was neither a great father nor a convincing family figure. He had a full-time lover throughout his long marriage, and was rarely around. Therefore, happiness, friends and family, and all other similarly unquantifiable stuff, was never part of my master plan either. I liked the general idea of being a godlike patriarch so long as I did not have to attend all those countless gruesome family functions; but it took me three decades to understand that families, like dogs, aren't just for Christmas day in front of the fire.

2. Storm and Stress

I have never let my schooling interfere with my education.
Mark Twain

By the age of 15 Necko's influence and my natural hyperactivity were increasingly channeled and starting to bear fruit. I had always absorbed information easily but was thoroughly disinterested in school. I devoured over one hundred books per year, mostly fiction and textbooks about proxemics, body language, facial expressions, hypnosis, graphology, massage, physiognomy, color analysis, psychology and other weird stuff. As a child my nickname was HCA (i.e. Hans Christian Andersen) because I was prone to exaggeration and frequently confused fiction with fact. I especially liked Karl May's adventures and the fairy tales of the Brothers Grimm. At fifteen I studied Erich Fromm, at sixteen I appreciated Dostoyevsky's *The Gambler* and *Crime and Punishment*, André Gide's *Lafcadio's Adventures,* Tolstoy, and Carnegie's *How to Make Friends and Influence People*. At seventeen I studied the existentialists, Kierkegaard and Nietzsche. By the time I entered Harvard I had probably read close to a thousand books—but very few from the syllabus.

My grades were subterranean until tenth grade. I suffered from chronic monotony-induced absent-mindedness in class. I was also hyperactive and fidgety. My oversized frame was hunched into chairs seemingly made for midgets, not for a budding giant. On the other hand, I performed well in those classes taught by strange and engaging educators. Several teachers thought I was intellectually challenged. Others thought I was gifted. Nobody thought I was normal. I hated authority and dull material taught by even duller teachers. I wondered what these introverts were doing in a profession that favored extroversion and interaction. They made fifty minutes seem like five hours. I hated them. They insulted my curiosity, tormented my soul and kindled my frustrations.

In tenth grade, my biology teacher, Mr Barclay, told my parents to place me into a school for the mentally subnormal (handicapped). I was miles below the bottom of the class, having received three Fs during the first three-quarters of the year. He was absolutely terrified of allowing me, the retard, to take the International Baccalaureate biology examination, afraid my zero score would wreck the average for the other, far more intelligent students sitting this high-level examination. My parents stood their ground and I took the test. I scored the second highest grade among twenty eager beaver, ass-licking pupils. He gave me an A for the last quarter of the year and a B-minus for the full year. I still struggle to see how three Fs and an A mutate into a B-minus average, but there you go.

My confidence of course grew an awful lot when I began playing sport at a very high level. For the first time, I also started getting useful grades regularly. By my junior year my grades, International Baccalaureate results and IQ scores were sufficiently high to get me a one-year, all expenses paid academic scholarship from the American Field Service to attend high school in America. Meanwhile the relationship with my parents was reaching new lows on a weekly basis. I was practically living with my eighteen-year-old girlfriend, experimented with hashish and used the parental residence as an occasional crash pad, cafeteria and Laundromat. I kept up my studies and sports and was involved in some petty thefts and odd jobs to assure some financial independence.

My scholarship assigned me to live with the Sampsons, a hardworking, caring but very uptight fundamentalist Christian Midwestern family in Livonia, Michigan, a Detroit suburb. All the privileges to which I had grown accustomed disappeared immediately. No more orgies in the mansion pool; I was not even allowed to bring girls to my room. No more late-harvest Riesling with foie gras at Schloss Kronberg, or Weizenbier with smoked ribs and sauerkraut in Sachsenhausen. No more ad hoc overnight trips to Paris or Amsterdam. I was decidedly homesick and never felt a more profound appreciation for my tolerant laissez-faire parents than during the first month attending Livonia Bentley High School, home of the Bulldogs.

What straightened out my head was a deep conversation with my American host mother, Geraldine, who told me about her recent breast operation and marital problems. She told me, "Young man, you have the world in front of you. Stop complaining and seize the day." That message hit home like an atom bomb. I was touched by her sincerity and her great attitude in an unrewarding environment and stopped sounding off like a wimp. I started enjoying my existence in deeply religious American Midwest.

What made the home of the Bulldogs eminently likeable was my instant fame as a foreign scholarship student who also happened to be all-state basketball material and halfway decent-looking. The zits were gone, and my figure was now athletic not gawky. The groupie and recognition factor was beyond my wildest expectations. In Germany, playing for the junior national team would get me extra pussy a few times a year. In a large public American high school, the top athletes scored with exceptional ease. Just because I could bounce a basketball a little better than most I got much more action than I ever thought possible in this God-fearing, law-abiding, hard-working, racist and prudish community.

My grades also went from honorable to spectacular—not because I had drunken from the fountain of wisdom in Detroit, but because we actually received grades for classes such as Steering Committee. Creative writing would produce an instant A if you could write more than two pages with less than ten major grammatical errors. You could have written "I am a moron" 125 times and they would have given you top marks.

I received several basketball scholarships and generated cash from hawking sporting goods given to us by Nike and others at AAU tournaments. I smoked pot with the homeboys and mastered in Ebonics. I learned to move as well as any of the brothers to the latest Motown tunes, and had my first innocent dates with the soul sisters. People love bashing Motown as Murder City, and yes, I had to carve up some derelict who tried to steal my valuable sneaker collection at Saint Cecilia Gymnasium with a screwdriver. But all in all, I was safe and in teenage paradise.

My absolute highlight in Detroit was starting once on the same all-star basketball team with Earvin "Magic" Johnson, the NBA legend. The game featured the finest Detroit players, all big-time college basketball material, against our team, which was composed of the best players from the suburban communities of Michigan. Our starting line-up featured four future NBA players and me. We were called the suburban all-stars, but I was the only white player on either team and there were not a whole lot of homeboys living in the Michigan suburbs at the time.

Somebody handed me a quality joint in the locker room, and by the time the warm-ups started most of us were reasonably doped. The preparation for the game was appalling. These future basketball legends were missing the simplest layups, Sam Vincent, Greg Kelser and Magic barely managed to get up from the bench as they were flirting with half a dozen groupies in the stands. Magic hit two air balls from the free-throw line, missing the rim and the backboard entirely.

Meanwhile, we could not stop laughing at the bozos from Detroit. The brothers from downtown were doing 360-degree slam-dunks, hanging from the basketball rim and swishing all their free throws with total perfection. They were deadly serious while we could barely walk in a straight line. They swore to beat us, especially their Nazi import, by at least thirty points. We just kept giggling and giving each other high fives for no apparent reason. "Can anybody on this team catch a basketball?" I asked myself. "We are going to get thrashed. This is going to be ugly."

That game was a complete revelation to me. Never judge a team by its warm-up drills. Once the whistle blew the clowning around was over and the game faces came on. We learned that some of the Detroit players had placed some heavy bets they would beat us. Our pride was at stake and they had messed with our manhood. Magic played out of his mind and made the most insane passes, which were finished off by thunder dunks by our sensational forwards and centers. These guys were still in their teens but already consummate professionals.

I have never received better and more spectacular assists in my life. I scored in double figures and looked promising to a dozen college scouts attending the game. However, while I played well, the entire credit had to go to Magic. He was constantly double-teamed, leaving me totally open under the basket. He delivered the ball exactly at the right time and with perfect precision. Ray Charles could have made those shots right under the basket. I swear Magic has eyes in the back of his head.

We won by thirty points and I thought we would face a riot after the game. Instead, we all picked up a bunch of Nike and Reebok sneakers to sell later, and went to the parking lot and smoked some more weed. The superstars like Magic went off with the plastic dolls and we went out to party.

*

Fairly stoked after one long, rough playground session downtown, I invited some of my friends from the inner city public school system to my suburban home in all-white Livonia. My host parents almost had a heart attack when I walked in with three oversized, heavily tattooed black guys. My friends did not exactly look like Salvation Army soldiers, but they had respectable manners. It took the Sampsons almost an hour to realize we were not going to trash the place, turn it into a coke den and rape the dog. They managed an awkward smile here and there, and even offered us lemonade.

The next day they told me they had quite a time with those interesting people from the inner city. They did remind me to please let them know a little in advance when my friends would be coming over again. Of course, I complied. I grasped their fears. Livonia is ranked as the whitest city in America with a 99.5-percent Caucasian population. The only black people they knew were the Cosby family.

My host parents Geraldine and Richard always had the best intentions, were sincere, caring and unpretentious. My much older host sister Susan tried to come on to me on several occasions. I had already "de-virginized" a close relative back home, which had caused some minor uproars in the family. This time I mustered the necessary moral rectitude to prevent a potentially explosive "family" conflict. In any event, firstly, I was getting all the action I could possibly handle, and secondly, I liked her a lot platonically. She was really bright and a whole-hearted Samaritan.

I especially liked my host brother Richard junior, because he talked and walked straight most of the time and spoke his mind. He hung with the dopers and greasers, which meant that hanging with Richard was a break from the self-important ruling class of jocks and homecoming queens. It also allowed me to score with budding biker babes. Richard, when stoned, would always want to shadow box with me for fun or just to annoy me. I had once just returned from a failed date with the ultimate prick teaser and was in a foul mood. Richard, on his second six-pack and well into a half a dozen doobies with his auto repair buddies, tried to show off his boxing skills. I said to him, "Rich, give it a break. I just had the worst date of my life with the hottest junior in the state. I think I need to go upstairs and whack off my tension." Way too inebriated and stoned to catch my drift, Richard clumsily hit my shoulder and attempted a kidney punch. I wasn't really angry, but I did not feel like playing the clown for the Simpson family's grease monkeys. I placed a well-measured love tap on his soft chin and he was out for the ten-count. The stoned greasers looked at me as if I was King Kong and then started howling with laughter and applauding. Richard recovered. We gave each other a big bear hug, the last joint made the rounds and we moved to attack the remaining Budweiser.

True to my arriviste upbringing and my quest for wealth and fame/infamy, I was less than successful in maintaining contact with these captivating people after returning to Europe. This ability to forget those closest to me and move on to new shores would be with me most of my life. I have always struggled with attachment and maintaining relationships. Separation was rarely an issue.

During my final year, I ran into an influential recruiter from Harvard who identified top athletic talent for them in the Midwest. I had barely heard of the place, but knew that several schools were offering complete athletic/academic scholarships. Harvard did not even offer to pay me some serious cash under the table for considering them. $10,000 for a no-show job for the summer seemed an alien concept to them. Indeed the recruiter seemed offended when I raised the subject. To add insult to injury, I was not even guaranteed to get in, had to take three SATs, a TOEFL examination and three achievement tests. I had also already signed a National Collegiate Amateur Association "letter of intent" for a full Oakland university basketball scholarship. The Harvard guy did not think that was very funny and believed I was jerking him around.

"Who in their right mind would go to a place like that?" I thought. Then I mentioned this recruiter and Harvard to my dad. Our relationship had improved visibly with 5,000 miles separating us. He offered to pay for Harvard if I got in. Unlike my sister's wish to study psychology, about which he was never pleased as he felt it reflected poorly on him, having a son at Harvard carried status, so no wonder he agreed to pay, despite the fact that it was very expensive. The dollar was still a real currency back then.

I had visited several other campuses by then and had met a number of scholarship athletes. The experience was alarming. Half the guys could barely spell their own name, passing grades were given and not earned and everybody over six feet three seemed to major in speech communications or physical education. I concluded, "If one cannot pronounce 'Speech Communications' without difficulty then one should not attempt to major in it." Attending the University of Detroit, San Diego State or Oakland University as a basketball major was not an option if your brain contained more than three functioning cells. Mine had four at the time, so I was out.

I had missed the last chance to take the achievement tests and was therefore not qualified even to apply to Harvard in 1977, so I had to park myself somewhere for a year. Germany was too drab and England too stiff, so I decided I wanted to attend the American University in Paris. Maybe because I lost my virginity at fifteen with a chubby but charming Pigalle street hooker, maybe because the application to major in political science took only one hour to complete, maybe because I was looking at some handy cash flow from a professional club or maybe because I liked existentialism, chateaubriand and the Crazy Horse—whatever it was, it was certainly sexier than majoring in basketball with eleven other retards.

It was sensational. The academic requirements were lightweight, allowing me maximum free time. My English literature professor and my French professor were excellent teachers. I was learning and having fun, living the light in contrast to unglamorous, suburban, Christian fundamentalist Michigan, ransacked by guilt and angst. The school paid me well to coach and play on their men's basketball team, which went undefeated that year for the first and only time in their long, illustrious history. My Paris basketball club paid for the apartment and basic living expenses. I was micro dealing in coke, and the occasional photo shoot would bring in more cash. I was typically dating loaded older women, so clothing, weekend trips and dinners were free. Well, almost free. My parents were also funding me, knowing full well that Paris was an expensive city. I was seventeen, living in the fast lane on a middle management salary but without the onerous tax deductions and housing costs. This was better than Detroit because I had far more money, unlimited freedom and nobody told me what to do. In short, I had all imaginable privileges and zero responsibilities. I was *The Prince of Paris*, at least in my own sophomoric mind.

The only person who told me what to do was my landlady, Juliette Maureau, an eighty-year-old avant-garde feminist, who had been a member of the resistance. We shared this vast apartment on the Bois de Vincennes. She would forever dig into me for not studying. "How can you not study Florian, ever? I simply responded, "I have never studied and look where it got me. I am living with you, *Cherie,* and I'm having the best time in the world." Like most women, Juliette liked to talk and I was an attentive listener. She would tell me about planting explosives under Gestapo vehicles during the war and torturing collaborators in the provinces. Suddenly, as if struck by lightning, she would drift into some distant land and lament the fate of countless married women who faked orgasms for their husbands for decades. She was fairly nuts but highly entertaining.

Her pet topic was the prevalence of homosexual and lesbian relationships within the French resistance, especially among the more literary types—not exactly run-of-the-mill cocktail-party talk. She was remarkably thin and her oversized bulging eyes were lit up like a Piccadilly neon sign. She was naturally wired. We earnestly discussed whether Simone de Beauvoir denied or actually lived out her extreme feminism in secret lesbian relations, before cracking up with laughter at our own pretentiousness.

Dinner for two at nine on Sundays was our institution. During benign weather, we would dine on the terrace overlooking the bois. On less favorable days the winter garden would have to do. Foie gras and Debussy was our favorite appetizer. The main course, usually chateaubriand with Cheval Blanc 1947, would require our undivided attention and the heavy composers would therefore get a rest. For dessert, strawberries covered in chocolate with Chateau d'Yquem could only be consumed in the presence of Chopin. During these lovely dinners, we managed to reconcile our human condition to our relative insignificance within the universe. We were happy.

My best friend in Paris was a very twisted Swede, Anders Kierkegrund, whose dad was a top dog at the Organization of Economic Cooperation and Development (OECD). I met Anders when I was trying to pick up his sister. She was kind of cute, kind of sexy and kind of smart, but not hot enough overall, and not outstanding enough in any single category to merit prolonged courtship. Her brother, on the other hand, was a deep well. Always properly dressed, polite and helping old ladies crossing the street, below his perfect outer shell Anders was a deviant. His real passion was motorcycle theft and I became his willing apprentice. Once we got bored with the bikes, we would neutralize them. That meant taking them down to the banks of the Seine and riding them full throttle towards the river before jumping off at the last moment. Whichever bike flew the furthest would designate the winner. I took plenty of involuntary baths in the Seine during my early apprenticeship. While I was a motivated student and quick learner, Anders usually reigned supreme.

This pastime came to a sudden halt in December when, after racing down the Champs Elysees at 90 mph on a hotwired 250cc Yamaha, I was apprehended in front of the Russian Embassy. I was able to talk myself out of this mess instead of spending Christmas in jail by claiming I was Thor Olaffson, son of the acting head of the OECD. I mumbled my story with great moral conviction and in a barely comprehensible Scandinavian singsong accent, every thirty seconds flicking my shoulder-length hair like some Euro-trash preppy to underline my appeal and importance. The show was first class. By chance I was wearing an Armani suit and an expensive cashmere coat my most recent girlfriend had acquired, because I had planned to go to the Le Castel nightclub later. I looked just like one of the spoiled sons of diplomats from the sixteenth arrondissement, who never carried their driving license or residency papers because Daddy's diplomatic immunity extended to the good-for-nothing children as well.

Because I had placed my very fashionable beige suede gloves on the ignition, the cops did not notice that the bike had been hotwired and they let me go. They kept the bike and I promised to get the ownership papers and my driver's license within the hour. We never heard anything so we chilled out after a couple of days. As usual, the signs were obvious. My time as a motorcycle thief was definitely over.

I would like to find out what happened to Anders. He is probably a protestant minister in Malmo, masterminding industrial fraud raking in millions just to keep his perturbed mind buzzing.

That same Christmas I received my Harvard College decision. Despite one of my written recommendations being from Necko, who had mistakenly written that I was a "seven-foot baseball player," I had been accepted. The admissions people are looking for people who they think might go on to show excellence, in whatever field. They want evidence of leadership, lateral thinking, drive, distinction, or all of these. I'd played basketball for my country and the sports element of my admission was clearly important and put me on their radar, but I'd also worked in my father's construction company since the age of thirteen and was fluent in four languages. I was no genius but had scored a prestigious academic scholarship as a senior. I had proficient grades and head read widely, in unusual areas. One of my other written recommendations was from the Harvard Basketball scout, whose last line—after all the stuff about my playing abilities—asserted that it was possible I might actually also graduate.

Having been accepted, the consequence was that my academic motivation in Paris immediately leveled off towards zero. My grades went from well above to below average. It did not matter. No one would ever ask for them. I got up at two in the afternoon, did my course work on the Metro if at all, attended at best one class, played pinball and hung out with my friends at cafes doing nothing for hours, played some hoop, then went to dinner, then to a club, then to a 24-hour cinema. At about three in the morning I would drop in on one of my girlfriends to crash or consummate the relationship. Afterwards I would smoke a cigarette with a glass of cognac before crashing at dawn.

Other days I would go the flea market, hang out with bums in squalid Belleville bars, before heading to Pigalle for oysters and Gewürztraminer. Later I would hook up with my basketball buddies for a night of club hopping and head to Strasbourg Saint-Denis to have breakfast watching the hookers and pimps return from the night's work. Back home at eight in the morning I let Juliette bitch me out for not studying and then settle down for eggs benedict for breakfast discussing the penis sizes of midgets with her.

Sometimes I would hold profound philosophical discussions with my less debauched intellectual friends around midday; go to one of the 360 museums followed by a visit to the notorious Piscine Deligny, weather permitting, to meet some rich bitches, although the problem with Piscine Deligny was that affluent aged queens were also on the prowl for handsome young men. These pederasts had to be avoided like the plague. After an early dinner I would go to the Opera, the Ballet or the Comédie Française, either by myself (cheap seats) or with an older female companion (great seats for free). A late cocktail at the Ritz or the George V would lift my spirits, and given that my companions might have to work the next day, I would respectfully call it an early night around 2 a.m. Before departing I would look into my date's slightly wrinkly eyes with great tenderness and tell them how much more meaningful my life had become since I met them.

When I was not escorting wealthy divorcees and philanderers or boutique owners, my favorite pastime was acting the worldly Frenchman and Latin lover and scamming on German and American tourist girls. I would tell them I was Alain de Geste from the Chateau Tonreve (which means "your dream") in Burgundy. Most thought my front was hilarious when they found out and kept hanging out with me; others thought I was a creep for lying to them and departed abruptly. Almost all these girls had steady boyfriends or husbands back home and were looking for romance and Latin love in Paris. It was a once-in-a-lifetime, non-stop free ride.

Yet I was tired, my brain was in a constant state of remission and I felt like a parasite. The endless partying, superficial sexual encounters and meaningless chitchat the French are so famous for were getting to me. The la-di-da French movies about nothing grew tiresome. Even the Comédie Française and Molière were leaving me non-plussed. Paris had become a cliché, a pretense that left me empty. I needed more substance, structure and intellectual nourishment, and I was going to get it at Harvard.

Part II
Climbing

3. Cum Laude

Some Harvard guy said that acid would open our minds, pot wouldn't hurt us, and cocaine was benign.
Chevy Chase

I entered Harvard College at eighteen going on fifty. My year in France had robbed me of the last vestige of innocence.

I arrived at my dormitory, Pennypacker Hall, wearing a full-length brown leather Gestapo coat, a white netted muscle vest and a diamond earring, and introduced myself to my Mormon roommate (who was the son of the governor of Utah) in perfect inner-city Ebonics. I had been a part-time gigolo, micro-dealer, professional athlete and cosmopolitan degenerate, and I was obviously nuts according to my roommates. I had already made far more money at seventeen than my classmates would earn upon graduation. I was the brother from another planet transplanted into a hostile and alien environment, the Paris playboy in the stark Unitarian Boston landscape.

Undergraduates were expected to study nine hours in addition to their class work. I had never studied more than a couple of hours after school, my entire life. Class attendance was required. I had never attended class consistently anywhere. There were big student protests for keeping the libraries open for 24 hours. What on earth for: To write the 100,000th essay on Paul Revere's brilliant communication skills or on Adam Smith's invisible hand?

At least half of the members of the freshmen class were virgins and three-quarters were men. The girls, on average, were not only beastly. They were largely sexually inexperienced, extremely uptight and self righteous and useless in bed, overall a dreadful combination. Nevertheless, I did score with several of the less handicapped creatures during freshman orientation. One called me a hedonist. Another called me a narcissist. What's wrong with having fun? It beats biting your nails over an organic chemistry midterm examination. And the only problem with self-love is that it's unrequited.

I was completely unprepared for this culture shock and was constantly on the verge of being expelled during my freshman year. My first midterm report card showed one B, two Cs and one incomplete. The incomplete was in expository writing. The professor commented that while I was supposedly enrolled at Harvard College she had not yet had the privilege of making my acquaintance. She said she was looking forward to meeting me before the end of the semester, probably to give me an F minus. If my grades didn't improve dramatically, I would be expelled in January.

To make matters worse, I was hustling silly white boys at the college billiard hall (gambling); I had seriously intimidated the billiard-hall attendant (violence); I was charged with plagiarism by the Romance Language Department in a segment of a paper relating to Vautrin, one of Balzac's antiheroes, which I had paraphrased from a renowned French literary critic (academic fraud, although I had no idea what plagiarism was); and I had the worst attendance record of the entire freshman class. My situation was so hopeless it was almost comical. They were going to ding me for sure.

My saving grace was my tutor, the saintly Ellen Porter. To this day, I do not know what she saw in me, but she managed the impossible and saved me. Heartfelt *mea culpa* admissions, profound moral introspection, even tears and Oscar-quality acting performances assuring my betterment got me a stay of execution. However, my ambition to become a multilingual diplomat was shot to pieces. I could hardly remain in the Romance Language Department as a vile plagiarist, and therefore switched to the economic department. I finally committed myself to capitalism.

In spite of the mess I was in, I had hooked up with this hot Afro-American girl, Lynne Valencia Perry, who would be my main woman for the next six years. She was a profoundly positive influence. Lynne helped me overcome my academic deficiencies. I took Afro-American history classes, and in return practiced German with her. She urged me to become involved in charitable causes. She softened my innate mercantilism and broadened my horizons. She was a lector at the Cambridge Catholic Church and I would attend services to listen to her resonating voice.

One summer I stayed with her family in an all-black, upper-class section of Houston. It was the perfect contrast to Livonia. Dr Perry senior was a star cardiologist under Michael DeBakey, the world famous Houston-based heart-transplant surgeon. These Afro-Texans had real money and loved to show it off. Their house could have been renamed the Golden Palace. The cutlery was gold-plated; the music room did not feature one item furniture that was not shining 18 carat gold. The family had converted to Roman Catholicism. Everyone in the family played at least one classical instrument. The more rebellious had ventured to play the saxophone. They had their own little symphony going with ten kids and both parents. Instead of playing the hoops, American football or track and field, the Perry children learned to swim and play tennis. Ebonics was strictly outlawed as the language of the ignorant, black lower classes. My jive was far better than theirs.

The ten Perry children attended the best "white" prep schools that Houston had to offer and some of the best universities in America. With the exception of the black sheep of the family, Maurice, they were all model citizens. Lynne was the valedictorian of her preppy white high school. She was smart, funny and danced well. She loved making fun of the klutzy, arrhythmic Harvard girls with their jerky moves and constant hair flicking.

Lynne's parents' attitude towards me ranged from threatening murder to almost full acceptance. Dr Perry once called me from Houston explaining that he had a loaded Colt in his hands and was coming up to see me if I did not stop dating his daughter. I took him seriously. These Texans, much like the Russians, are dangerous people. But I was not about to give up on Lynne. She had been the best thing in my life. For a while they cancelled her allowance to exert extra pressure. However, Lynne was loyal and could not be bullied. She did some temporary work to stay liquid. In the end the Perry's love all their children and gave in. The generous allowance was restored.

Surprisingly, even our parents got on well. My parents knew Lynne had an excellent effect on me and Lynne's parents got on well with them. I was obviously the black sheep in this equation. There was a lot of common commercial ground and similar bourgeois social and cultural ambition. Race was at best a tertiary issue after a couple of years. Lynne, on her visits to Germany, was well like even by my extended family and the old Nazis. Wealth, education and success were the relevant common denominators, not race. It was truly amazing how the descendants of slaves and national socialists could function so well together.

Lynne's parents earnestly tried to convince me to become a doctor. I politely declined their well-meant suggestion several times. The Perrys wanted all their ten children to become doctors and most did. I could not see myself studying feverishly until my early thirties. They came to our engagement party and were well liked by our friends. The Perrys are solid, ambitious citizens. Like the Neckermanns, they preferred not to address deeply disturbing issues and resolutely swept muck under the carpet. I understood their reservations against white folks in general and me in particular. I am glad I never had to walk in their shoes in the segregated South.

Lynne dissed me after six years due to my chronic infidelity, and married a tender and caring German doctor, a much better man than me, a few years later. They have two children. Dr Perry-Bottinger became a famous cardiologist with appearances on *Oprah*.

Back at Harvard, in the fall I donated some olive trees to a Kibbutz to feel better about myself. I had never performed any social work in my life and Lynne was constantly urging me to self-improvement through community involvement. Without a doubt, she planted the seed fort my future charitable activity in Liberia. This concept of helping poor or disadvantaged people was totally alien to me at the time. I could not see myself getting involved in any of these bogus curriculum-vitae-building causes.

By sheer accident, one afternoon in Harvard Yard I ran into some Phyllis Brooks House Prison Counseling Program recruiters. This sounded intriguing. Many of the inmates being counseled at Walpole Maximum Security Prison were violent, and some were bordering on criminal insanity. There were few takers. They accepted me right away, no questions asked. I was finally going to see a maximum security prison from the inside without having to commit a major felony. I would be able to hang with truly evil characters, not the punk-ass, switchblade wielding North African dope dealers I knew in Paris.

Given my fluent French, I was assigned to a former hit man and bank robber for the notorious Montreal Dubois crime family. My new best friend had been in several bank robberies and had committed a couple of murders in New England. He was a career criminal and professional assassin, who had graduated to the US Marshall's ten-most-wanted list at the height of his career. He was in for 39 to 54 years without the chance for parole. It was his first exposure to the American penal system, explaining in part his absolute ignorance of English. Given that he was 45 at the time, and looked like he was going on 65, I seriously doubted whether he would ever taste freedom again.

The tutoring was badly needed. According to our liaison officer, there were no other Canucks at Walpole and my guy Jean Christian (JC) was under constant threat from the Aryan brotherhood, the Irish mob, MS-13, Bloods and lesserorganized local hoodlums. Thus far his reputation had protected him from severe violence—the rumor was that JC had whacked over twenty people in his career—but sooner or later other inmates would begin to question his impressive credentials. His life achievements would not shelter him from gang rape or other savage acts forever. During the late seventies there were more than twenty murders among the Walpole inmate population per annum.

Given a prison population of only 900 inmates, the probability of being murdered while serving a 39-year sentence at Walpole, was easily 90 percent. Not being able to communicate and form alliances made JC even more vulnerable. The way things stood, JC was going to get whacked at Walpole for sure. Speaking just a little English would allow him to materially improve his chances of survival. He wanted to live and was a quick learner.

The prison conditions were appalling. I saw rats the size of small dogs, the toilets overflowed after heavy rainfall and some of the canned food was twenty years or older. Several meetings had to be cancelled because riots were a regular occurrence. I did manage to teach JC Basic English, though I did not find it easy to understand his Montreal gangster dialect. The police ended up nabbing his equally devious brother, also a top-ten guy, so these overachievers are now reunited and their odds for survival have improved even more. JC was smart but a bona fide bad guy through and through. He personified true evil. If I could do it again, I would work with the victims rather than the villains. JC caused way too much direct and indirect collateral damage during his life to merit my unmitigated love.

Lynne was strictly against drugs so I cut the habit for a while and began to scrutinize all the amazing opportunities Harvard offered. Instead of dealing dope, I was elected to be a paid director of the Harvard Cooperative Society, a $100 million retailing organization which also had on its board the legendary Professor Michael Porter, the competition guru. I then started speculating in stocks and formed a successful investment partnership with my friend Michael Kagan. Mike was one of the managers of the Harvard basketball program and seriously into stocks. He helped me open a Fidelity discount brokerage account. I put all my eggs into his first recommendation, a hot tip, Sunbeam Electronics. The company received a whopping takeover offer four days after I had placed my trade. I made $7,150 doing absolutely nothing. The rush of almost doubling my money within only minimal downside risk was better than smoking smack.

I was totally hooked on investing from that point onward. Instead of hanging out with rich divorcees and degenerate playboys in posh Paris nightclubs, I got serious about making money and career advancement. I was elected secretary of the Harvard International Students Organization and president of a prestigious Harvard Finals club. I quickly learned to stay away from classes that involved small study groups and those where attendance was closely monitored. It took me two semesters to figure out how I could achieve a maximum grade point average with minimal input and attendance. Most of the time students were needlessly duplicating their efforts. If one studied the course material closely, going to lectures made very little sense. If you focused your attention exclusively on cramming for midterms and finals, you would have lots of free time in the interim while scoring more than passing grades.

However, there was one class I did make a valiant effort to attend regularly—Nazi Germany and the Holocaust, aka Krauts and Doubts, run by Professor Hunt. I had met him previously, and as president of the influential German American Society he was quite familiar with Necko and his role in Nazi Germany. He encouraged me to attend the class and to conduct primary research into the subject matter, interviewing those that had experienced the period at first hand.

This sounded potentially and marvelously explosive. I would get to sniff around my family using Professor Hunt as my alibi. I would ask penetrating agonizing questions. I would penetrate the collective unconscious of the German mind and drag out gruesome details of complicity and despicable mercantilism. This was going to be intense. When I grew up, any discussions about the Nazi era were avoided at all costs. Our German public school devoted two meaningless hours to this dark and sinister episode in German history. No one in their right mind would admit to any ties to this debauched regime, yet millions had of course been involved and the elite, without the slightest doubt, knew exactly what was going on.

However, the first class of Krauts and Doubts was a real shocker. Professor Hunt introduced me. He described me as a descendent of a German family that had "witnessed" (i.e. "participated in") the events in Nazi Germany from 1933 to 1945. He asked me to stand up so everyone could see me. He added that he expected me to gather valuable, primary information from surviving family members and to provide a contrast to the insights provided by survivors of concentration camps and their descendants, who were also attending the class.

A third of the class actually voiced their disapproval after his introduction. They did not murmur, these children were hissing me. I turned to the guy next to me as I sat down and asked him what that was all about. He replied to me in a tone that implied I had raped his nine-year-old sister that morning, "You are part of the problem. All Germans are responsible for the damages inflicted on the Jewish people in general and my family in particular." I was stunned. This was totally wild. How could I respond to such an insane theory? What were they teaching these kids over at Hillel, the finals club for orthodox Jews?

I was born fourteen years after the war ended. My best friends at FIS were David Gower and Angelo Romain. My best friends at Harvard were Steven Larab and Mike Kagan. I could not care less if they were Jewish or from outer space. They were interesting, wired characters and I took a sincere interest in their history and met their families. Unlike most Germans my age, I had studied this dark period. (Sheepishly I have to admit that I also had two close friends at Harvard who were not Jewish: the most entertaining, wittiest character on campus, Costas Zombanakis, a Greek, and Marco Bodor, a sharp-minded Croatian American.) While Necko had clearly been an opportunistic Nazi swine, my deceased maternal grandfather Hans had been an allied spy and an active member of the opposition, so I felt I was not entirely evil, and not perfectly Arian, genetically speaking, due to my distant Mexican/Semitic roots.

The animosity towards me mellowed dramatically during the course of the year. By the end of the semester, only one radical Jewish jihadist in my study group kept being a racist pig and attacking me personally in section discussions. Let us call him Shalom Weiss.

My attempts to reconcile with Shalom did not work. He firmly believed I was the reincarnation of Ernst Kaltenbrunner and needed to be punished and insulted incessantly. The Florian-bashing continued to such an extent the teaching fellow, a Semite himself, had to intervene to discipline Shalom for his below-the-belt personal assaults. "Enough is enough; this guy is gonna pay," I promised myself. During the last study group of the year, I turned to Shalom and engaged him in a conversation in front of my fellow students. Some of my classmates had been debriefed about my plan.

"Mr. Weiss, the class is almost over and just to show you how racist, vicious and hypocritical you have been, I am going to open your eyes and show you how undeserved your savage and very personal assaults have been. Until today, I have never told anyone that my maternal grandfather died in a concentration camp. Tell me Shalom, how exactly does that make you feel?" He looked at me with complete astonishment. Guilt and his own stupidity were written all over his face. He looked at his notebook in a state of moral turpitude, wriggling uncomfortably in his seat. After a few seconds he lifted his eyes meekly and asked me how my grandfather died. I replied, "He fell off a watchtower, you hypocrite."

At this point, one half of the class was completely silent and in a state of shock. The other half, mostly the Jews whom I had debriefed, roared. If looks could kill, Shalom would have atomized me in nanoseconds. But for once, beet red and breathing heavily, he was at a complete loss for words. I never told my classmates, and certainly not Shalom, that my grandfather, my grandmother and her unborn child and my uncle were either recklessly killed or murdered by American soldiers in 1948. It was too personal and therefore none of their business.

*

I was becoming increasingly aware that various blocks had to be attained and put in place in order to construct a successful career path in the financial world I wanted to join, to learn the ropes from the best and then dominate. It was important to get some traineeship, and after my freshman year, I spent the summer working in South Africa. My parents had some investments there, and knew the South African politician Howard Odell. I worked in the Carlton Centre in Johannesburg for Nedbank, the largest private South African bank at the time, compiling and interpreting statistics in their economic unit, which was the best in the country. Full apartheid was still in operation, and the work was very much about developmental economics, which of course becomes more interesting set within that particular context. The South African data as a whole suggested the South African blacks were far better off than their peers in Botswana and Malawi. Yet a detailed analysis of several homelands or Bantustans revealed poverty, literacy rates and violent crime could be worse than in other sub-Saharan African nations. I went to Soweto, although it was strictly *verboten,* and saw crime and violence beyond even my imagination. Ciskei, a homeland territory, was far poorer than Zambia, Botswana, Namibia and even Angola.

As a black American, my girlfriend Lynne could come to South Africa as "Honorable White," enjoying all the privileges of white South Africans, even staying at white-only hotels. The Economic Intelligence Unit at Nedbank employed both Blacks and Whites. The blacks were perfectly capable and welcomed me to their homes in the townships. This was illegal by South Africa's apartheid laws. I participated in anti-apartheid protests in South Africa, and Lynne and I went on several protest marches in the United States, which was highly unusual for an Aryan capitalist working for the major South African bank—but not speaking up would have been hypocritical and against my beliefs.

Also at this time I co-founded an investment partnership, Interinvest, with Michael Kagan. Interinvest prospered from 1979 until 1982 in spite of a sharp market correction. We focused exclusively in takeover candidates and risk-arbitrage situations. The general idea was to develop networks and contacts to sniff out companies which were worth far more than the sum of their parts and therefore likely to be acquired at a hefty premium to our purchase price. We made solid returns with this approach during a time when the general market was tanking. I was also beginning to build a formidable knowledge and contact network, which would give me a powerful competitive edge many years later in my career. My focus on sensitive information would also get me in trouble more than once as I became a baby tycoon.

The largest investor was the guy from the next room in my freshman dorm, Carlos, who came from a Greek shipping dynasty, and his brother Nicholas, who would later marry a Bond girl. Carlos was an even bigger nut than I was. The first time I met him he was banging on my door asking if I knew where to get needles so we could shoot up some heroin. Although I had snorted and smoked heroin, I told Carlos that intravenous action was not my scene. If he wanted to score some needles in a hurry his best bet would to visit University Health Services where he should fake food poisoning or some exotic infection to get a blood test, and when nobody was looking he could easily grab a few.

Carlos converted to Islam and became a full-fledged Mujahedeen, worked on Wall Street and edited literary magazines. He reminded me of my sister. They would have made a great, totally insane couple. He went on to have an affair with the wife of Bobby Kennedy Jr, whom I would also get to know. Carlos allegedly died of a self-inflicted heroin overdose in a dumpy hotel in Peshawar. That explanation for his death was downright absurd. Carlos both loved and hated himself too much to kill himself, either by accident or via a deliberate golden farewell shot. He always had to prove something to himself, stand out and shock. He was mellowing out and had things to look forward to. He was also an ultra-sophisticated master user, a bona fide narco pharmacist. Carlos was whacked because he was investigating explosive subjects and extremely dangerous people while working for CBS 60 Minutes. He got too close and became a severe risk. Nothing is easier to arrange in these countries than a death by overdose. Carlos was simply the wrong guy at the wrong place at the wrong time with the wrong people. His time was up. End of story! Nicholas, lower key than Carlos, would introduce me to potential investors two decades after he became a founding partner in Interinvest. Mike Kagan became a very successful mutual fund manager in New York.

To keep things really interesting, by the start of sophomore year I had signed a lucrative contract with a professional basketball club in Germany, BC Giants Osnabrück. From then until I graduated, I commuted between Boston and Germany to play ball, mostly for extended weekends. I frequently had to reschedule examinations "for prescient personal reasons." My brother died in a car accident. Contra rebels in Nicaragua murdered my beloved sister. Two aunts died of breast cancer, and three uncles also died—from heart failure, colon cancer and lung cancer respectively. My father had two debilitating strokes and had to be fed by tubes once. I reached a new low point when my mother was confined to a mental asylum after a nervous breakdown. My grandparents each died at least twice from old age. In total, within three years there were fifteen fatalities and four severe accidents in my family, all of which required my urgent presence in Germany. My abysmal attendance record, however, was not entirely unique. Actor John Stockwell, who starred in *Christine*, had a supporting role in *Top Gun,* and directed several commercial successes like *Blue Crush* later in life, was for all practical purposes a full time model and actor during college. Another and endlessly more gifted college student during our time, Bill Gates, dropped out during his junior year and never graduated.

On campus, to keep busy I acted a reasonably demanding part in Dürrenmatt's *The Physicists*, which showed at Harvard's Experimental Theatre, I took some drawing and fine arts classes as well as several graduate courses in German literature, demographics and birth control, and I became president-elect of the SPEE Club, an elitist male-only Finals Club, whose most famous members included JFK and Bobby Kennedy. I enjoyed Harvard's diversity, learned how to digest mountains of information, developed analytical, business and leadership skills, and made several lasting friends. I got into far fewer fights and became a little more humane and socially aware. I even managed to graduate *cum laude* in economics.

4. NYC

An unfulfilled vocation drains the color from a man's entire existence.
Honoré de Balzac

A few professional basketball contracts were dangled in front of me when I left Harvard, but I was beginning to think incisively. I adored the game, and yes, they were lucrative deals for a young guy, but why would you accept a seven-year income stream, even at that level, in preference to a forty-year income stream? It would have been a sort of dream to play in the NBA, but it was one that was easy to pass on. There was no real angst in the decision, especially as the other dream to "out-Necko" Necko was attaining increasing definition. Having recently divested himself of his business concerns, Necko was mellowing into a life without the mercantile drive, and managing it rather well. This meant that the family ruthlessness had to find somewhere else to reside, and I was exceptionally willing to throw open my door and give it a comfortable home for another generation.

I took the first steps into the darkness in 1982 when I applied for a management traineeship in a big investment bank. Out of 2,000 applicants, I was one of five who were successful. I had been an elected and paid director of the Harvard Cooperative Society for two years, a $100 million retail organization, where I oversaw the pension fund and investment committees. Naturally it helped that I already had a functioning and profitable company in the investment world (which, ironically, my then ethical side made me sell before I took up the post), in addition to the years working for my father in school holidays, plus the South African training, plus the languages, all of which meant that I had experience that very few other applicants brought to the table. In fact, I probably had more trading and investment experience than most thirty-year-olds in the business. As I say, I had become very aware of what I needed to do to succeed, and for a number of years had built the right blocks accordingly, whether it be experience, leadership, benevolent work and so on. I didn't fall into success. My ascent was carefully planned and executed.

It was probably the most prestigious traineeship going, certainly better than the one offered by Goldman Sachs at the time. It involved fifteen months in the offices in London, Frankfurt and New York, looking at equities, debt, commodities, investment banking, sales, the whole capital markets show. They wanted the program to produce the next generation of leaders, and ultimately to be the source of the future chairman of what was the biggest brokerage house in the world. The other four successful applicants were a woman from Oxford, who couldn't even pass the licensing exams we all had to take, a very smart guy from Panama, a Frenchman, who turned out to be a capable merger and acquisitions specialist, and a German nerd, who was too introverted and not bright enough to leave much of a legacy.

After all, the technical and opaque equities, futures, commodities and options permits had been attained, I was assigned to the brokerage division of a high-net-worth brokerage office in the heart of Mayfair, London. It was an insanely *nouveau riche* scene. I was 22, driving my Porsche or Mercedes to the office, lived in a big house all by myself and wore a $30,000 Rolex. While the world around us was maligned by double-digit inflation and unemployment, we were a new generation of movers and shakers, the nascent London yuppies. Later on, we were working on Eurobonds, commodities and investment banking, a very lucrative and rapidly expanding playing field at a time when Thatcher and Reagan were creating an environment in which the sharks could feed without obstacle or hindrance. The momentum was awesome. Interest rates were declining each month, markets moved rapidly upwards and the economy was beginning to grow by leaps and bounds. Even better, our industry was enjoying ever-increasing profits and astronomic bonuses.

After the traineeship, I became one of the youngest securities analysts ever for the bank in New York in 1983, moved the Porsche from London and got a fancy apartment overlooking the Hudson and Broadway. Compared to London, New York at that time had its foot permanently on the gas, with none of the "old school tie" crap impeding the corporate desire to be agile, sharp, analytically and brutally efficient. It was a gold rush going on right next to the crime and depravity of the South Bronx, Harlem and the Lower East Side—from my point of view, vastly entertaining. Over the decade, the wealth pushed up and out into the wider city, and everything changed very quickly.

Whether at work or play I was having a whole lot of fun. For no reason or many reasons—the Neckermann connection, my exotic Germanness, Harvard, great prospects, rich, smart, hedonistic—I became a highly visible member of the Junior International Club (JIC) loosely affiliated to the big Manhattan nightclubs. Basically a conglomeration of wealthy Euro-trash and rich New Yorkers, it was the self-declared most exclusive party hub in town. The club would issue formal invitations saying "Florian Homm and Ingrid Rockefeller invite you to a private party at Studio 54," but I would rarely show up, half the time not even realizing I was hosting a party for the JIC or that I was on the invitation.

Ultimately I was partying way too much, and after nine months I got fired from the analyst position because I was repeatedly found asleep in my office overlooking the Statue of Liberty and Manhattan Bay, unshaven and drooling. This was not the behavior becoming of a proper corporate Wall Street citizen. They didn't have a problem with my work or research quality—my attitude and lifestyle were the problem—so when the research division fired me, I walked across the 49th floor and scored a new job as a financial advisor and commission broker in the Foreign Office, which effectively meant I was the closest thing to an entrepreneur you can be within the corporate structure, running my own franchise. They'd asked for a reference from their colleagues across the way, the last line of which simply said "He's quite an individual and could do well fending for himself." I'll take that any day.

Throughout this period I was in my physical prime and remained addicted to the hoops. All tall people should thank God for basketball. Competitive sports were a superb influence and protected me from intellectual and physical nihilism. High-level athleticism requires persistent discipline and hones competitive instincts. Those who can transpose their athletic prowess into a business mind frame later in life are often remarkably successful.

When I first learned the game as a goofy 12-year-old, my German coach said they should break all the bones in my body and reassemble them in order for my movements to become less awkward. I had simply grown too quickly and was an uncoordinated klutz, who was often the subject of ridicule.

If you do anything diligently for five or six hours per day, you will probably turn out as a virtuoso in about five to six years. This is called the "10,000-hour rule." By the age of 18, I had evolved from the klutz into making a living off basketball having represented Germany in international contests.

Forgetting the money aspect for a second, sports is awesome in tearing down race, class and cultural barriers. I played the hoops in Africa, China, the Caribbean, Mexico, Europe, England and the States. I played in slums even seasoned cops would refuse to patrol. I played in front of 20,000 spectators and I played against international superstars and NBA legends with some aptitude. I met many great guys along the way.

Via basketball I learned to assert myself. Given that many of my teammates were hard-core ruffians if not downright criminals, the constant exposure and de facto combat training made it virtually impossible for me to feel intimidated later in life. That would become intensely useful in my career as a hostile raider, greenmailer, short seller, and nightclub and bordello owner.

During the summer of 1984, time out from investment banking involved playing in several amateur/professional leagues like the Michelob Professional League at Manhattan College, the legendary Rucker's tournament in Harlem and the West 4th Street Summer Pro League played at the cage in Greenwich Village. Virtually all the players were college standouts, playground legends or NBA second stringers. In my best game I scored 33 points against a Detroit Piston benchwarmer called John Bostic, a complete bricklayer albeit a monster of a man. OK, it was not his best day and he even air-balled a few free throws, but at least I was in grand form.

After the game a 300-pound, heavily scarred black bear with grotesque tattoos on his neck came up to me and invited me for drinks. I was curious. What did this brute want from me? It turned out Vincent and his best buddy, the notorious East Harlem drug dealer Smokey, wanted to recruit me for their team in the St Mary's basketball league in the South Bronx. At the time, the South Bronx was a strict no-go zone for anybody remotely resembling a white person. It was clearly competing with Bedford Stuyvesant ("die in bed sty") for the most fucked-up, dangerous community in greater metropolitan New York. Dope dealing was conducted on an industrial scale through several drug wholesale warehouses. Smaller merchants would have their stalls on the pavement. Gangs controlled every block in the area. Drive-by shootings were so common the cops barely paid attention, and even stopped investigating them. Every fifth building was burned down for insurance fraud. The place was murder. I perked up.

The league was filled with college superstars and several high-profile NBA players such as Gus Williams and Rodney and Scooter McCray, who were playing in the league while waiting for reassignments to new NBA teams. Plus there was plenty of pussy, spending money and snow to go around if I was into that. Vincent slipped me two $100 bills and promised to pick me up at my Central Park South apartment to escort me to practice.

Vincent's vehicle was a $200,000, pimped up, thirty-foot custom-made van. It featured whacky TV and stereo systems, glass coke tables and reclining chairs big enough to serve as beds during orgies. I had never seen anything like it, not even in MTV videos. Vincent had several roles in Smokey's organization. He was obviously the coach, but he was also responsible for "marketing" and logistics in Smokey's coke and smack conglomerate.

Our team was stacked. It included Art Green, formerly of Marquette and NCAA champion, Tony Price, who took the University of Pennsylvania to the

Final Four and drafted in the second round of the NBA, and Pookie Wilson, an NBA-caliber guard and playground legend who would routinely score 30 points per game. We ruled that bush league. The games were all well attended and clouds of ganja smoke drifted towards center court by the end of the first quarter. Given most of the fans had never left their borough and only knew white people from television, I soon became known as "Larry," after Larry Bird, the Boston Celtics legend and the only tall white person these folks seemed to know. Although Bird was one ugly hick from French Lick, Indiana, I was flattered by the comparison because he was a basketball god and a great leader.

Lamar, one of my teammates, formerly from the University of Las Vegas (a great institution of higher learning with a 10-percent graduation rate among football and basketball scholarship students at the time) asked me where I was from. I told him Germany, and he replied, "So you're a Nazi?" That was the first time anybody called me a Nazi, simply because I told them I was from Germany. I was slightly disoriented. It took me about an hour to explain that Nazi Germany had ceased to exist at the end of the big war and Germany was now both a democracy and a staunch ally of the United States in NATO. He did not fully buy into my history lesson because he kept asking me about wolf packs and that nasty little guy with the "stache" (Hitler) who smoked the Jews, and kept eyeing me suspiciously for at least two more weeks. When he finally saw me dating a well-known six-foot-one mulatto runway model, Charmaine Williams, he told me, "You might still be a Nazi, but you obviously like black pussy, so I guess you're not into that gassing niggers after all."

As he opened up to me a little more I told him that I came from an ancient German family dating back to knights and dragons, somewhat simplifying my historical roots. He grasped the image perfectly and started to call me "the Count." That name stuck. I was no longer the great white hope, the Flying Dutchman or just Larry. I was soon rechristened "the Count" by all my teammates.

Due to Smokey's and Vincent's guardianship, I was completely safe in large swathes of East Harlem and the South Bronx. When I parked my Porsche in the hood, my tires and engine would not be removed. Instead, I usually found a few amateurs in miniskirts sitting on the hood looking for a hot date after the game. Nobody would fuck with the Count or his ride. I was definitely connected and protected but I stayed away from their business operations as far as possible. I had no ambition to become Scarface after my brief forays into the industry in Paris. I took my Porsche to get to games even though I did prefer being picked up by Vincent in his magnificent pimp van after he had finished his drop-offs in central Manhattan and Wall Street.

One morning, I had just exited our headquarters with four investment bankers and the CEO of Germany's largest utility company, when I heard somebody yelling at me. "Yo Count, Count, motherfucker, over here niggah, it's Vince, come and greet yo coach." From the corner of my eye, I saw Vincent pull over in his oversized pimpmobile and move his impressive frame towards the astonished bankers and corporate executives. I could see the fear in their eyes as Vincent got closer. He seized up the situation at once and said, "Chill, snowflakes. I ain't gonna mug you. This is my homeboy Count. He scored twenty against Rod last night," and gave me one of his famous spine-cracking bear hugs.

Over lunch, the German CEO was intrigued by the incident. My colleagues were afraid we might lose a big bond issue, but I managed the situation. When asked who this strange man was who almost broke my back and called me "niggah," I told him I play in charity basketball tournaments to support disadvantaged children in St Mary's Parish in the South Bronx and that Vince was my coach. I also told him we had recently donated $5,000 to the children's library. He was clearly impressed and congratulated me for my Samaritan acts and generosity and my association with people who had been less fortunate in life. We closed the deal. My colleagues didn't know what to think, especially since some of these sleaze balls must have been sourcing their rocks from Smokey Inc.

My last tournament of the season with Smokey's team was in East New York over a four-week period. Although I was connected in parts of Harlem and the

South Bronx, East New York was an entirely different country. I had no protection there and my Porsche was in the repair shop. The tournament was important to all of us because one of our teammates had been shot there and this would be the third annual competition commemorating his death. Not showing up for the opening game, was not an option. Everybody would be there. I had to go.

It was a Friday afternoon and I had just finished a lame research report on German retailing. I had to head home and change my clothes—wearing a $1,000 suit and carrying an Etienne Aigner leather briefcase in East New York was not advisable. Even the kiddie gangs couldn't resist the temptation of such an attractive target. I changed into black pants, a tailored Italian shirt and my snug custom-made black leather jacket. I looked like a packed upscale calabro 'Ndrangheta gangster.

I got a subway towards Bushwick Avenue where Vince was supposed to meet me and get me to the playground. In the mid-1980s, the deteriorating New York subway system was notoriously unsafe. Bernard Goetz, the famous subway vigilante, was whacking people for understandable reasons, and even an oversized thug like me needed to be careful.

Fate struck. Three delinquent members oft the National Association for the Advancement of Colored People (NAACP) mugged me. Their leader seemed like a really bad, black version of me, standing about six feet six, albeit seriously battle worn from too much crack and cocaine in his brain. His irreverent attitude and mildly detached, threatening smile was disarmingly familiar. Even his nose was straight like mine. Was I tripping or was this really happening? Had I descended into the netherworld and transformed into an ignorant, emaciated, black heroin addict mugger? Was this God's revenge for my life of debauchery? My Afro-American doppelganger was mugging me, the count; his white mirror image.

After handing over my wad of twenty-dollar bills at knifepoint, the ringleader took note of my fancy lizard boots and my leather jacket and confiscated them with a truly ingratiating million-dollar smile. He then proceeded to share his infinite wisdom upon departing, "chew know disis not yo hood cowboy, nex time ill take yo mony and cut chewup juss fo fun." Even though he was a demented jive talker, the dude had a cool, winning smile, so I decided to christen him Smiley afterwards.

I had been robbed at Carnival in Rio about a year earlier, with my girlfriend Lynne in tow. The young robbers there paid a high price for a low-price Seiko watch. Two favela thugs had concussion and one had a respiratory impairment requiring medical treatment from a perfect shot to his larynx. I could not get my watch back because the runner was carrying it. It made no sense to pursue him unless I wanted a bullet between my eyes.

This time my odds for a gratifying non-verbal resolution were vastly inferior. Even if I wasted one of these subway pirates, I was certain to get cut or stabbed by the other two. I was in top form, at least verbally, addressing my muggers as Sirs and Gentlemen and offered one a possible admission to an Ivy League school if we were to become better acquainted over lunch at the New York City Harvard Club in the near future. These dudes thought I was seriously mental but they did not inflict any physical punishment on me. They laughed their ass off and wished whitey "happy days" before carrying off 500 bucks in cash and $1,500 in quality merchandise, which they would probably hawk for a Benjamin Franklin.

At the time I was upset but not terribly angry, and thought Smiley was simply doing his job. I decided to try and ignore the incident, but failed miserably. I have this mean streak and it is difficult to suppress at times. I wanted revenge, maybe a bloodbath, a little castration would also do. I therefore scored a tired .38 caliber unregistered Cobra from a nice Italian "fellow" and continued taking the subway on my trips to East New York.

On a sunny Sunday afternoon I finally scored. Who was coming down the subway aisle: my doppelganger Smiley, albeit with a different support cast. He saw me, took a double take and broke out his sinister ear-to-ear smile. "Silly whiite muddafucka. I tol chew lasstime too stay ouwde hood. Wad you got fomee tooday, a Rolex fomy daddy or maybe dat cute dimon eeding fomy bitch? Don look ad me like sum alien. I ax you a quession, wondabread."

I took out a small wad of one-dollar bills and handed them to him. Then I grabbed my shopping bag and got out a brand new pair of Michael Jordan size-13 sneakers, a prized possession in predominantly black neighborhoods at the time. Smiley seemed to approve, but he was visibly stressing over the one-dollar bills, possibly because he was either unable or unwilling to count past ten. As I handed him both shoes with my left hand, I stood up and pulled the Cobra out of one of them with my right. I rammed the cocked gun into his mouth, smashing a few front teeth and cutting his big fat upper lip. His knife-toting cronies immediately backed off, given that I appeared sufficiently motivated to pull the trigger. These guys were no heroes. They specialized in robbing old ladies in wheelchairs or little Chinese shop owners. They were now calculating odds like me and did not like what they were seeing.

At this point I noticed that Smiley was wearing my $500 lizard boots. This enraged me, and I turned the gun on his cronies while he was trying to put his severed lower lip back into place. Both of these heroes were sprinting down the aisle like Speedy Gonzalez, fully expecting double taps in their backs. Luckily for them, I don't even like guns and don't enjoy shooting humans—I only enjoy shooting pheasants and grouse for culinary pleasure. I pistol whipped my doppelganger, cracked his nose while tearing some facial tissue near his beak. What a mess, there was blood everywhere.

Smiley's knees were shaking and he was about to collapse, barely hanging on to a pole in the middle of the carriage. I rammed the gun into his crotch with full force. Smiley collapsed on his butt with his head on his chest. I told him to take off my fucking boots. He was totally helpless, not responding and holding his crotch in obvious pain. Then I asked him very calmly, "Who is laughing now, Smiley?" I pushed the Cobra against his head acting as if I was going to give him the final love tap. He started whimpering and seemed in another world. While I was celebrating my moral victory, Smiley started urinating violently. Much to my dismay, the flood of urine rapidly found a home inside my precious boots. I abandoned the boot recovery project, left him with twenty piss-soaked dollar bills, exited the subway, changed platforms and headed back to civilization. I was a little shaken up and observed some bloodstains on my coat.

Returning to midtown, I scalped some first-rate tickets at Madison Square Garden to watch the Knicks lose by twenty points. Then I headed home to my pad overlooking Times Square, the bright lights of Broadway and the Hudson River. Annette, a wild girlfriend from Berlin, was visiting. She had endless legs, a Bardot mouth, natural blonde hair and blue-green eyes. Her Arianism contrasted beautifully with Lynne's Negritude and the Cajun gestalt of another Harvard friend, Colette Creppel. After the episode with Smiley & Co., our sex was a little twisted that night. What a joy it was to sleep in so many different flowerbeds. And what a glorious Saturday it had been.

There was no Smokey/Vincent repeat. I met Pookie at a tournament at the 128th Street Police Athletic League facilities in Harlem and asked how plans were shaping up for next season. He looked at me in total disbelief and told me, "Count, you not know this? The shit was all over the *Amsterdam News*. Smokey was shot in his face point-blank, and Vince is deep undercover somewhere in the South."

I was dumbstruck. Smokey, the smooth and gracious urban entrepreneur was no longer with us. This aspiring Afro-American multimillionaire was only in his mid-twenties when he met destiny. I liked him a lot. Unlike me, he had barred expletives from his vocabulary. He was gallant, soft-spoken and polite, always impeccably dressed, very organized and obviously intelligent. He had smoked some competitors during his race to wealth and fame; now somebody had smoked him. "A bloody shame," I thought at first, and then, on further reflection, "What goes around comes around." Smokey was no saint and he had played with fire for too long.

*

As a commission broker on the Foreign Office desk I made about $10,000 a month hawking US securities to drug cartels, corrupt politicians, clandestine foreign exchange dealers, money launderers, wealthy families and tax evaders all over South America and the Caribbean. I even charged this Colombian flower exporter a 5-percent sales fee for a two-year Certificate of Deposit. A Mexican President, Colombian coffee exporters, Peruvian foreign exchange dealers, commodity producers, traders, top army brass, legitimate entrepreneurs, families and corporations, shady banks, Jews and old German boys (fugitive Nazis) were among our clients. Not surprising given the wealth of information, the office was managed by a competent former CIA executive.

Let me share the depth of our depravity. The US and its ubiquitous financial institutions have always been and continue to be the largest money laundering machines for Latin America, the Middle East and much of Asia. Rogue investors from the developing countries, who deposit their wealth on American soil, face very no risk of being revealed to their governments back home by American authorities. These deposits are very welcome and presently rather crucial for the survival of the US banking system, especially in those regions bordering Mexico. The only freezes occur when America is either conducting warfare (Iraq, Libya) or boycotting a specific nation like Iran. Meanwhile the US is attacking every country in the world with a low tax rate, a decent financial infrastructure and a solid financial position, Switzerland and many Caribbean nations, which cater to private investors. The US employs, just like the French and Germans, criminal measures such as bribery as well as political and economic pressure to obtain constitutionally protected customer data from these countries.

Our Foreign Office in lower Manhattan was one of the nerve centers of US money laundering in the Americas. Technically, we were not violating any US laws at the time, and that was all that mattered to us, but we were definitely violating the laws of many of the countries we were operating in. No other office within the vast international network produced more commissions per broker than us. I built my customer list in two ways: firstly, I made sure that the most interesting leads would end on my desk after client requests would be allocated to various brokers after advertising campaigns. That basically meant appropriating leads placed in the mail slots of other brokers in the office and developing them as my own clients. The other formula for building a sizable business was extensive travel to some of the most dangerous places in South America. My reasoning was that if the client had lots of money but lived or worked in hell, there would be far less competition pitching him for his account than if he were living in popular places like Rio de Janeiro or Punta del Este. Moreover, these clients would appreciate a banker who would take significant risks to develop a long-term connection.

Therefore, my top three business development zones were: Peru, largely controlled by the Shining Path Maoist Guerillas; Panama, controlled by General Noriega and his cronies; and Colombia, largely controlled by FARC and other terrorist organizations.

In the early and mid-1980s, Peru was a strict no-go zone for anybody with any common sense and respect for self-preservation. The Shining Path easily controlled more than half of the country and violent attacks in Lima were commonplace. The Shining Path detonated the Bayer industrial plant, blew up central power stations and the offices of the ruling party. They committed thousands of murders. Prominent foreigners were highly priced kidnapping targets. The Peruvian economy and Lima itself, meanwhile, were on its last legs. Just 1 percent of the population owned 99 percent of the nation's wealth. The majority were uneducated and dirt poor, with no prospects for improvement. Unemployment was over 50 percent. Malnutrition was the rule, not the exception. Peru was a pitiful sight, a fully-fledged banana republic.

My Peruvian client list was initially largely made up of black market foreign exchange dealers who supplied Peruvian companies with badly needed foreign currencies at more competitive rates than the absurdly unrealistic official exchange rates. Differences between official and black market exchange rates were as much as 50 percent, making the bigger black market Forex dealers wealthy in just a few months. They were ensuring that companies could continue to remain competitive and pay for imports with hard currency. It also allowed the wealthy Peruvians to exchange their useless local currency for US dollars and then ship these funds to safer harbors abroad, mostly in the US.

It quickly dawned on me that if I treated the Forex dealers like gods, they might ultimately introduce me to their most potent and much larger clients. Everything I was doing was blatantly illegal by Peruvian law at the time. That, however, did not bother me in the least. Just because certain laws are in place does not mean they are just or make any sense. My grandfather had been a major black market operator, my father a minor one. Milton Friedman, the most prominent economist of the last century, had the following to say about black markets: "The black market was a way of getting around government controls. It was a way of enabling the free market to work. It was a way of opening up, enabling people." And that is exactly what I was doing. I was helping develop free markets in Peru and enabling people to move their money out of the country.

So I would launder money for the sake of capitalism and civil and economic liberty. American independence is based at least partially on a revolt against the prohibitive and monopolistic English taxation system, and import and export restrictions. Black market operations in New England and the Southern states have a long tradition. American traders have for centuries made a fortune evading English, Spanish and French duty controls. In my deranged mind, I saw myself as a freedom fighter for Western capitalism.

Based on 24/7 customer service and bending over backwards for clients, I had gained the trust of the biggest Peruvian Forex dealers. I was helping them channel their funds via our Panama office and investing it in secure and attractive investment-grade bonds. Word got around that I knew what I was doing and could be trusted. The Forex dealers opened up and introduced me to their senior business and government connections. In time I became the trusted financial advisor to the head of National Security, the number one general in a top cocaine processing and producing region, and ultimately a consultant to the Federal Reserve Bank of Peru.

My last trip to Peru was especially memorable. On a Friday I had advised the Federal Reserve Bank to invest a substantial amount of their total foreign currency reserves in a seemingly mad leveraged transaction. I convinced the governor of the bank and his deputies to take $100 million of their reserves and invest it in ten-year US government bonds yielding 12 percent at the time. That in itself was a lucrative investment, given that inflation was dropping and the bonds would certainly increase in value. But anybody could propose such a simple bond investment. My angle was to convince them to borrow another $300 million at 6 percent for two years and invest the loan in the same ten-year bond yielding 12 percent. They would earn, net of our excessive fees and commissions, over 25 percent per annum. If interest rates and inflation kept declining, they would earn substantially more. Our commissions on the transaction would come to over $3 million, of which I would receive roughly $1.2 million. Not a bad payday for a twenty-five year old for a few days' work in the mid-1980s. We drew up preliminary contracts and I was in constant communication with the institutional desk in New York to close this deal.

It never came to fruition. I had simply been too dewy-eyed. Our major competitor, a major American bank, stole the idea and got the deal because they were smart enough to share 50 percent of their fees with the Central Bank governor and his deputies in a special purpose offshore account in the Bahamas. I had been too greedy. I should have thought of this myself. I was still young, very ethical and very naive.

On the weekend I was flown in a military aircraft to Ayacucho, the Shining Path stronghold. Ayacucho has 33 fine churches and vestiges of civilization dating back an astonishing 15,000 years. At the time, however, it was easily one of the most dangerous places on earth. I was picked up by a colonel in an armored vehicle to meet the general himself at his compound. The general was in a talkative mood. Apparently, he had negotiated a truce with the Shining Path leaders in his region (this meant he would be sharing rather than fighting over the profits from the regional cocaine trade), which would allow him a more tranquil, profitable coexistence in one of Peru's leading cocaine-producing provinces, Huamanga. Unlike the sleazy bankers, the general kept this word and became a major client. What I did not know was that I had been followed and spied on virtually nonstop during my last three trips to Peru. Seemingly, there had been a leak about my meeting with the central bankers in Lima, and flying to Ayacucho courtesy of the Peruvian military was not exactly a low-key move.

Returning to Miami in first class, Peru's national security chief was sitting next to me and was kind enough to inform me I had made it on the Shining Path's "most wanted" list as a major foreign collaborator. He strongly encouraged me not to visit Peru until things had calmed down. He simply could not guarantee my safety. Only a week later, the Shining Path threw a hand grenade at another banker from our office visiting Ayacucho. The guy barely made it out alive.

Peru has since recovered thanks to its strongman president and very effective leader Alberto Fujimoro, who is presently in a Lima jail. Two decades of uninterrupted economic growth based on sound free-market policies have made Lima and even Ayacucho livable cities. A middle class has emerged and is here to stay. Last year Peru eclipsed Colombia as the largest cocaine producer in the world.

While Peru was on its last legs, I was the second highest commission generator out of 183 graduating brokers. I was making more money than the top graduate of Harvard Business School would make upon graduation in 1987, but I was bored with burning and churning high net worth individuals for maximum commissions. I couldn't see myself as a commission prince, selling dreams to wealthy Latinos and constantly figuring out how much I could rake them for. I'd had three years at the same bank, I was 26, the job content was becoming truly brain dead, and I had learned how to sell. The curve had flattened and it was time to move on.

5. Sharking

Capitalism is not about free competitive choices among people who are reasonably equal in their buying and selling of economic power, it is about concentrating capital, concentrating economic power in very few hands, using that power to trash everyone who gets in their way.
David Korten

Capitalism is the legitimate racket of the ruling class.
Al Capone

It is a common route for baby sharks to return to school after a period swimming on their own, and it is a path I also took. Especially in the US, you are nobody without "MBA" stamped on your forehead. Arrogant as I am, I applied only to Harvard Business School and Stanford, and found myself back in Massachusetts at the top graduate business school in the world. What the prospectus says is that you will learn about operations management, managerial economics, advanced accounting, international business and so on. What all this translates into is teaching the baby sharks how to bite hard. This was about connections and making money—big-time, eight-figure money, nothing else.

About 800 brainwashed developing capitalists enroll at Harvard Business School each year. The vast majority in 1985 were visibly bland and at best light grey, mostly unmemorable eager beavers trying to get the biggest slice of the money pie into their mouths as quickly as possible. In that sense I truly belonged, but what made the place so soulless was its conformity and the small, controlled worlds in which these people moved. The dress code was preppy and yuppie, class discussions were temperate and largely monotonous. However, the general IQ level was high and several professors were truly brilliant, especially Michael Porter, who is an authentic genius with genuinely revolutionary business ideas. As well as being academically insightful, he is a very successful commercial businessman in his own right, having built a large consultancy.

Everybody was looking to hook up in investment banking or consulting, which was ironic in that by the time we graduated two years later, we were only a few months away from Black Monday. Ass-licking professors was the favorite pastime for many, and most professors liked it. There were exceptions among the students, like Koreans who could not speak a word of English, my roommate JD, a French major from Fiddlebury College (Middlebury) and a micro entrepreneur who was accepted off the waiting list, some charity workers who wanted to switch sides, a few professional assassins from special operations, and yours truly.

I spent most evenings after studying flipping beer cans and taking brain damaging bong hits with JD and his fiddlehead friends, passing out on our stinking sofa after watching *Hawaii Five-0* reruns. JD's anxiety level was far higher than mine, given that he knew shit about math, accounting, finance or economics.

How was I going to explain to my classmates that I had worked principally in money laundering and tax evasion? I was already a seriously strange dude to most of them. As it turned out, they were too self-involved to give a shit anyway, so I talked a lot about international capital markets and left out the really juicy and incriminating stuff. What made me feel better was that some of the special ops guys and navy seals were equally uncommunicative about their former clandestine activities in the Philippines, Nicaragua and Guatemala. I might have been a rogue and a minor hoodlum, but at least I wasn't an authorized killer.

Having been sufficiently debriefed about the Harvard experience during my freshman year at college, I was nevertheless not fully prepared for business school. Class attendance was mandatory, so the family fatality stories would not work here and tardiness would be punished severely. I arrived at the Section A classroom at 8.25 a.m., a whopping five minutes before schedule, proud as a peacock for my superior punctuality. When I entered, I saw that everyone was already sat down and had probably been there since 6 a.m. There was only one seat left in the whole multilevel auditorium, generally reserved for the eager-beaver, ass-kissing Baker scholars and idiots like myself who did not know that the seating system is such that where you sit on day one is where you sit for two semesters. I had landed in the worm deck. I was so close to the professors I could smell which toothpaste they used. The problem with the worm deck is that the professor could see your notes and whether you were paying attention. Taking a nap during class was out of the question. You had to look bright-eyed and bushy-tailed all the time. I was so stuffed I could have cried. Possibly this was poetic justice for years of abusing the system during college, doing the absolute minimum to achieve the maximum result.

By the third semester, however, seating was no longer fixed. I could sit anywhere, and making an early comment in class satisfied the oral participation requirement and allowed me to study the cases for the next day while the class was still discussing some useless matrix management structure.

I found myself doing particularly well in areas like organizational behavior, and career management. In fact, I was so switched on that remarkably, and in spite of my natural rebelliousness, I became an official tutor for several subjects and was asked by two departments to consider an assistant professorship. Me, the absentee derelict scholar or the idiot *savant*? I had to laugh. And then I refused, because the positions offered low hourly returns and too little financial upside.

I was also the president of the Investment Club and vice president of the Venture Capital Club. I had moved to the Spee Club on 76 Mount Auburn Street. Bobby Kennedy Jr and the son of the acting president of Colombia were my floor mates, which was certainly an intriguing constellation. Bobby Kennedy junior invited me on several occasions to spend the weekend at the family compound in Hyannisport. But I reclined, being far too busy throwing coke bashes for my club mates or scamming on hot Wellesley, Smith, Mount Holyoke and Harvard College girls with my old college friend Costi Zombanakis, who was attending the Kennedy School of Government.

Cocaine is just about the most addictive drug on the planet. In one experiment, a chimp was trained to hit a bar in his cage to be administered with a dose. At regular intervals, the number of times the chimp had to hit the bar to get the coke was increased. The experiment was abandoned when the chimp whacked the bar over 12,000 times to get a single hit.

Sigmund Freud, a heavy user for over two decades, admitted "I take cocaine in very small doses … I partake of it regularly and against depression and against indigestion, and with the most brilliant success." This is a total lie. "Small" and "regular" doses of cocaine are an oxymoron. Dear Siggi, I hate to break the news to you: you are a coke monkey.

In total, I consumed considerable doses of cocaine off and on for about eight years. If I add up all the money I spent on coke and all the money I made "prescribing" it for my affluent patients, I definitely came out ahead, financially speaking.

I have also experienced with opium, heroin, hashish, ecstasy, crack, LSD, mushrooms and speed. My only knowledge of morphine is as a painkiller; it is unequaled in that role but is simply too pleasant and addictive for casual, recreational use. I was never into pharmacological substances and prescription drugs. My appetite for drugs is actually rather limited, and after intensive study I can conclude that they are overrated. Opium is too heavy for my liking and turns me into a zombie. Strong weed is better than most hashish. Mushrooms can turn into some truly weird and unpleasant trips. LSD and Ecstasy fry you brain. Why would you want to do that to yourself? Heroin can be snorted, but requires intravenous injections to achieve full impact and then makes you puke. If you use an infected needle, you probably get AIDS and die. There are faster and better ways to commit suicide.

Free diving, hiking in the Sierra de Santa Marta and FARC controlled areas in Darien (the lawless border area between Panama and Colombia), adrenaline-pumping car crashes, being chased and shot at by opium dealers in the Golden Triangle, very creative, physical emotional sex, kite surfing three-story-high waves, jumping from 60-foot cliffs, getting thrashed by world-class heavy-weight boxers, even parachuting and bungee jumping are all far more exciting and interesting. Plus drugs are totally passive and expensive. And if you do not want them to negatively impact your net worth, you may have to consider merchandising them to sustain your hobby, which is a bad idea long term.

During all the years I took cocaine, I never let it interfere with my studies, sports, sex or business. I was never detained or arrested but even at my most enterprising times I was never more than a minor dealer. Nor did I hang out at schoolyards to hook middle-school pupils or keep coke whores as concubines. My customers were only ever demented, rich and spoiled young urban professionals with more money than sense. Sort of like me.

While attending Harvard Business School my favorite professor had me figured out. We had a long one-on-one session in his office and he told me that I was kidding myself about cocaine and that I was an addict. He knew, because he was an old Wall Street cokehead himself, albeit a reformed one. He also told me that he would like to hang out with me because he was convinced I would become filthy stinking rich. However, he did add that I might also go to prison one day. He was genuinely concerned and his analysis and conclusions would prove infallible. I was an addict. Whether I would become stinking filthy rich and flirt with justice or rot in the slammer, only time would tell.

I did not completely ignore his advice, but at that time my merchandising business was growing a little bit too fast and furious and my friend Charles had just introduced me to some heavy Irish/Colombian connections. Not only could I score nearly pure coke in unlimited amounts at great prices from Murph and Angel, the income potential far surpassed anything I could get from Goldman, McKinsey or Fidelity by a factor of three or four after tax. Contemplating this dilemma during a 48-hour non-stop coke binge the answer presented itself. After the obligatory eighteen-hour somnambular recovery spell, I managed to crawl down the stairs of my Cambridge town house to meet a few friends for a late Sunday night dinner. I tried to talk, but I was drooling and uttering complete gibberish. It seemed like my entire face was paralyzed and I was permanently speech-impaired. It took me about five minutes to recover my vocal abilities and full use of my facial muscles. I stopped using cocaine that day.

*

After my first year at business school, I worked for Bain Consulting in Munich and London during the summer of 1986, but while I thought the job and the people there were intellectually stimulating, the work itself was not hands-on enough for my liking. The two cases I was working on were a major global credit card group and a fledgling German retailer. The former was a bona fide growth story on an international expansion binge. The latter was fighting for basic survival. I was being paid a whopping $20,000 after tax for six weeks of work. While I was collecting a lot of data and drawing endless charts, the teams were small and highly motivated. Everyone was brainy. Plenty of time was spent on radical and creative analysis.

The big dogs running the London and Munich offices were working eighty-hour weeks and making about as much as senior partners in top law firms. Consulting is a low risk, reasonably well paid advisory function. Even the absolute top consultants were nowhere to be found in the *Forbes, Fortune or Manager Magazin* lists of the richest Americans or Germans. The deal monkeys or commission merchants at Goldman were making far more money.

Clients were billed by the hour like lawyers, which turned me off. I wanted a big slice of the action. That meant equity, a fat share of the profits, insane venture capital returns, anything with unlimited upside. How was I going to become a Deutschmark billionaire with such a lame compensation system? I would barely crack low two-digit millions if I was lucky by my early sixties. Even worse, I would work like a dog and have absolutely no fun. One day I would hire the best lawyers and consultants. I was too in love with risk and adventure to join such a predictable guild.

During my second year at business school, I worked for Fidelity Investments as a shipping analyst. To hold down that kind of job in addition to the supposedly monstrous workload given to Harvard MBA students was absolutely unheard of. Certainly, I was working outside of the system by doing this, making some cash flow while paying the not insignificant HBS fees. That money, plus the Bain dollars over the previous summer, meant that I never had to sell my soul to some company who might pay the fees in exchange for having me work for them on graduating. I never needed a student loan. I cherish freedom and independence above all things, and that means I hate owing anybody a dime, including banks, family, friends or the government. I made a killing in several shipping stocks and came out of Harvard Business School with a Cambridge town house, a Manhattan apartment and my cash reserve larger than before.

On the whole, HBS is one of the planet's most soulless places. As always, there are exceptions, but generally speaking, if you want to be a better person, make the world a better place, have fun and meet interesting and fascinating people, avoid the place like the plague. If you want to develop a powerful network and become a zillionaire, apply.

Six years of Harvard had forced me to actually learn something. I was less flaky intellectually and could hold my own in terms of analysis. I was street smarter than most and still irreverent and fun loving. I also knew I was certainly not going to get stupid rich by billing hourly like consultants or lawyers, or on a transaction-fee basis like investment bankers while ass licking my way to a partnership. I was going to do it by learning how best to invest my ever-growing cash pile and build my own companies. I wanted to understand industry and company dynamics so I could someday build my own company and sell it. Rather than waste excessive energy on more redundant case studies, I focused fully on the recruitment process. As a result, I had multiple lucrative offers from several investment banks, top consulting firms like Bain and McKinsey and investment managers like Fidelity and T. Rowe Price.

In late September 1987 I joined Fidelity Management and Research in Bean Town (Boston) as a fund manager and analyst, even though their pay package was inferior to the investment banking and consulting offers I had. However, what was vitally important and extremely attractive was that some of the sharpest investors worked there, including the icon of fund management, Peter Lynch, and I would have the chance to interact with them and learn from them on a daily basis. Lynch was and remains a legend. During his tenure of Fidelity's Magellan Fund from 1977 to 1990, he saw annual returns of 29 percent on assets that grew from $20 million to $14 billion. They were a truly global outfit, the largest mutual fund management company in the world with lots of exposure to all sorts of industries, and I would be learning from the likes of Lynch. It was going to be beneficial to be around people like that.

My recent abandonment of drugs was twinned with a determination to lead a dutiful corporate life. On my first day, Fidelity gave me my own fund (one of their most volatile, high Beta Funds, the Fidelity Broadcast and Media Fund), which was unprecedented. Twenty-one days later, on Monday 19 October 1987, the Dow Jones Industrial Average declined 22.6 percent in the largest single-day drop in history. The world financial industry was in a profound state of shock and uncertainty. Even the relatively stable mutual fund industry was heavily impacted by Black Monday.

At Fidelity, redundancies in the Operations department were announced. However, the Ivy Leaguers in asset management would be left unscathed and selective hiring was still going on. Seasoned fund managers were probably making on average twenty-five times more than the average person in Operations, where the mood was especially somber. These guys disliked us as a rule. Right now they really hated us.

My own situation was picture perfect. I had sold numerous positions leading up to the crash, raising cash because most of the valuations were idiotically high. I was going to divert this cash to less expensive media stocks in Europe and Asia and some high yielding convertible bonds. The fund had almost 40 percent cash on the day of the crash. It was a mix of luck and skill. No other Fidelity equity fund, out of 100-plus funds, had more portfolio protection that day and performed better relative to their benchmarks. Consequently, I was in a great mood and very upbeat while some of my less fortunate colleagues were worrying about redundancy and checking the balances in their savings accounts just in case. I have always loved down markets. They create so much opportunity.

A few days later, the fund management squad was facing the Operations team in the Fidelity intramural basketball league. In the past, the Operations guys would annihilate the research and fund management geeks by at least forty points. Their team was made up of former competitive athletes, mostly from South Boston, aka Southie, Boston's rough Irish working-class neighborhood. I had joined the fund management team along with Frank Bracken, an intensely built six-feet-four former college football player, who had also been a high school basketball standout.

With two heavyweights on the team, Frank, I and our physically illiterate teammates were beating the pride of South Boston fair and square. The Operations guys started playing incredibly dirty while triple-teaming me. I got elbowed in the jaw and undercut on layups and dunks, hitting the concrete floor on several occasions. One guy squeezed my balls as I jumped for a rebound. This was turning into ice hockey and the referee refused to or could not control the game. He was either blind or dating someone on the South Boston squad. It was time to end this child's play.

As the guy who had just mangled my testicles crossed half court, I tripped him while pushing him to the floor with my left hand for more impact. His hard, abrupt landing could be heard in the stands. I made sure the incident looked like a complete accident, a picture of innocence offering to help him up. He refused my helping hand and got up to challenge me with raised fists, mumbling some gibberish in a thick Irish brogue.

I seized the guy up quickly—not bad, about 230 pounds, six feet four, a few ugly tattoos and fairly bulky arms lacking muscular definition; probably slow, a brawler rather than a boxer, no doubt the class bully in high school who now drank too much beer. In all street fights, making the first move is critically important. If you seem distracted or unprepared, you are more likely to connect a stiff surprise knuckle punch to your opponent's larynx, literally leaving him speechless and breathless.

But this was the Fidelity corporate basketball league. I simply couldn't be seen as the instigator. It could affect my career prospects and therefore the net present value of my future lifetime earnings. I needed him to make the first move. "Aggravate him, get him to commit but do not throw the first punch, stay calm," I said to myself. While I faced him off, I told him quietly and resolutely he better pick up his pink redundancy slip in the mail tonight. This guy was clearly pissed off but not quite ready to rumble. "Almost there," I thought. "How did it feel when the ref fucked you up the ass before the game, flamer?" He was visibly struggling now. I gave it another shot. "Dude, are you going to hit me," I said, pointing at my chin, "or are you going to go home to mommy and cry like a little bitch?"

Involving mom in these discussions almost always works with Latinos and hard core Catholics. The pride of the St Patrick's Day parade took this apelike, telephoned roundhouse swing to take me out. As a seasoned pugilist, while his fist moved slowly towards my head I could not help thinking "How slow can one human being hit another?" As this whaler of a punch passed by in ultra-slow motion, I ducked into him, compacting my power from my ankles, through my calves, into my thighs, stomach and back muscles, chest, arms and fist, connecting two lefts to his forehead and cheek and landing a cracking right uppercut to his soft chin. The connection was profound, but this guy was still standing. My hand was reverberating from the impact. He raised his hands to fight, mumbling, "Is that all you got, faggot?"—and then slowly tipped backwards to the floor.

The idea of annihilating one guy in a few seconds and hoping that this will deter his buddies from mauling you only works in the Harvard Law School basketball league and in Eddy Murphy movies. Experienced bruisers and combatants are very rational at what they do best: messing people up. As long as the odds are in their favor, they will do what it takes to complete the job. They are not easily impressed by superior one-man pugilism. Unlike in the movies, where they line up orderly to take shots at Bruce Lee, nobody here was waiting their turn. Four bulky Southies collapsed on me simultaneously, willing and able to inflict permanent damage.

I felt somebody grabbing my hair trying to introduce my face to the cement floor. Sucker punches were landing on the side and back of my head. I did not like the idea of concussion, a broken nose and jawbone. I was even less enamored by reconstructive facial surgery. Somehow I got hold of the guy's arm trying to flatten my face and bit into it like a bull shark on crystal meth. God was with me as my teeth easily tore through the skin and hit an artery, albeit a small one. I had remnants of his hairy skin, meat and blood in my mouth as I noted this small fountain of red shoot up about four feet in the air. It was difficult to miss as the blood started landing on some of his friends piled on top of me as well. This stalled the action for a split second and I desperately looked to my teammates, hoping for reinforcements.

Fat chance. These guys were on the sidelines, biting their fingernails and literally shaking. They had never been that close to naked violence in their entire sheltered lives. I knew home girls in East Harlem with bigger balls than those sea cucumbers. I rammed my head under one guy's chin causing a nasty crack, but I knew I was done for. I could not keep getting lucky with about 1,000 pounds of Irish republican aggression thundering down on top of me. "See you in surgery," I thought to myself.

Then Frank had a flashback to his old rowdy football days in Texas. Frank was top fit then, able to bench-press over 300 pounds. He was probably on steroids too. He also had a very useful deviant streak. He left the geek squad on the tramlines and started tearing bodies off me. Even the referee had recovered his sense of duty and was helping Frank restore order. With bloodstains all over the floor and Frank in on the action, the Southies were recovering their wits. Even Saint Patrick was getting up from his heap of misery. He seemed dazed but generally intact. Somebody stopped the blood gushing from the guy's arm with a towel and rushed him to the hospital. We were declared winners by default as we were ahead by a few points when the fight broke out. I had timed it well.

My reputation at Fidelity as a pugilist was firmly established. Some colleagues refused to look at me directly, obviously intimidated, fearing I might sucker punch them if they disagreed with me. Others were noticeably impressed and approved my audacious self-defense. A few days later, I saw Saint Patrick in the elevator. He had not been fired. I was glad for him—he wasn't really a bad man, just a mid-level bully who ran into the wrong guy on the wrong night. But I couldn't help cracking up looking at the three table-tennis-ball-size welts on his face.

*

This was not the only intense interaction I had with someone of Irish ancestry at this time. After I had been at Fidelity for a about a year, I met Susan Elaine Devine.

I had previously been engaged to three women. One was a hot mulatto model, who proposed over a nasty curry in her flat in London; another was Lynne Perry, who told me it was about time to get married and I disagreed; the last was Colette Creppel, whose parents had ceremoniously announced our engagement to several hundred of their closest friends at a New Year's party at the New Orleans' landmark Columns Hotel, which they owned. The problem was that neither of us had proposed, and in fact had never even discussed marriage. I liked the Creppels. They were just trying to egg me on in their charming Southern way.

I suffered from profound difficulties with commitment and monogamous lifetime attachment. Oscar Wilde said—and I thought there was much truth in it—, "One should always be in love. That is the reason one should never marry." Being a "Fidelity" man during the day was vaguely comical, given the fact that I didn't believe in the concept. There was too much empirical evidence that showed high-status males had multiple wives or additional mating opportunities in the ancestral environment. I was not going to put up too much of a fight against what comes naturally to many men: multiple sexual partners. It comes naturally to some women too, of course. My mother had set a fine example and taught me well.

Regardless, numerous superficial sexual relations were leaving me increasingly hollow, and I began to define what I was looking for. Most men devote more thought and energy to their car purchases than evaluating their future wife. Not me, I am the *Überflieger*, the self-declared over-achieving master of mental masturbation and extrospection. I devised a multiple-dimensional matrix analysis of the perfect wife during working hours at Fidelity, with formulae and outcomes based on age, looks, intelligence, humor, strength, wealth, maternal qualities and so on.

She would have to be European and Latin at the same time. European women generally have more class but overcomplicate things and take themselves too seriously, while Latinas are warmer and know how to have fun. She needed to speak at least four languages. I could not imagine myself touring the world with someone who needed to have the menus translated wherever we went. Of course, she had to be strong, kind and patient. She would need a sense of fatalistic humor to tolerate me on my dark days. She needed to be happy with herself because I was certainly not planning to spend too much time at home. I would prefer a sole inheritor with an unrestricted trust fund and a large future inheritance. Of course, she had to love me more than herself and be eternally faithful.

My ever-growing matrix and regression computation produced an R-squared above 80 percent. All I had to do was to find and seduce someone who matched my modest selection variables.

I met Susan at a cheesy Boston nightclub called Zanzibar. It was a sad Tuesday night and the Daughters of the American Revolution were holding some sort of outing. Unaware of the dress code (suit and tie) I was wearing a short-sleeved shirt with "DOO-DOO" (a truncated Shakespeare quote) written on the front in large letters. I was reasonably tanned from a short vacation in Bermuda and looked seriously out of place among the pasty, chalk-white New Englanders. Scouring the scene, I observed nothing but seriously overweight fake blondes with black turtleneck sweaters and pearl necklaces.

Resigning myself to solitary confinement for the night, I then noticed this slim and shapely five-foot-eight sensation at the other side of the dance floor. She was wearing a tight black all-body outfit and a shiny leather belt tightly strapped around her slim waist (this was the late eighties, let's not forget). She also had a gorgeous face with prominent cheekbones, a cute sexy mouth and stand-up tits. She obviously had rhythm because those hips were moving just fine with the music. Her hair was dark auburn and she had sparkling and penetrating blue eyes. And she was not wearing a single fucking pearl, thank God!

Susan was obviously there with some balding guy, who was grabbing her elbow as if she was his misbehaving seven-year-old daughter. As I contemplated how to drag her away from this gnome, our eyes met across the dance floor. We connected. I smiled. Susan smirked when she realized I understood her predicament. Then she drew her head back in laughter just enough for me to observe her perfect, aristocratic, ceramic neck. She turned towards me, elegantly removing her suitor's elbow grasp, assessing me, and granted me an approving, all-knowing nod.

I took a deep breath and fought my way past Baldy and half a dozen asexual, pale-faced Waspy admirers. I approached her and asked her, in perfectly pronounced Portuguese, "*Gostaria uma Caipirinha?*" (Would you like a Caipirinha?) She looked slightly intrigued and responded, "*Sim, por favor.*" I had noticed her authentic samba moves on the dance floor. The Daughters of the American Revolution were unable to move those body parts like that. She would obviously know the Brazilian national drink and welcome a change of companionship.

The gamble had paid off and I had broken the ice. When she told me her last name, though, I laughed. Who on earth had a name like Divine? Nobody.

She was making fun of me, I thought. I simply did not know that Devine is a very common Irish name. She was slightly taken aback, much more used to responses such as "Well, your name really suits you." She was clearly thinking "What planet are you from?" but was also sufficiently intrigued to tell me where she worked, although not so much as to give me her number. "Not great, but doable," I said to myself after she left. I like a little fight. It turned out the woman had principles. It took more than two dates to get her to commit.

She was twenty-six, barely younger than me, and still lived with her parents. She was relatively virginal, but she was not ten years my junior nor did she have a decent investment account, let alone a trust fund. I spent more money buying cigars in a year than the value of her cute antique collection or her yearly salary. However, she more than fitted the bill on most of the other criteria. The European ancestry was twinned with Brazilian charm—hence the authentic samba moves—which was the perfect cocktail of sensibilities as per my matrix. I was in love with Susan, my angelic opposite. And she was in love with the bad boy, the enterprising and entertaining rogue. We were married six months later in Gruyeres, Switzerland.

While her dowry and trust fund were non-existent, she more than made up for it by helping me accumulate great wealth. She also became my sounding board and moral compass keeping me out of trouble most of the time. When I became a European partner of legendary investment firm Jonathan & White, Susan was holding down about three jobs at the European operation at once. She not only helped me build this operation, in which I was a minority partner. Later she helped me build Value Management and Research AG into an international $500 million stock-exchange-listed capital markets group. We complemented each other superbly, had two great children, many dogs, and were soul mates for almost twenty years. Susan was my best deal ever and in retrospect the only which really mattered. Necko himself, a consummate judge of a deal, said to me that even I, a reckless and mindless Casanova, had for once made a wise decision. She was inherently cheerful, *bien dans sa peau* as the French say, and could easily laugh at herself and ridicule me even better. I loved that woman within the constraints of my emotional straightjacket. The gods were kind to me. I was almost happy.

She also aged ridiculously well and looked easily a decade younger than her actual age. I had never included "benign aging ability" as a determining variable in my matrix analysis—I was only using the absolute age parameter. I could have kicked myself. Analysis is a tedious task, and the results can always be improved. It is easy to make mistakes. Live and learn.

*

Overall, Fidelity was an enriching experience as fidelity. My Broadcast and Media Fund was rated the number one select mutual fund by Lipper in 1988, and outperformed its benchmark by ridiculous margins under my management.

The focus of Peter Lynch was something to behold. He was habitually in the office on Saturdays, his theory being that every time he came in at the weekend he would have a little bit more of an edge over anyone who didn't, and if you multiply that over twenty-five, thirty years, you have a serious competitive advantage. I remember one Saturday I was in the elevator with him and another famous manager, who also had an illustrious career and was Lynch's assistant, Jeff Vinik. Jeff was carrying all these gifts, and Lynch said to him, in his strange faltering way, "Uh, Jeff, are these all the, uh, Christmas gifts that you didn't, er, take home from the office yet?"

"No, they're my wedding gifts from colleagues," said Jeff.

"Oh, uh, I didn't know you got married," replied Lynch. These guys had been sitting next to each other for fourteen hours a day for years.

"Peter, you were invited."

Fidelity Boston offered a steep learning curve. Twenty percent of the managers were not only brainy but also hard-working. And the brightest people all seemed to be remarkably strange. One extreme introvert had been a mail chess champion. Another was an amateur, ultra bulky weightlifter. One manager's principal aim was to go to rabbinical school. The nerd factor was very high and as a womanizing European playboy, I was as strange and out of place as anybody there. But if you could deal with all the oddities and had eyes and ears you had to learn a lot. Nothing even remotely comparable to Fidelity existed in Europe or Asia at the time.

After two years in Boston, I spent 1989 and 1990 in the London office. London had mutated into the undisputed epicenter of European financial power and creativity, albeit still New York's little sister on the global stage. The London office had one intensely bright man, Anthony Bolton, who ran Fidelity's Special Situation Fund with such success from 1979 for nearly thirty years that towards the end of his stewardship it had to be split because it had become so big, potentially too big to continue to be successful. General consensus has it that he is the most gifted UK investor of his generation. What I got from Bolton was something of his analytical insight into how to dissect European accounting.

The problem with London, though, was that once you took Bolton out of the equation, you had a hell of a time trying to find the next really bright star. There was too much pretense and conformism there to cultivate world-class investment talent. The Fidelity London people were *long* on form and very *short* on content, the exact opposite of the Boston weirdo geniuses.

Nevertheless, I was within the light cast by the brightest and most controversial of them, and I was enjoying London a lot because the entrepreneurial scene and the players were no longer so blue blood. The days when the partners' rooms at Cazenoves or Barings were Shangri-La were dead and buried. You could smell the dust in there, and thank God, there were more Cockneys, Jews and foreigners in the City than ever. I had a big problem of content as well as form with the clubby old-school crowd. There was an element of blue blood in my own genes, but I didn't give a shit about that in the way these dinosaurs did. Is it important to the deal who your daddy was or where you went to school, what clubs you belong to and where you play golf or tennis? That is noise. It distracts and it is a bloody waste of time and energy. How are you going to nail an all-important investment banking deal while you are sucking on your public-school tie? You think you got a chance against the new breed of ultra-aggressive, intensely focused, mega-mercantile, no bullshit, razor-sharp street-smart financiers? Cut the blue blood Ivy League/Oxbridge crap, get rid of the airs, and let's do business. Show me the money or go back to your dining club garden party.

Crucially, the fully mature Thatcher/Reagan axis was pumping so much power into money-hungry sharks feeding on both sides of the water that the old school knew they were simply no longer agile enough. While the old farts sold out or retired, we were being given the right tools and an environment in which to use them recklessly. The major Wall Street sharks were using an army of lobbyists to dismantle the Glass-Steagall Act, a very reasonable piece of legislation, which separated commercial and private lending from investment banking. Capital adequacy requirements were constantly lowered to give the proprietary trading desks ever more flexibility and leverage to maximize short-term profits. Natural restraint, self-containment and ethical etiquette are alien attributes among sharks engaged in a feeding frenzy. We were *empowered by* a society and its elected politicians in love with spending, addicted to debt and single-mindedly focused on material values. It never occurred to us at the time that many of us would pay a high price for our recklessness, either financially or in terms of shattered families or both.

But Wall Street firms and their professionals were not the only ones to blame for the pursuant excesses and the most visible disasters of the last thirty years: the Savings and Loan crisis, the Internet bubble and the mortgage disaster. Government debt and payment obligations went from a net creditor position to $90 trillion in consolidated debt in four decades. Nobody forced US households to abandon all self-restraint and indulge in unlimited financial recklessness. Household debt increased to $14 trillion, or by 600 percent, between

1985 and 2007. During the same time the US household savings rate declined from 12 percent to negative. Meanwhile average household income adjusted for "real" inflation barely budged, even with the prominence of two parents working.

Beginning with Jimmy Carter, every single Republican or Democratic administration was altering or rigging the most critical economic indicators (inflation, GDP growth, unemployment, productivity, etc.) to make the economic situation appear far rosier than it actually was. Social security is a classic Ponzi scheme, and US government accounting is opaque, archaic, misleading and Enron-like. Without artificially low and manipulated inflation figures the US mortgage crisis could never have evolved into a full-scale global financial disaster.

America's most powerful special interest groups were easily as active as Wall Street in making the politicians dance to their tune. They were less visible but no less effective in screwing up America's economy, balance sheet and income statement while decimating the middle class.

The US National Security Complex has succeeded in engaging America in countless conflicts resulting in the greatest ever military, espionage and domestic security budgets, fifty percent greater than even during the Cold War. Reliable studies confirm 737 US military bases in 62 countries and the presence of US military personnel in 156 out of 193 countries around the world. The cost of the Iraq/Afghanistan wars is approaching $5 trillion, or $50,000 per American household. According to Chris Hellman of the National Priorities Project, the US National Security Complex spends at least $1.2 trillion a year. That is exactly how much the US federal government generated in total revenue in 2010, adjusted for Social Security and Medicare contributions. Not one dime is left to spend on anything else without incurring additional debt, deficits and payment obligations.

The law enforcement lobby has engaged America in a pointless $4-trillion war on drugs (another $40,000 per household) and generates incarceration levels unmatched by any other country on the globe. One in five Americans has a criminal record. Many states spend more on incarceration than on higher education.

Medical and healthcare costs have exceeded core price inflation every year for decades, primarily benefiting American doctors, healthcare providers and the pharmaceutical industry. Meanwhile Americans have become the most addicted people on earth consuming half of all drugs with only five percent of the global population.

The big food groups have benefited from sizable subsidies, as Americans became the most obese people on earth. Illogical, poorly structured agricultural subsidies have ended up encouraging unhealthy, addictive foods to be more affordable than healthy foods. Hyper-profitable oil majors were receiving government handouts. Even the left-leaning teacher unions have done their part in America's degeneration leading to absurd increases in the cost of private and public education well above the rate of inflation with no discernible improvements in math and language competency. College tuition costs have increased four times faster than core price inflation during the last decade alone. Are Americans turning into idiots, asks Professor and United Nations advisor Jeffrey Sachs, with the average American adult now spending 13 years in front of the television.

So Wall Street bankers and their professionals are not the only ones to blame for America's and the western world's financial misery, below average US educational standards and an increasingly second rate infrastructure. While the alleged culprits of the global crisis—commercial and investment bankers—are in rather poor financial shape and struggling, the big pharmaceutical, food, oil and defense companies have never been more profitable or cash-rich.

When the great bull market started in 1982, the new generation of financiers saw bountiful upside in upsetting the corporate gravy train on both sides of the Atlantic. The Establishment had become fat and stupid since the 1950s. Corporate overheads were absurd, companies were overstaffed at all levels, and managements were entrenched and complacent, supported by crony board members and left alone by sleepy shareholders.

Performance mattered very little, and as a consequence, profit margins and cash flow were pathetic. Our carving knifes were leveraged buyout financings, proxy fights, bridge financings, extraordinary shareholder meetings, controlling share blocks, little interference from regulators and very lax enforcement of any securities laws. The point was to own stakes in companies where a lot of fat could be shed, to produce higher profits leading to much higher share prices.

It was pure Darwinism. Only the fittest species would survive. This rule applied to companies, managers, investors and financiers. I was becoming increasingly voracious, tough and lithe. My knowledge was growing fast, and I had professional contact with energetic characters, players and hard-core operators like James Goldsmith, John Malone, the Barclay Brothers, Ted Turner, Jim Slater, Michael Green, Robert Maxwell and Tiny Rowland, who wanted me to look at their companies a) because I worked for Fidelity, and b) later because they felt I had something to offer. Big sharks often keep baby sharks by their side under close supervision, in case they want to bite Daddy's tail. Terry Smith, who wrote *Accounting for Growth* and exposed major British companies as accounting frauds, was a close contact at the time and a fantastic source for short-selling ideas.

However, I was increasingly uncomfortable with being told what to do or how to do it, and despite the fact that my learning curve was steep, I was always in search of a my own challenge, a battleground where I could apply my skills to maximum advantage. And a perennial problem of mine is that if I am not challenged, I move on. I struggle with authority and the authorities all my life. And where does a shark go? It goes where the fattest, unsuspecting fish are sitting without knowing what's going on, and where there are fewer other sharks. While the big sharks and their pilot fish were scouring the Anglo-Saxon markets for targets, continental Europe was largely ignored.

I knew the real music, at least for me, would play out on the Continent, which was truly still in the dark ages and still didn't have either an initial public offering (IPO) market or a NASDAQ (security dealers association), for instance. Short selling was in its infancy and hostile takeovers were simply not done. The analytical lessons learned from Peter Lynch about dissecting industries, and from Anthony Bolton about dissecting companies, would be incredibly valuable when applied here. And within Europe, German, Austrian and Swiss companies were the blinding opportunity because as well as being outrageously mispriced they were greatly undervalued relative to their global peers. In light of inevitable harmonization of shareholder structures, securities legislation and accounting conventions, these companies would not remain mispriced much longer. I wanted to go to the Continent to feed. There was very little competition. I resolved to become one of the biggest sharks in those quiet, well-stocked waters.

I ended up getting fired from Fidelity by Richard Trader, the London head of personnel, for running a fully registered parallel organization, an asset management company called Interinvest Ltd, while still an employee. Fortunately, I had seen that the discovery of this fact was a potential outcome, and to hedge my exposure I had already signed up to be senior vice president at an old private Jewish Swiss bank, Bank Julius Baer, with offices in Frankfurt.

Although the urge to set up on my own had been there since the age of about 18, I was also correct in the analysis of myself that I wasn't quite ready yet. There were a few more blocks to put into place, and when I did strike out, I wanted to take some serious clients with me—institutional clients and other fat tickets, who knew I'd be capable and who would walk with me. I wasn't going to start a company and struggle, just for the sake of starting a company. When I did it, I was going to fly from day one.

Peter Lynch wrote me a lengthy, extremely positive personal recommendation, which I would abuse intensely for institutional marketing purposes for the better part of the next fifteen years. That was obviously callous and insensitive. Thanks and sorry, Peter. "Trust me, it will not happen again."

I increased my compensation package by fifty percent, was a director rather than a lowly analyst and fund manager, scored a flashy metallic blue BMW 5 series and moved into a villa in the best neighborhood outside Frankfurt. I was just 30, and was excited to apply my state-of-the-art financial arsenal to the unsophisticated European markets. The strange accounting practices, the pathological aversion to rocking the boat, the tight and secretive alliances—these were all elements of continental business that I felt were not just conservative but backward, and I wanted to mess them up.

However, I had a tough time re-adapting to Germany, as all my Germanness comes out when I'm there. I get upset if the living room's in a mess, or nervous if somebody is late. It is such a highly regulated society that when the few of us who worked late left the office at midnight, say, we would be harassed by the police who thought we must have been robbing the place. One of my friends, AVP Michael Uhlemann, was reprimanded by the Worker's Union for working 60 to 70 hours per week. The Union's reasoning was that if Michael worked regular hours, the bank would have to hire another, unionized employee. This was not an especially shark-friendly environment.

While London and New York were booming and everyone wanted to be rich—and the richer you were, the better—in Germany the jealousy factor was big and a problem that simply didn't exist in the UK or the States at the time. I felt that very keenly, especially because I was one of the best-paid 30-year-olds in Germany and additionally had a fat bonus plan at Baer, which was uncommon at the time. I was the youngest guy in the best neighborhood on the best compensation package with a beautiful, cosmopolitan wife and a fancy new car. They hated me. They also hated me because it all came easily to me, and I found myself being undermined a lot by my colleagues.

The jealousy, spite and vindictiveness was of course annoying and quite wearing when you're trying to move at a good lick, but what was truly unpleasant was to see how the operation was run. Private banking is the nucleus of low-energy, amateur consensus idea flows. Bank Julius Baer wanted to be more than they were—they had cash coming out of their ears from their successful private management business, but they wanted to get into mergers and acquisitions, they wanted to be institutional, they wanted to get into research, and to try for all this was the reason they had the office in Frankfurt. They had brought me in as an international rising star to staff and develop the institutional asset-management side. They were carps wanting to be sharks.

In one sense it represented a much needed opportunity to practice real entrepreneurialism with no real downside, and the fund we ran immediately shot up to become the best European equity fund—not only because we ran it extremely well, but also because the competition was poor. A vital component of the success was the fact that I hired Kevin Devine, Susan's older brother, to come and help me build a brand new computer program that would provide revolutionary analysis and remarkably accurate predictions.

Kevin was a genius. He had received perfect SAT, GMAT and MCAT scores, graduated from Dartmouth, attended Harvard Medical School and received his MBA from Stanford Business School. That's not just smart. Three decades ago that was one in a million smart. I had rescued him from a dead-end geek job at Hewlett Packard in Paris. He was also my best friend (until he married my brother's ex-wife Ute). He and I were the perfect combination: the cerebral but distracted professor and the focused, street-smart capitalist. Kevin could translate my analytical concepts into highly functional and effective investment software programs. Besides being a genius, Kevin was also a world-class programmer. Like his sister, Kevin was deeply religious, and unlike me he could differentiate right from wrong. We made a superb team.

We harmonized the different accounting languages across Europe years ahead of the pack. The concept was both simple and revolutionary. It was also incredibly challenging to execute. At the time, every European country had its own accounting standards. The English would significantly overstate their earnings in their published accounts, whereas German and Swiss companies would basically present ultra-conservative tax returns to their shareholders, dramatically understating their profitability. Translating Lufthansa's accounts to UK accounting standards would produce a price to earnings ratio of three, and translating British Airway's accounts to German accounting standards would show a loss.

Creating software that would find its way through all these different accounting conventions focusing on cash flow and hard assets would give you an in -depth, reliable understanding of relative value and appeal across European companies and industries. This analysis would not only allow you to identify the best, hidden European equity values, it would also be a starting point for identifying the best short-sale candidates by finding those companies that were overstating their earnings with accounting gimmicks. What made this exercise even more relevant was that European accounting standards would certainly be harmonizing over the coming decade. As a consequence, investors would be shifting more money into the undervalued companies while reducing their exposure in the more overvalued ones promising outsized capital gains. We already knew tomorrow's winners and losers today. All we had to do was position our portfolios accordingly.

Most valuation analysis fails to get beyond the most simplistic price/earnings formula—what do I care about that? That's useless. What I wanted to know when I looked at a company was how has it behaved over the last hundred years, in what range, does that help me predict its future share price, does that help me find the point at which I want to own it? It is all about cheap entry. I wanted to find the rare nuggets in this seemingly limitless analytical field that would make me rich.

Another radical piece of investment software Kevin and I developed was based on the simple theory that company and market valuations trade within relatively predictable bandwidths. For example, over the last fifty years the US market had traded between one and three times replacement value. The German market consistently traded between two and five times cash flow, whereas the UK market would typically trade on a dividend yield range of 3 to 7 percent. When valuations approached upper and lower quintiles, you needed to position yourself on the short or the long side.

I had developed such a valuation model for the shipping industry while at Fidelity. In the mid-1980s, shipping companies were trading at two times cash flow and 50 percent of liquidation value. Their historical range had been between 1.6 times and 7 times cash flow, and between 0.4 times to 1.7 times liquidation value. Not only were the actual operating cash flows depressed, the whole sector was trading at low historical levels and a steep discount to replacement value. What would happen if the cash flows recovered and the cash flow multiples expanded as well? This sector would easily appreciate 500 to 1,000 percent in a few years.

I had got this point across to Peter Lynch and a few other fund managers at Fidelity and the firm went from having virtually zero exposure to owning hundreds of millions in shipping assets. We owned material stakes in the sector as the group returned to investor favor. The companies appreciated on average 620 percent over a three-year period and I looked smart. Peter was even smarter. He got in at the bottom in 1987 and 1988 when everybody hated the sector. He started phasing out his positions in 1989 and was gone by 1990 when all the usual lemmings were falling over each other to buy the more profitable but by now overvalued shipping companies. Peter used the market's euphoria and exited the sector completely, realizing hundreds of millions of dollars in profits for his investors.

Kevin and I ended up with state-of-the-art intellectual databases, which gave us a grade-A competitive lead. Today, investment professionals call this discipline "valuation based range trading." When we developed the concept, no one had even heard of what we were doing, let alone given it a name. We had found the Golden Fleece. Word got around, and the valuation characteristics that we developed were eventually taken over by UBS Warburg for all their pan-European research. M&G, the number one UK unit trust house, offered us £1 million for the program, a handy sum in 1995. Kevin and I looked at each other and said "Naaah," and politely turned them down. It was worth so much more if you knew how to use it right, and it would make both of us serious multimillionaires in the coming five years. Still, it was flattering to have the interest.

Culturally, Baer was clearly at odds with such an innovative, high-end analytical methodology, because to some degree our approach was born out of an irreverent base that demanded lateral thought and whose mantra was "assume nothing, doubt everything." I was absolutely the wrong person to work for a Swiss, ultra-conservative family-owned bank. It was as though Barings had hired Hunter S. Thompson to write their market reports. I barely lasted two years there. What really pissed me off was how clueless these guys were about basic equity investing. I had gone from eager student to teacher, so my benefits in terms of experience and knowledge acquisition were nil. My learning curve was flatter than the Utah salt plains and I did not like it. Why would I hang around? It felt like a big part of me was dying, not blossoming.

Something else in me was also on the point of dying. These years were the last of Necko's life, and in fact he became surprisingly human and lightened up considerably as he mutated into a Nice Old Man. His business had been sold years before and the Deutsche Sporthilfe was no longer managed by him. To the dismay of the sycophant bystanders, my mother Uschi and he became very close, and he supported her against my father during their separation process. He was her greatest ally during the divorce. He developed a sense of self-irony and would laugh freely from the heart. Who says old dogs can't learn new tricks? I guess there was little left to achieve and he had finally allowed himself the time to deliberate. My own deliberations, after my exit from finance later in life, would also make me a more giving, more humorous man.

Necko taught me to leave excuses for the losers and to assume responsibility for my own destiny. We are what we do and we can be whatever we want. Life is far too short to spend contemplating all the misery you may have suffered at the hands of others. "Get a life, do something else, grow a beard, but for Christ's sake stop moaning" became one of my favorite lines.

I remember him taking on a walk with Susan and me in the park near his home on a lovely Saturday afternoon. We passed a young couple walking their dog. They greeted us with a nod, as was normal in a small tightknit community. To my surprise, Necko went over to them, shook their hands warmly and engaged them in a conversation. This went too far. The couple looked perplexed. They had no idea who this strange old man was. Necko thought they had recognized him. I thought to myself, "If I ever get famous, God, please shoot me if I start believing everybody knows and recognizes me." But it was a sunny day and everybody had the right to be a fool, especially a charming old peacock like Necko, who had accomplished so much during his life.

He did not want me to see him on his deathbed. He wanted to be remembered as a conqueror, not as a defeated old man on his last legs. He died of lung cancer in January 1992. His funeral was attended by 20,000 mourners, including Chancellor Helmut Kohl, and countless other celebrities. It was a wet, miserable day. The "Ave Maria" requiem was overpowering. I cried like a young dog that had lost his master.

The cheap shit, however, left me nothing. In his defense, his oldest son Peter was handling the disbursements, but to have delegated the responsibility to his avaricious son was meek. Maria, his loving caretaker for two decades, was also stiffed, escorted me to Necko's basement where the unwanted and unsalable items were stored. There, like a common thief, I scored two plant pots and an engraved silver cigarette case from some equestrian tournament to remember him by.

That day I resolved to accelerate my career. I was sure I would never inherit a dime. My fortune would be greater than Necko's, I swore to myself. There was no upside in divulging my master plan to anybody, not even my closest friends and family. Only Susan had a vague idea where the trip was heading: right to the league table of the richest Germans. Besides, it was no one's business but my own. Actions define men, not words. The game had begun and nobody was going to stop me. I would become an unmitigated success even if it meant collateral damage along the way. Achieving love and happiness was an elusive, abstract concept. I had not seen it anywhere in my world. I had no idea what it looked or felt like, so why strive for it? That left money and power to aim for. The fast ride to the edge of the cliff had begun. I felt sure that when I got there, I'd be flying.

Financially things were heading in the right direction. My offshore bank accounts had ballooned to several million dollars—not bad for an employee in his early thirties. I had a house in the top suburb of Frankfurt, a townhouse in Cambridge, an apartment in New York City, seven rental apartments and a beach house in the Médoc and a multimillion-dollar off-shore bank account. Susan had no idea that we were already fairly loaded. She thought we were struggling with barely enough cash to cover the monthly bills. She was driving this ancient Fiat Panda. When it snowed, the flakes came in through the air vents, and if you looked closely, you could see the road under your feet. Surprisingly I was monogamous for the first time in my life largely due to Susan's emotional brilliance. Meanwhile Kevin was keeping me on the straight and narrow path at work.

At that time I did not have the faintest idea how ridiculous my wealth maximization actions were. I was praying to the god of money 24/7. When I was not making money, I was saving it. I was whining about excessive telephone charges resulting from constant overseas calls to her mother in the States and told her we might even have to get rid of the maid (who only came once a week) if we could not control our expenses. Yeah, I was a little man but we ran a tight ship. I needed that capital to grow. I could not let her waste it on phone therapy sessions with her mother, because I rarely showed up at home before ten in the evening and usually worked on weekends. Plus, digging into working capital rather than living off the interest and dividends would be both unforgivable and unprofessional for an aspiring tycoon. My plan was to spend three to five more years as an employee and then take my performance record and reputation as a capable, seasoned moneymaker—and some juicy clients—to start my own asset management operation. It did not quite work out that way.

I stayed in Frankfurt and moved up to an equity stake in the European operations at my next employer, Jonathan & White, where I was a minority partner. They were based in New York but had large European exposures. These guys ate, drank and breathed security analysis and "value investing," the principles of which underpinned every fund they had. They were the real masters of discount shopping, the direct descendants of the father of value investing, Professor Benjamin Graham, the so-called "Dean of Wall Street," who had begun teaching it at Columbia Business School in the late 1920s. Warren Buffett, one of Graham's disciples, applied the same paradigm on a grand scale to become at one point the richest person in the world. I was learning again, but what I learned about value investing was that although to some extent it appealed to my mind, it certainly did not suit me temperamentally.

Properly applied, no other equity investment technique will produce more superior, risk-adjusted investment returns over the long term. Although less than 10 percent of investment managers apply the technique with discipline, rigor and consistency, those who do will not only experience above average capital appreciation, but they will also have a fair amount of free time on their hands.

And this is where I had a strictly personal problem with value investing: I am a hyperactive nut case and at best marginally sane. As a consequence, I get bored easily. I need constant adrenalin shots to stay amused. Value managers are typically even-keeled people, who make terrible jokes like the partners at Jonathan & White. They barely have a pulse and are neither greedy nor fearful. They possibly lack emotional depth and are all about intrinsic value, free cash flow yields, low price earnings to earnings growth ratios for the more audacious, relative bond and dividend yields, sum of the parts values, and so on. Value investing is a lot like contra-cyclical bottom fishing in commercial property—an undemanding discipline. This is not quantum physics or fuzzy logic. If you do it long enough, it can actually become rather dull while you will become progressively richer.

I had always been the odd man out in capital markets, prop trading, hedge fund management and securities analysis. I am not Armenian, Lebanese, Indian, Chinese or from London's East End. I am not five foot six, I do not come from Brooklyn, and I do not have dark curly hair and close-set eyes.

Fortunately, there were many ways to make money that are better suited to my aggressive, wired and impatient nature. I needed higher returns faster. I couldn't wait four years to cash in on a position. I needed numerical satisfaction, the quicker the better. I needed the rush in my brain and my wallet in order to feel alive. One such technique was activist investing.

I had been at Jonathan & White two years when, true to form, I was raiding a cash- and asset-rich baby-food producer with a wide-open shareholder structure—the perfect asset-stripping candidate. An upside of 100 to 200 percent was virtually assured in six to nine months if one caused enough trouble. Galactina AG (later Asclia AG—they changed their name, paid big dividends and the share price tripled) had much more cash than its market value, valuable land holdings and other hidden assets. All these were listed on the balance sheet for one Swiss franc *pro memoria*. This was to make sure the company did not forget they owned them because these assets had all been written down to zero to optimize taxes. All you had to do was to accumulate a sizable position and then expose this ultra-conservative, asset-rich company to investors, and you would be rich. You would be even richer if you managed to carve it up and sell the parts. This was the consummate no-brainer.

I gained control of 35 percent of the outstanding shares with several accomplices and had come into the possession of some very useful and highly sensitive information. An extensive internal study revealed management was deliberately misleading investors about the company's true worth and cash flow because they were planning to take it private themselves. Another document showed that one board member had been paid 700,000 Swiss francs for a high-school quality, handwritten, five-page report. I immediately sent these documents to my connections in the Swiss media to enhance my bargaining position and attract other investors to support my cause. One major Swiss financial paper published the evidence. The media reaction was surprisingly positive for once. For once, I was the good guy exposing abusive management practices within the Swiss Establishment, and most journalists sided with me.

However, the media ruckus got totally out of control. My mug shot was all over the place. My senior partners did agree with the investment, but scolded me for making my moves without informing them at every twist and turn. They were getting requests for newspaper interviews and had no clue what was going on. Moreover, Jonathan & White was managing material funds for other Swiss public companies. One such outfit, an equally opaque and undervalued potential target, asked them "whether Homm is going to ambush us next." Most if not all of my senior partners hated being surprised and upstaged by one of their juniors.

Neither Jonathan nor White was amused. I got fired for all the usual reasons (lack of communication and coordination, not following etiquette, too "rogue," conflicts of interest ...). Because I had only been there for two years, I was not able to walk away with more than a few clients: a giant food company, a major publisher, and the scion of a famous Viennese medical family. I also had not had enough time to set up a corporate structure for my new company, or to recruit talented traders and analysts. I was nevertheless an extremely strong swimmer now, and was pumped up to get in the pool by myself and make a big splash.

There was another reason why I felt a sense of urgency to swim on my own. For some reason, which I never got to the bottom of, I had always believed that I would die aged 50 and that everything—*everything*—had to have been tasted and achieved by then. If you take the length of that working life as running between the ages of 18 and 50, then the simple computation was that in 1993 I was precisely halfway down the road towards the darkness which had only very recently enveloped Necko. It was time to make a real fortune. Fast.

Additionally there was a fear of monotony, of becoming stale, to some degree precisely because I had several million in the bank and could have stopped then and there. When you stop learning you stop moving, and that's a sort of death. If your lights are on, you stay young, and you stay even younger if the lights in your heart are on. Of course, the hard part is the "heart" part. My heart was single mindedly focused on Susan and to a lesser extent on Kevin and my mad sister. I was still fixated on the trip, and although some of the better emotional things in life were beginning to be crowded out because of that fixation, it hadn't yet got to the point of chronic value disintegration. I was experiencing character slippage and was moving ever faster away from the boy who fed the deer in the forests outside Oberursel, but I believed I was still a safe distance from the edge.

If all that hadn't persuaded me that the day had arrived when I could at last go marauding, then the logic of a final reason was perfectly irrefutable. When you have been fired more than once for non-conformism rather than for poor performance, you need to be your own boss. If you're going to work for an asshole, it might as well be yourself.

My newly-wed mother and father

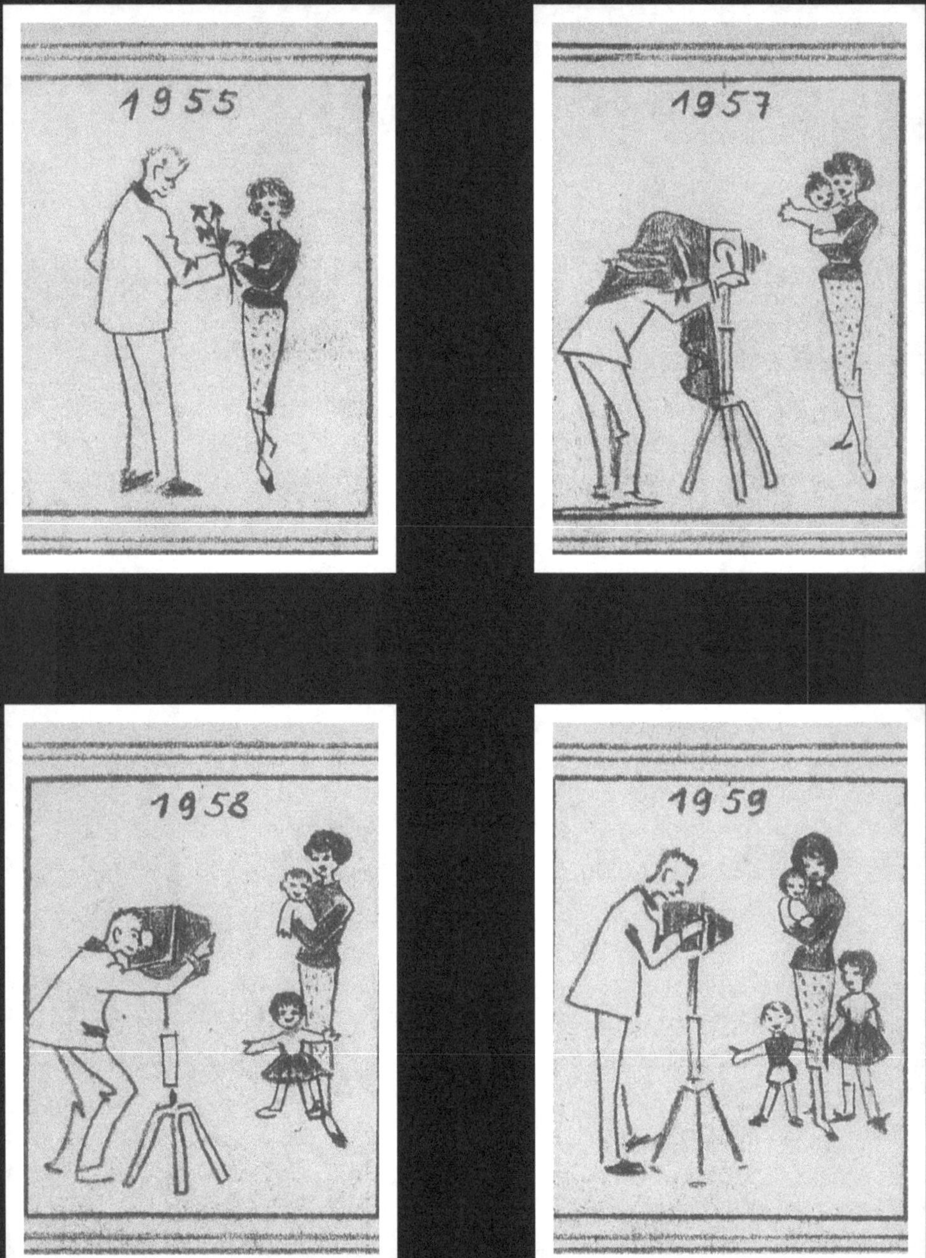

My birth announcement, drawn by my mother

Me, at the tender age of 16

The beginning of a great passion

My Comp Card, 1979

Toronto, Canada, May 1977

Graduating from Harvard

My first office

Wedding with my wife Susan

Christening of my son Conrad in the Catholic church in Königstein

Can Girasol, Palma de Mallorca

The Homm familiy at a family reunion at Kronberg Castle

Me and Oskar Lafontaine (former Minister President of the state of Saarland) on the "Sabine Christiansen" talk show

Me, as major shareholder of the soccer club Borussia Dortmund

Borussia Dortmund stockholders' meeting, national league season 04/05

Me and Howard Marks, famed for being the biggest cannabis dealer in the 1970s and 1980s and author of the best-selling biography *Mr. Nice*

Inauguration day and art exhibition of the primary school of the
Liberia Renaissance Foundation, which I support

Welcome to Duazon, Liberia

Part III
Cruising

6. Adventure Capitalism

Entrepreneurs are simply those who understand that there is little difference between obstacle and opportunity and are able to turn both to their advantage.
Niccolo Machiavelli

I named the new company Value Management and Research (VMR) after Fidelity Management and Research, my former employer. It sounded virtuous, sincere, professional and trustworthy. In short, all the things I was not. It was a market-penetration vehicle, and very much a pioneering venture. There was a hedge fund element at a time when there were only about twenty hedge funds in the whole of Europe, and none of them was managed from Germany. Pioneering is fun.

VMR started in my billiard room, mainly to keep overheads low early on, but also because I can't stand commuting, which I regard as inhumane and a pure waste of time. We soon moved into a top-floor office in the lovely medieval town of Königstein, at the foot of the Taunus mountains near Frankfurt. It had a sweeping view of the castle from out of the cathedral sized window, and a sobering perspective of the porno video store and loan shark's office downstairs. We squeezed eight employees into 700 square feet, but within five years we were employing over 100 capital market professionals in the Frankfurt headquarters alone. Our international investment-banking group, with offices in Madrid, Luxembourg and Los Angeles, was now managed from a very posh and respectable ultra-modern office building, which we shared with Dow Chemical. We owned our own stock-exchange-listed highly profitable bank in Munich.

Initially, my wife Susan was running the fund accounting, operations and office administration functions. Her efficiency and hard work did wonders for our profit margins. That way she compensated for her non-existent trust fund. In 1994 she was replaced with three full timers as she was eight months pregnant with our son Conrad. Her brother Kevin, after having been my number two at Baer and also a minority partner at Jonathan & White like me, became an equal partner in the firm upon arrival. He lived with Susan and me for almost a year before he bought his own house on the same street.

Kevin wrote first-rate software and sourced state-of-the-art hardware to handle all the computations. I was useless at programming but a creative project designer. We tested sixty-nine financial variables across 5,000 companies, in seventeen countries and in twenty-eight sectors, using our proprietary valuation models. Our computer speed- and memory requirements were immense. Our aim was to identify which factors would show the highest correlation to share price performance. Once those factors had been identified, we would determine at which range valuation you needed to own or short a given company, sector or market. We would back test the data sets intensely to identify the most reliable correlations and valuation triggers and to avoid qualitative and quantitative errors in our models. This was all about probability and anti-cyclical investment behavior. The results were outstanding. These systems allowed you to find the perfect parameters, which would tell you when and at which price to buy a company, a sector and sometimes an entire market. As these got better and better, all our long-only funds rocked and received numerous awards—best European pension fund for three years, best European equity fund, best Germany fund, and so on. Our assets under management grew exponentially. The systems were less reliable and accurate for identifying over-valuation, especially selling short growth companies.

To gain an extra edge in hedge fund management, I had also invented something called "competitive verification" in the late 1980s. The philosophy behind CV was based on the fact that CEOs and CFOs lie much of the time. When they are not lying, they have no idea why their business is performing, and nor do they have any clue what challenges they might face in the future. The standard company visit or CEO contact is totally overrated and often a waste of time.

Much more could be learned by dissecting subsidiary company filings, monitoring insider sales, getting useful hints from competitors, customers, employees and suppliers. The most important information could be sourced from antagonistic competitors, major customers, commercial lenders, former employees as well as esoteric trade publications nobody would read besides geeks like us. CV was all about snooping around the company and identifying real weaknesses and potential risks. Indeed, CV is very similar to the work performed by hardcore investigative journalists, ruthless consultants and industrial spies. Our operating philosophy was: go deep, don't trust anyone, do your own work and draw your own conclusions. Our best analysts were, without exception, all former investigative journalists. Digging up piles of dirt came natural to them.

Academically, CV is based on the teachings and publications of Michael Porter's *Competitive Strategy* and *Competitive Advantage*. Both books are absolutely required reading for anyone looking to manage a larger company. I had been on the board of directors with Professor Porter at the Harvard Cooperative Society for two years and watched him in action. His insights were mind-blowing. CV went further than Porter's approach, as we would use snitches, detectives and disgruntled employees with an axe to grind to get our competitive information edge. For some inexplicable reason, nobody had ever applied Porter's game-altering concepts to fundamental securities analysis or short selling in Europe in a highly structured manner. I was the first.

Another undeveloped element, and the biggest of all, was Germany's capital market, virgin territory for anyone looking for a feast. There were a lot of fat cows running around the yard with no guards and no fence. There was little or no financial regulation. Equity stakes only required disclosure once you passed the 25 percent ownership threshold (this figure was 5 percent in the US and 3 percent in the UK), insider-trading regulation was still in its infancy and the market for IPOs was virtually non-existent. There had been about eight IPOs on average during the previous ten years and the average company coming to the market was some low-growth industrial dinosaur averaging almost fifty years old.

Meanwhile in America, the average company going public was only five years old and there were hundreds of new issues each year. Research quality was dilettantish and superficial. Financial disclosure was opaque at best. German, Swiss and Austrian financial reports were similar to tax returns, often understating a company's true profitability. This gave you a plethora of buy candidates to choose from. The British tended to overstate their earnings providing numerous, easy short-selling targets. Many major companies did not have English language annual reports. Just understanding Italian, Portuguese or Spanish gave you a competitive edge. I saw Germany as one giant capital market opportunity. And the market was dirt-cheap after a very ugly, prolonged crash and the competitors were relatively clueless. The only real negative was my personal tax rate, just under 60 percent. I should have operated out of Zug in Switzerland like my client Señor Rico. I reckon I'll be smarter in another life.

Being a devout student of Machiavelli, I set everything in motion for maximum advantage. There were two competing organizations that wanted to dominate the market for growth stocks in Europe: Germany's Neuer Markt (new market) and EASDAQ, modeled on NASDAQ. Working both sides of the equation came natural to me.

NASDAQ was the largest market for share trading in public American and international growth companies in the world in the early 1990s. Microsoft, Google and Apple are all listed on NASDAQ. No equivalent or remotely similar structure existed in Europe at the time. Many European, Israeli and even Asian growth companies would list their shares on NASDAQ because American investors were vastly more sophisticated and familiar with investing in high growth, high technology companies than the stodgy Europeans.

Why did major European growth companies have to go to America to be funded? EASDAQ and the Neuer Markt wanted to keep growth companies at home and provide more local and regional access to risk capital. It would be much better and profitable for the European banking sector and investors if these attractive growth companies could be funded at home. The Neuer

Markt, EASDAQ and NASDAQ were consequently all competing to attract the most promising European growth companies.

Given my broad US capital markets experience, I was selected to join the Neuer Markt task force charged to define its rules and regulations. Meanwhile, VMR was a founding shareholder in, and I became a board member of, the body that oversaw the evolution of EASDAQ, so I had my hands in that pot too. I was the only person in Europe able to bet on both horses in a two-horse race, and since I did not have the faintest idea which venture would ultimately succeed, I did indeed place large bets on both horses. In fact, we even held a 50-percent stake in a US broker and dealer with extensive dealing and listing capabilities on NASDAQ. We were incredibly well positioned.

What followed is history. The Neuer Markt kicked ass, given Germany's mountain of wealth and insatiable virgin appetite for growth companies. EASDAQ faltered somewhere along the way as other European nations launched their own NASDAQs, but I didn't mind. We made money on it while it lasted, and much bigger money on the Neuer Markt. At the height of our power, we had more than a 10-percent market share in all IPOs in Germany. The list of future IPO candidates seemed endless. We were underwriters, placement agents, pre-IPO advisors, pre-IPO investors, PR service providers, research providers; you name it, we milked that cow every which way. The capital market activities were already highly profitable, but our information edge directly benefited fund returns, our private banking division, and boosted our proprietary trading profits.

There were dozens of companies going public every year and our research department was analyzing every single one of them. The imaginary Chinese wall between corporate finance and securities research was rather porous if not almost non-existent in Germany at the time. Insider regulation was still young and ineffective. Few operators were more connected than we were. Obviously, Neuer Markt regulation was progressive by German standards but still light years away from the strangling constrictions of the American securities markets. By advocating very light regulatory standards with minimal penalties,

I had made sure my investment decisions would not be restrained by stringent market manipulation and insider trading rules. Any reader who has experience of international finance at a sophisticated level will be wholly unsurprised by this strategy; any reader who has no experience of international finance should understand that beyond a certain level everyone operates in an area that is to some extent grey, with the black-and-white world of regulatory frameworks always one step behind.

In 1995 to 1996, I scored my first major public home run short selling and exposing Bremer Vulkan (BV), the largest German shipbuilding group, aptly named the Burning Mountain of Bremen (*Vulkan* is German for volcano). I did not "bust" BV as many analysts claimed. It of course blew up but I was only the messenger and prime financial beneficiary. The company had the most unintelligible financials of all time and prohibitive off-balance sheet debt, very much like the United States of America today. When you finished doing the numbers properly (which required going to dusty offices to collect data from subsidiaries), it became clear they were basically living off subsidies provided by the state of Bremen while their financial reports were designed quite imaginable. I concluded that BV was consistently teetering on the brink of insolvency. The next step was to verify the order outlook with their competitors. A major European rival confirmed that all Bremer Vulkan yards were without profitable orders and were now attempting to move from primitive, loss-making container-vessel construction into highly specialized cruise ships.

BV announced that they had won two sizable orders for cruise ships from Costa Crociere, another public company based in Genoa, Italy. We interviewed Costa Crociere and got lucky because the chief financial officer that day felt like talking. He had no idea we were planning a short raid on BV. What we learned about the contracts was awesome: if BV could not finish the vessels in time and to perfect specifications, the penalties were so onerous (1 billion Deutschmarks) that it would certainly bankrupt the entire BV group. The BV group had one impressive military unit, specializing in high-end marine vessels and technology. In the case of bankruptcy, this well-performing division would have to be sacrificed to satisfy creditors. Given the Italians had secured state guarantees, the state of Bremen would have to step in and pay them for any financial damages which BV itself could not manage, possibly triggering a crisis at the state level. The Italians were certain BV would incur heavy losses building these high-tech cruise ships but the cost of the vessels would be so low they could wait a while longer for delivery. We had found the mother lode of short selling: a bona fide bankruptcy candidate. Hundreds of thousands of shares sold at 100 Deutschmarks or more per share could be bought back for a few Deutschmarks in the future if the group went bust.

What was senior management at BV thinking? It was risking everything on one fatal management decision that committed them to building two vessels in an area in which they had no prior experience or expertise. Failure was certain and would mean wiping out a 108-year-old shipping tradition and would cost over 23,000 employees their jobs. The carnage for the subcontractors, many of whom would not get paid, could be even greater.

We went two levels deeper and checked with several cruise operators and competing vessel builders in Germany and Scandinavia. The consensus was the Italians were shrewd and would not lose money, but BV would never deliver the ships on time and on budget. We then made some perfunctory checks on the financial condition of Bremen, to verify whether the state government had a half a billion to a billion Deutschmarks lying round to shove into BV's coffers to keep them afloat. At the time, Bremen was in a terrible financial mess and would probably not be able to bail out BV via a cash injection, emergency loan, equity stake or debt/equity swap, if and when the fan started appropriating shit.

Finally, we hired informers and detectives who would keep us updated on the work in progress on the two Costa Crociere vessels. To no one's surprise in the industry, BV were botching up the Costa orders in grand style, yet financial investors did not yet have a clue. BV reported steady progress and profits obviously fudging the numbers. Quality issues, faulty designs, material shortages, all resulted in gargantuan cost overruns and major delays. At BV, screwing up was the norm, while getting things right the exception. We borrowed several hundred thousand shares and sold them at prices between 80 and 110 Deutschmarks. At the time, my former colleagues at Fidelity owned a whopping 12 percent of the capital, with Templeton Growth Fund owning almost 20 percent. Borrowing the shares via our prime broker in order to sell them was easy.

I also knew the guys biting their fingernails in the Fidelity corporate basketball-league did not have the stomach for heavy investigative work. They would prefer staying at the lush five-star Bremer Park Hotel and meeting with management in their executive offices. By contrast, I had got access to the shipyard posing as an American tourist and aspiring maritime engineer, and was hanging out with workmen at local dives to make useful contacts and source primary information. My front was credible. I got smashed on one occasion and talked German with a perfect American twang. I was knowledgeable enough about maritime engineering after being a shipping investor and containership owner for years. I was certainly no engineer, but I knew when to sidestep discussions that are more technical.

The Templeton and Fidelity "analysts" were buying into management's propaganda that the Costa orders would lead BV into a new era of heightened profitability and growth. This was going to be a dirty street brawl and the nerds had no expertise in this area. I even talked to Anthony Bolton and his poorly informed Germany analyst about BV to get him to sell his shares before the implosion. They did not believe me and declined to follow my advice. I had useless discussions with the Templeton analyst as well and mailed our research to all the fund managers there who owned BV shares.

Approximately 90 percent of people suffer from a normalcy bias or consensus syndrome. They also suffer from an authority complex. They naturally trust people in positions of power because they are followers rather than leaders themselves. They are naturally gullible, have never been taught and are unable to read between the lines. Most are blind believers in authority and never question the information they are fed. This is one of the reasons America gets away with shoddy archaic accounting practices, manipulated economic data, colossal deficits, mountains of unconsolidated debt and inflation-adjusted payment obligations. Look at Madoff: the warnings were ample and well documented, but the majority preferred to trust the stated figures, the auditors and those in control rather than trust information from competitors, clients, suppliers and employees. The same warning signs exist on US debt and the US dollar and entitlement obligations. Believing no one and forming your own opinion after diligent, multilevel, lateral research is one of the few surefire ways left to earn outlandish returns.

The vast majority will suffer dramatic losses rather than act on perfectly rational information and sound analysis. Fidelity and Templeton held on to most of their shares until the bitter end, losing hundreds of millions of Deutschmarks for their fund holders, preferring to trust a clueless management when they had first-rate investigative research at their fingertips.

Well, the money was not really lost. It had just gone from Templeton's and Fidelity's funds into our pockets. I did get several other less gullible major holders to reduce or sell their holdings and the share price pulverized within months.

At the height of this short squeeze, one mad retail investor publically offered, via several newspapers, a 100,000 Deutschmark reward to find the villain who was orchestrating the BV share-price demise. I called this lunatic to identify myself and collect the reward. I could easily prove to him that I was the guy he was looking for. I even volunteered our research. Needless to say, I never received the money even though I was fully entitled to it. I should have sued the bozo.

We made out like bandits buying back the shares at much lower prices well before the company formally declared bankruptcy. Timing was always an important consideration. The faster BV would crumble, the higher our annualized return. So we shared our insights with anybody who cared to listen. If you could make $20 million in either six months or two years, producing a return on investment of 200 percent and 50 percent respectively, which path of action would you choose? Would it not make perfect sense to pick up the phone and talk to a few shareholders like Templeton and Fidelity and to debrief a few lazy journalists? I was only doing what any investment professional was paid for: solid, in-depth research. Of course, I was a lot more proactive. It was only logical that I should get paid handsomely while others were sitting on their hands.

It turned out BV had embezzled over 900 million Deutschmarks in federal and state subsidies resulting in criminal and civil charges. Several members of the Bremen Establishment appeared to be involved in this scam. Guess what happened in the end? Two of the executive board members settled out of court and everyone else got away scot-free.

These regulators keep missing the point. If you are part of the Establishment, you can wreak complete havoc and get away with it. The worst you can expect is a wrist slap. However, if you are an independent, anti-Establishment guy or organization, the whole system, including the lemming journalists, descend on you on the slightest alleged infraction.

The morale of the story is simple: it is better to form your own educated opinion than believing what the compulsive liars in the corporate propaganda department tell you and the market. That is why at least 60 percent of all financial analysts and reporters are failures, and why few equity managers outperform the indexes over the long run. They are lazy, gullible and unimaginative in their research. They cannot fathom a contrarian thought and are always concerned about their short-term performance relative to some meaningless index and their peers, instead of concentrating on absolute returns and loss limitation. Most importantly, they can't think the unthinkable such as US government default, zero growth, deflation, financial repression or traumatic hyperinflation. "Always form your own opinion" became one of my maxims after Bremer Vulkan.

Competitive verification still offers superior returns. The white-shoe firms like Fidelity, Jonathan & White or Templeton are nowhere near executing this concept. Peter Lynch was the first and only boss of mine who actually asked me to talk to customers and competitors whenever I could. His request did not fall on deaf ears. I believe any quality company report should analyze customers, competitors, pricing power, barriers to entry and competitive position. Why they still do not include all these critically important elements continues to baffle me, but clearly part of what prevents CV from getting more prominence in investment circles is the time-consuming, costly, exasperating, unglamorous, underwear-sniffing that it entails.

Sometimes, these and other highly unpleasant elements threaten to take over proceedings completely. At such times you need your shell, the protective armor that is an essential part of the job and has been cultivated over many years, to be in first-rate condition. At Harvard College my close friend Steven Larab took a semester off and moved to New York City to "broaden his horizons." He came from a practicing Jewish conservative family in Australia and had led a sheltered existence until he arrived at Harvard. His IQ was abnormally high but Steven was a little bit too crazy for his own good. He was a manic-depressive. He was also spending too much time with me, and I probably tainted his virgin soul.

While in New York, he met and consorted with members of the Gambino crime family and the Brighton Beach Russian mafia. He was renting the very glitzy and decked-out apartment belonging to Steve Rubell (the owner of Studio 54) on the Upper East Side, and his best friend in the city was a coked-out criminal lawyer working for Carlo Gambino. Coke abuse and freebasing were rampant and Steven was losing his marbles. He even moved over $1 million in uncut diamonds for a member of the Russian mafia who had undergone plastic surgery to avoid murder. Steven fell long and hard and ended up in McLean Psychiatric Hospital affiliated with Harvard Medical School. Upon recovery, he joined the Israeli army and married a caring, loving, orthodox Jewish woman. I was not invited to the wedding, probably because I was both a Goyem and a bad influence. After a few hiccups, Steven restored his faith and mastered his trials and tribulations well.

Before he entered the funny farm, he introduced me to this assortment of low-life friends. Consequently, I spent several time with the made members of New York's waste disposal department. It was disconcerting to see these guys in all walks of life waste disposal, gaming, cement, construction, transportation, unions and even securities firms, plus all the usual nasty stuff from heroin dealing to human trafficking. I was offered half a dozen custom tailored Armani suits by their legal representative. The suits were fashionable and worth about 10 thousand dollars, but I had the good sense to refuse them. My regular interaction with the "brains" in the organization also gave me an insight as to which mob groups were involved in which securities markets.

In the early nineties I was sponsoring Ben Tower, the majority owner of a Technology Group, a small but promising stock-exchange-listed IT company based in Manhattan. Ben Tower became one of my few friends. I respect his courage, backbone and loyalty. I admire his intelligence and perseverance. At the time, he was desperate for funding. He had no credible investment banking partner, promoter or broker/dealer funding his growth, just a bunch of shysters trying to extort outrageous fees for non-existent fund-raising services. His prospects were exciting so we funded him, did not charge excessive fees and introduced him to numerous juicy capital market and fund management contacts. We were successfully promoting Towers and the share price doubled to $1 per share.

Once the share price reached that level, all our promotional efforts failed miserably. Even though our clients were buying hundreds of thousands of shares, the price did not budge a cent. We had run into fierce opposition from short sellers and market manipulators. It got worse. The guys we were facing made a living by illegally short selling young and promising companies and then extorting large sums of cash or shares from the owners and management to go away. Thanks to Steven Larab's introduction, I knew damn well how these extortion scams worked. Our homework showed that our opponents were heavily connected and might employ more than rogue financial techniques when push came to shove. It occurred to us to report the incident to the Organized Crime Unit of New York's finest, but concluded that by the time an indictment was reached Towers firm would be dead and buried—possibly along with its chief executive.

The guys were offering to buy millions of Towers firm shares at a ninety-percent discount to the prevailing market value to cover its naked shorts, locking in millions in illegal profits. The normal underhanded threats could not be missed and were part of the early negotiations.

While Towers was toughing it out in New York, my reputation as a financier and promoter was going through the roof in Germany. The once mighty Bremer Vulkan conglomerate had just crumbled, giving me a reputation as a ruthless, unscrupulous profiteer. I was known in some quarters as the antichrist of finance. Celebrity status as a hardnosed raider or rather a degree of infamy as a short seller was altogether useful. As long as our track record was stellar our market following kept growing. Just building a small five-percent stake in a company could lead to a 30-percent share-price increase as speculators followed our initiative. Often enough we would use this momentum and dump our holdings on the blind investing public that were attempting to follow our moves and were still buying shares. Because I am vain, I was generally amused by the media attention. However, one-sided and completely negative portraits have always bugged me.

VMR was on its way to being valued at half a billion dollars; not chump change, even by New York mob standards. We were managing over 1 billion Deutschmarks, owned our own bank, broker dealer, an institutional sales desk, a large securities research firm, a private banking subsidiary, even a PR organization. We could influence people, move companies and markets, even in America.

At the time, Towers was risking his life, I was one step removed from the immediate battlefield. I had done some more homework on our opponents and concluded that they were definitely not connected in Germany, so I felt relatively safe. Towers was endlessly more vulnerable. If he did not sell the shares, he might get whacked. Without its driving force, the share price would collapse and on our opponents would profit handsomely covering its illegal short positions. Moreover, we and our clients would lose a small fortune. Agreeing to a deal would mean surefire destruction for Towers and the technology group—these guys would never go away until all the value had been squeezed out of the company. We decided to go to war.

I organized a sophisticated short-squeeze plan using a dozen off- and onshore vehicles to buy the stock from several different countries and entities. It looked like everybody under the sun had suddenly decided to own Towers[2] firm. All our funds were asking for physical delivery of the shares, causing the scumbag short-sellers considerable distress in settling their bogus trades. Then we listed Towers' firm on the Frankfurt Stock Exchange with tremendous fanfare and organized European investor roadshows. The PR department got Ben numerous articles in influential financial journals. The German retail investors were buying the shares in droves. Swiss Banks were buying. The share price doubled within five days. By now, our opponents had done their own research and wanted to meet us, urgently.

They were no longer confronting an up-and-coming New York entrepreneur but a powerful notorious financier and legendary short seller to boot. We kept squeezing the mobsters and the shares doubled again. Our opponents were losing millions. As a result of our second short squeeze, the tone of the negotiations changed noticeably. The underhanded threats ceased completely. We had played hard asses all along and the enemy was bleeding. Finally, our opponents closed its short position with a hefty loss.

Towers' firm experienced several growth spurts thereafter with the share price increasing eightyfold over five years. This multibillion-dollar company was now called World Tex. By 2000, two big investment banks had become Ben's principal financial backers. World Tex did not survive the Internet meltdown on Wall Street and 9/11. His headquarters near the World Trade Center were directly impacted by the attacks.

A couple of years later in 2003, Ben Towers and his partner, another gifted serial entrepreneur and I acquired Penthouse Media Group. Unbeknown to my virtuous wife, I had made her a sizable shareholder, which technically made her an investor in pornography. In 2007, Penthouse Media Group purchased an online dating service for $500 million and later changed its name. The Internet holding company is owner for numerous Internet companies including online-dating websites, online sex, swinger personals community websites, and the flagship site has 30 million active members worldwide. In total it has over 30,000 websites and approximately 405 million registered users in 185 countries. It is also amazingly profitable. Ben is a major owner and is its CEO. Having funded and backed him against mob financiers, he returned the favor by making us lots of money in Penthouse. Ben has had his ups and downs, but has come out on top. He is still the American Dream, albeit with a few deep scars from his battles and a divorce. Unlike me, Ben never lost his internal anchor. Mine was mostly external, represented by Susan and Kevin. He was always a caringly active dad and did not let the money, the bimbos and power go to his head. I have a lot to learn from Ben.

*

Amongst the many positive sides to venture or early stage investing (precious few of which the media ever focus on, such as the employment it can generate, or the wastage it prevents) and most rewarding is the emotional returns that can sometimes accrue alongside the financial returns. Since my mid-teens, I had been a keen student of the Jewish people and their customs and studied the lives of many important Jewish financiers (Goldman, Saffra, Rothschild, Wertheim, Warburg, Soros …) and principal philosophers (Fromm, Wittgenstein, Lessing, Hillel, Horkheimer, Spinoza …).

I am not completely mercantile. I will reflect on my actions and occasionally listen to wise people around me. Those who know me well are fully aware of a social conscience. I have hired people with zero prospects and large families to support. My driver, Herr Hinze, was 61 years and unemployed. My personal secretary, Miss Ballmer, in her mid-fifties and seriously overweight, was the victim of a corporate restructuring. Both were fully capable, but nobody gave them a chance because they were considered too old and over the hill. They would also be more costly and difficult to fire given Germany's labor laws, which favored the older employees. They both did a great job and fully deserved the opportunity they received. René Müller, of Fortune Management, was without a job and no tenable prospects for an equal lucrative employment when his employer was in trouble. He had five children, some with special needs, to support. He asked me for help. I backed him financially and helped him launch a group of companies. Thereafter, he became a multi-millionaire with no financial worries whatsoever. Burkhard Brauch, VMR's manager in Spain, had been embroiled in a messy financial scandal while working for Morgan Stanley. He was a young father and a friend from Frankfurt. Unemployment in Spain was rampant at the time. I hired him and gave him a second chance when nobody else would touch him. I have trained people in finance with no background whatsoever, like Alvaro Guzman, who become one of Spain's most respected and celebrated fund managers, and others who were down and out, like DR, who was jobless after the dotcom crisis and became a rich man in less than three years.

The single most positive aspect of venture or early-stage investing is that these companies often employ and train thousands of people, improve efficiency and often contribute to society. There has always been a degree of social awareness, albeit somewhat crippled. Ceteris paribus, I would prefer to sponsor companies that leave a positive imprint on society rather than invest into established arms manufacturers, junk-food producers, private-prison companies or alcohol distillers. I am not a "jewophile" but I do have a tiny Jewish bias, which includes philanthropy and charitable thought. It just so happens that when you are focused on finance, media and technology, if you dream about 1,000-Swiss-franc banknotes at night, if you like finance, probability and philosophy then you will meet a lot of them, and generally I like them. All three elements, wealth maximization, social awareness and Semitism, were united when I discovered JDate.

From 1997 until 2001, I was the angel investor, principal financier and advisor of JDate, by far and away the largest Jewish internet dating-site in the world. That equated to a market share of about 15 percent of all the eligible Jewish singles on the planet. JDate would enable Jewish singles to meet each other around the globe. JDate has enabled thousands of marriages (undoubtedly also many divorces) and is a brand name in the Jewish community. The parent organization, Spark Networks, which grew out of JDate, presently has about 40 million registered users worldwide.

I met Alon Karmel and Joe Shapira at the Cumberland Hotel in London to consider a venture capital investment. Very low on my agenda, I had scheduled the meeting for two in the morning with a cut-off time of 6.00 a.m. when I had to get to my first breakfast meeting. Either a deal was going to happen within four hours, including all the necessary contract work, or the Tel Aviv duo would have to fly back to Los Angeles to hawk videos for a living.

Joe and Alon were clearly out of money. JDate had a paltry 27,000 non-paying members and had failed to raise funds from any of the established angel investors and venture capitalists in Silicon Valley. It occurred to me these guys were desperate and I could score a stellar deal. At the time, the concept of Internet dating was inconceivable to the masses and especially the average financier, who was too old to operate a computer, never mind grasp the enormity of the change the internet would bring to every aspect of our lives.

Luckily for me, I knew how guys and dolls ticked, and Joe's software was better than average. Although their slide presentation not only sucked but also was insulting to a demanding investor—I would have fired an associate at VMR if he had presented me with such garbage—Joe's story was interesting. He had started JDate because he was seriously overweight with limited financial means and had trouble getting dates in Lala-land, very much like another thirty million single dudes who looked more like Rodney Dangerfield than Tom Cruise. Joe was not pretty to look at but had a great heart and a wicked sense of humor. That part of him would come across much better on the Internet than in a trendy Los Angeles nightclub. He was not exactly dating Cindy Crawford at that time but he was definitely getting laid using JDate to meet women. So if JDate worked for Joe, it would work for almost anybody. I was sold on the concept. I reckoned JDate could be a gold mine if it was properly funded and promoted.

If the company could get to 100,000 paying members, I could make at least $10 million by flipping it to a larger player. Given my appetite for risk and with no competition on the deal, I scored 35 percent of JDate for a ridiculously low sum of $350,000. JDate grew much faster than I expected. Within eighteen months, we had listed the company on the Frankfurt Stock Exchange and raised $40 million in the process. My eternal lawyer and friend Adam Kravitz was placed on the board of directors and became the chief financial officer to assure that the funds raised would not be squandered entirely on private jets, super yachts and Bentleys. Adam was only partially successful as Joe and Alon frequently confused the company's balance sheet with their own wallets. When I joined the board, the share performance went into overdrive and it was time to cash out.

The peak valuation exceeded $300 million and our stake had appreciated over three hundredfold. My personal options as a board member netted $10 million. Alon and Joe walked away with a fortune. Adam did remarkably well. Making me lots of money always touched the essence of my soul and elicited the most exaggerated expressions of gratitude. Alon and Joe became my heroes as I was realizing profits. We almost became friends, which was a challenging feat for me. Needless to say, once JDate took off, Joe was dating one cover girl after another. Given that he became famous in the world of wealthy internet entrepreneurs, he no longer needed liposuction and fake teeth to score in Beverly Hills.

By 1999, I had been a controversial, experienced money manager for more than twelve years. I had raided, shorted and greenmailed numerous companies, and invested in many others such as JDate which had extremely positive outcomes for thousands of people. I had received several prestigious investment awards. I was far from being a virgin in my industry. Socrates said that "Knowing that you know nothing makes you the smartest of all." Unfortunately, I suffered from believing I knew more than I did. What follows shows what delusions of wisdom can do. It also tells you that what goes around will ultimately come around.

I had met Dietrich Walther, the former CEO and majority shareholder of Gold-Zack, at Bank Julius Baer. He was one of the most innovative and creative financiers I had ever met. At the height of his prowess, he was a multibillionaire. He was also my mentor. We had a regular dialogue and he taught me about finance and accounting. I once translated his annual report from German into English over a weekend.

As he was building his investment empire, we met to discuss a deal. He wanted to take a stake in VMR. He liked our research and our highly profitable asset management operations. The price he negotiated for 25 percent was ridiculously low, less than the following year's pretax earnings. He was an awesome negotiator and an even better buyer. Although we would be giving the shares away, having a member of the top hundred largest listed German companies as a strategic shareholder gave us instant credibility and opened doors that had been closed previously. It would allow us to become vastly more profitable. The remaining 75 percent of VMR Kevin and I still owned would be worth a lot more than the 100 percent we owned previously. We could live with cutting DW a great deal. VMR was floated on the Frankfurt Stock Exchange in October 1998 and appreciated 700 percent in the following seven quarters.

The relationship was so harmonious and mutually beneficial that we decided to merge, creating a fully integrated, international capital markets group worth well over 2 billion euros. In reality, Gold-Zack, with a much larger market capitalization, was taking us over in a friendly manner. I had become the heir apparent to overtake DW's ubiquitous empire when he retired in a few years. I saw little downside in the deal. I would earn even more than before, easily ten million euros a year, and ultimately manage one of Germany's most powerful capital market groups. I could finally work with and attack the largest German and European companies. Until I became CEO, I would learn from DW and be introduced to his extensive and mighty network. My shares would appreciate and become absurdly liquid if I ever decided to cash in my chips. I would become a billionaire in time, probably within ten years. We saw little downside, so Kevin and I agreed: let's do it.

I also knew that Walther had one of the sharpest financial minds to ever come out of Germany. I was fully aware he knew every accounting gimmick going, and many which had not yet been invented. Kevin and I knew we would have to see his internal accounts before agreeing to the "merger." We were seasoned forensic accountants and hard-core investigators. We would strip Gold-Zack to the bone and discover all of its corpses before signing anything.

To cut a long story short, Walther was insulted and told us to fuck off. He told us the published accounts would have to suffice. The deal blew up, but to our total consternation, Walther did not withdraw his takeover offer. The mentor had turned on his own student, his designated heir. Daddy shark was going to have baby shark for lunch while all the goldfish watched. Reasonably experienced in hostile affairs ourselves, we managed to keep him down to slightly over 40 percent, and just about managed to stay in control of our own destiny.

He acted insolent about our lack of faith in his accounts, and I acted outraged that he wouldn't show us his underwear, but really, we kept on talking as if nothing had happened. Anybody else would have freaked out and hired scores of lawyers, detectives, investment bankers and PR agents. Normally lawsuits and counter-lawsuits would have been filed. Walther sicked a sleazy PR clown on me to tarnish my name—I had helped float this self-important blowfish's flimsy business on the Frankfurt Stock Exchange, and now he was accepting money to darken my reputation in the media—but I ignored the move. "More noise than anything else," was my interpretation. I concluded that Walther had wanted to teach me a lesson for the future: never underestimate the big bad wolf.

We got together two weeks later, and both came to the same conclusions. So things got a little ugly in the media. The press is like a pack of street hounds. When something moves, they start barking. They'll bark at something else tomorrow. We concluded: Let's move on, find a solution and make some money.

In retrospect, he had schooled me completely. While I was thinking about my upside, he was one step ahead of me at every turn. If the takeover succeeded, he would be able to retire and would have one of the brightest up and coming European financiers at the helm of his financial conglomerate. If the deal went sour, he had only used a little paper money to buy real assets and profits. If thinks went hostile, he knew full well we would take him out at massive premium to his entry price. He was now greenmailing us. His scenario analysis and experience were simply more advanced than mine. We found some alternative shareholders and Walther walked away with a net profit of 160 million euros. Daddy shark had just devoured his babies.

I have kept in touch with him on an irregular basis. Some of the guys he chose to run his conglomerate were demented alcoholics and the once mighty Gold-Zack went out of business in the 2000-to-2003 stock-market crash. I still like him, albeit strictly within my limited emotional range. He founded one of Germany's premier business schools after retiring from capital markets. Why he decided to raise more baby sharks in his free time remains a mystery to me. Maybe he did not deliberate enough.

It took me three proposals before I got married, and now I had rejected my first commercial proposal. About a year later, we started flirting with Germany's premier stock-exchange-listed venture capital group, Knorr Capital Partner. The merger would create the second largest listed European venture capital group with a combined market value of close to a billion euros. Once again, the deal made perfect sense, but this was more a merger of equals than a takeover. The deal had the added beneficial side effect that one of Germany's largest banks, the mighty State Bank of Hessen (HELABA), had injected a 40-million-euro equity stake based on the assumption that we would merge with Knorr and create this venture capital/fund management behemoth.

They guessed wrong. We kept the capital and dinged the deal. Not only was Knorr's Enron-like accounting way too liberal for us, we were very apprehensive because it would be virtually impossible to cash in venture capital stakes in a protracted bear market. Knorr Capital Partner went bankrupt because, just like Gold-Zack, they had debt they could not refinance, they believed too much in their own bullshit and retreated to the bizarre realm of optimism, disbelief, delusion and hope. The almighty HELABA bankers sued and threatened us. They lost. The Gold-Zack experience had taught us valuable lessons: never underestimate your opponent and do not agree to a marriage until you have figured out all the angles.

Our balance sheet was now in pristine condition and ready to weather any stock market deluge, whereas Knorr not only went bust, they dragged down a lot of their employees as well. Unlike VMR, where the employees and partners had cashed out, Knorr and his disciples were stuck with millions in debt, resulting from leveraged employee share ownership plans. Over 80 percent of the independent stock-exchange-listed financial firms in Germany did not survive the 2000-to-2003 bear market. VMR was among the proud survivors because it had cash, no debt, steady income, and had closed or sold all cost-intensive, cyclical operations.

We had floated the company on the Frankfurt Stock Exchange in 1998 and I began selling shares when the valuation passed $400 million, even though the shares kept moving up. I forced our chief financial officer, Matthias Girnth, to sell VMR shares in the employee incentive option plan. My orders in 1999 were crystal clear: sell at least two thirds of VMR shares or find a new job. Matthias thought I was nuts. We offered complete capital market services in Frankfurt, had built and developed the first internet bank in Munich, owned a highly profitable private client wealth manager in Luxemburg, a licensed broker dealer in the US and had streamlined all back-office functions in Madrid. Profits were going up every quarter. Some thought we were living in *Schlaraffenland* (the land of milk and honey) where our cups and plates would overflow with exquisite wine and sweetmeats served by plump cherubs.

I knew better, based on years of data mining and empirical valuation analysis. There was no way we, a diversified capital market group, could sustain being valued at almost ten times book value for more than a few years. Our valuation could only be sustained if world equity markets continued their breakneck appreciation indefinitely and we continued to generate a 100-percent return on capital employed. This was, of course, utterly unrealistic.

The crash of 2000 to 2002 was inevitable. Companies were no longer valued on hard financial variables but on page impressions. Valuation parameters that worked for dozens of years and had moved within defined bandwidths (EV to operating, free or gross cash flow, EV to replacement value, return on capital, EV to sales…) were temporarily replaced by flaky and meaningless criteria, which said nothing about profitability and assets. The traditional criteria, likewise, were on whacky valuation grounds. The US market had never been valued higher relative to tangible book value and even the UK market was offering pathetically low historical dividend yields. Profitability measures such as return on equity were sky high. Backlog orders of toys (private jets, serious yachts, helicopters and exotic luxury cars) were at all-time highs (a surefire contrarian indicator for market tops) and brand new internet millionaires, who had floated companies with no sales and revenues, were spending thousands on mediocre champagne and trashy women in Monte Carlo and Saint-Tropez nightclubs.

We had had fantastic tailwind for six years but were now heading into a hurricane on a rowing boat. The market was also well on its way to more uniform accounting standards and other smart managers were beginning to use range valuations as buying and selling triggers. European markets had evolved and regulation was rearing its ugly head. Our competitive edge was dwindling and I was not going to confuse rapacity and fortunate timing with ingenuity.

All the easy money had been made. It would be more competitive from here on. The party was over and the first drunken brawls were erupting. Why stick around and fight a vicious bear market? Who in their right mind would voluntarily sail against the wind for three or more years? Thank God, my brother-in-law wanted to be the number one after having been in my shadow for almost a decade. He wanted to bring precision and stability to this opportunistic, unpredictable and constantly mutating capital-markets enterprise. He was an engineer, not a mercantile financier. He thought there was Newtonian order to the universe; I believed in chaos theory. I wished him luck and gave him the reins.

*

Even the most negative circumstances can sometimes lead to remarkably positive outcomes. A critical reason why I was willing to cede control in 2000 was because in the winter of the previous year I had been diagnosed with multiple sclerosis by Professor Martin, one of the top neurologists at the University of Frankfurt. My sister had suffered from a severe form of the disease, and before it killed her she had been confined to a wheelchair, could barely speak and required 24-hour care. It is about 30 to 40 times more common among siblings than in the general population.

I had too many lesions in my brain and a large one in my neck to doubt the diagnosis. My entire left arm and right foot were numb. I was failing simple coordination and eyesight tests. I was also eating buckets of cortisone, which was turning me into a zit-faced, 260-pound zombie. I was done for. I would die before even reaching 50, pissing and shitting all over myself in the years leading up to my death.

I was devouring data to find a solution. I studied all the available treatments. I kept digging into alternative treatments, human growth hormone, homeopathic medicine, bone marrow transplants, nutritional additives, vitamin cures and so forth. Of course, this empirical study was condemned to the obscure shelves of esoteric medical literature. MS is a multibillion-dollar industry. There are no profits in recommending MS patients to change their lifestyle, soak up vitamin D in sunnier, drier and more joyful environments. The research indicated that lifestyle and weather change was easily as effective as the most advanced medical treatments. I began speaking with MS sufferers who had changed their lifestyle completely and moved to sunnier and drier places both in Europe and in the States. Many spoke about the unexpected positive results.

The weather in Königstein ranged from foggy to misty, and ultraviolet radiation did not exist ten months of the year. When it did, I was working 100 hours a week in an office or travelling. Between 1990 and 2000, when I was working like a total maniac, I barely saw daylight let alone sunlight. I even had a sofa bed in my office. I took less than a week's vacation per year during my empire-building phase. My ex-wife argued the total vacation time over the whole decade did not exceed five weeks. (She forgot to include the "working vacations" and some three-day weekends.) Smoking over 100 cigarettes a day and not much exercising did not help. I was damaged from the battle. I needed to do something radically different if I was to survive, literally.

Vitamin D strengthens bones and reduces osteoporosis risks. It modulates neuromuscular function, reduces inflammation, and influences the action of many genes that regulate the proliferation, differentiation and apoptosis of cells. It is produced in the skin after exposure to ultraviolet B light from the sun and occurs naturally in a tiny range of foods. I began taking supplements, and embraced the sun. I refused to have any more vaccinations, even though it prevented me from travelling to several countries in Asia, Central and Latin America. In addition to genetic factors there is compelling evidence indicating that vitamin D deficiency, frequent vaccinations, lead and other minerals in our bodies are highly correlated with MS.

After retiring to Mallorca, I refused to acknowledge the disease. I stopped studying the subject, never discussed it and told my brain my infliction was gone. I went on a radical health diet and became an exercise freak and sun-worshipper. I imagined before going to sleep I was getting better each day. I tried forcing my mind to signal my body I was perfectly healthy. I imagined that the numbness in my limbs was declining. I stopped all medicines completely. I exchanged cigarettes for cigars, reducing my toxic chemical intake by 93 percent at a stroke. I had all my lead and gold fillings removed and replaced with ceramics. For eighteen months, I changed absolutely everything in my life except my wife and children.

Two decades later, I am nowhere near using a cane, even though some numbness in my right foot remains, but I can deal with that. Most of the lesions are gone and I have made it past 50 in reasonably good shape, some bladder functionality problems aside. Despite the fact that MS often causes erectile dysfunction, I have also been known to get a 100-percent natural erection on special occasions.

I was off to my Mallorca palace with the family to embrace retirement. The charm of the island, besides the health benefits of the sunny and dry climate, is that although no single element is outstanding, it is a conglomeration of extremely fine elements. Its coastal road isn't as spectacular as the one in Amalfi, but it's damned good; its restaurants aren't as good as those in Paris, but they're damned good; its cathedral isn't the biggest in Spain, but as the fifth biggest it's still damned impressive. It has vivid natural beauty and some wildlife, especially inland, and that has been important to me ever since my childhood adventures in the forests near Oberursel.

On these and many other criteria the place scores consistently high marks, and when you add them all up, you've got something close to paradise. In addition, there is a very appealing mix of types, so that a very arty crowd is combined with a hard-core entrepreneurial tycoon element. What Somerset Maugham said about Monte Carlo is just as true about Mallorca: "It's a sunny place for shady people." I don't consider myself "shady," but it does give an interesting extra dynamic or texture to the atmosphere of a place. It's nice to rest in the shade once in a while.

Once I was settled, I sold all my remaining VMR shares. Kevin stuck it out, stabilized the firm during the market crash and covered my behind, preserved cash, fired almost everyone and sold asset-rich, profitable but utterly unimaginative and lethargic VMR to a risk-loving entrepreneur. Kevin has two children, no dog, goes to church regularly, loves Germany *über alles* and appears to be getting on OK with his calculating wife. He is a great guy, but he should move to a sunnier, more fun-loving place.

I had just turned forty and my wealth had increased twentyfold in the previous decade. A Mediterranean palace, a castle on the Mosel River, a grand master painting collection, a motor yacht, a Rolls-Royce convertible and other titbits had been added to the family fortune. My longstanding love affair with money and my vision of riches had become reality. The gods of wealth, power and vanity had answered my prayers. I had no idea I had been praying to a false pantheon.

Part IV
Crash

7. Absolute Capitalism

Moderation is a fatal thing. Nothing succeeds like excess.
Oscar Wilde

Retirement is overrated. If one is not absolutely prepared for it mentally and emotionally, the suffering can be tremendous. I became even more of a hyperactive lunatic. During the first months I painted the garage door, built one guesthouse for our bears and parrots, another one for human guests (never used), bought a tennis machine, speedboat, chess computer, motorcycle and 58 books. While my wife had a job raising the children, I had nothing to do.

This was my normal day: I would spend two hours ranting at my tennis machine while attempting to improve my pathetic backhand, followed by a thirty-minute swim to strengthen my back muscles. Then I would play two games of chess against the computer while talking to an imaginary opponent. Our cook would serve a highly nutritious light lunch with one glass of German Riesling that very much pleased my palate, after which I would retire for an undeserved fifty-one minute siesta. Upon waking, I would engage Andre, Fyodor, Erich, Soren or Friedrich to intrigue and amuse me and then go for a light jog to fortify my calf and thigh muscles, followed by a dip in the whirlpool.

After a seven-minute, lukewarm shower, I would take the motorbike or the speedboat out for a late afternoon spin. Upon returning to my estate, I would greet the departing gardeners and harvest a few fresh oranges for the following day's breakfast. When drinks had been served, I would kiss my beloved wife at 7.30 p.m. before dinner, after which we would take a thirty-minute digestive stroll through the property passing parrots, ducks, bears, rabbits, sheep, goats and various other wild and domesticated creatures which we kept for amusement. I would engage her in backgammon or mindless, esoteric discussions. While she was putting the kids to bed, I would watch peripherally interesting documentaries on public television or CNN for sixty minutes. We would have sex twice a week; Wednesdays after the kids went to sleep and Saturdays after a fancy dinner at a Michelin-star restaurant.

I would make up stories for my kids and I temped as basketball coach at my son's school on Tuesday and Thursday afternoons. The company of children does wonders for one's soul, and although my body was being nourished, my mind refused to cooperate. I should have been happy, or at least content. After more than a year of a healthy diet and stringent exercise, I was top fit and my life seemed orderly.

Unfortunately, I was also closer to a nervous breakdown than I had ever been. A psychological disconnection within me was not only failing to heal, it was being exacerbated. I had become a family man, but there was nothing in my history or my makeup that could tell me what to *do* with that. Family bliss was never part of my vision and had no role in my absurd value system. For two decades, I had been conditioned to get my kicks in other ways. The emotional returns from being a father and husband simply did not accrue because I was closed off to them. At the time, they were not my gods.

I was missing the simple thrill of trading and investing vast amounts of money, moving companies and changing destinies. I was not yet ready to abandon worldly ambition and the quest for wealth and fame. My juices were still boiling inside, because the Necko dream had been only partially realized. I was a lost soul in paradise, and as a child and disciple of the market, my false gods were wondering where I was. What a waste.

The terrorist attacks on 9/11 were a pivotal moment for the markets. My instinct told me that something serious was going on, not just in the markets (which were already weak), but in the minds of people in the marketplace. I felt that there was a fearfulness and unpredictability that could easily lead to mispricing. Initially I lost money on my long trade position because there was another market tumble after the second plane hit. At that point I thought this is going to have all kinds of ramifications, not least economically. Maybe we'll get an accelerated bear market, a properly messy situation in which I can operate. Any fool can make money when the market is rising. A rising tide lifts all boats. It is very difficult and sometimes almost impossible to distinguish oneself in a benign environment. That would be the perfect chance to launch another empire.

It's so illogical to me that people get into markets during good times, when everyone else is buying. Of course, the proper thinking dictates that messy markets, even disasters, provide the best opportunities. After the mess, things stabilize and move up. Both Necko and my grandfather Hans Lang demonstrated awareness of this fact during the war and even more so during the lawless, chaotic years afterwards. I made most of my money by starting businesses during market crashes. The competition is rattled and passive during tough times. Agile, differentiated operators can pick up disenchanted and frustrated clients more easily. There was an immense opportunity right in front of me. I couldn't resist the market's call any more.

The signs were obvious: the markets were sickly. All predictive valuation parameters were out of whack in 2000/2001. The European hedge-fund universe had grown tenfold to over 600 vicious competitors in less than a decade. I was convinced the smartest of them would only make modest returns or preserve capital during a market crash. I knew how to make millions from disasters. If we played the markets right, we would stand out, leaving our competitors light years behind. It was high time to get back on the money train.

I finally stopped crawling up the walls, returned to actively managing my own funds and began cashing in on the market's decline with a vengeance. During my early exile, I had noticed VMR going from ten times book value, an absurd premium to intrinsic value, to a deep liquidation discount as a result of the market crash. The shares were trading around 1 euro and I had sold my stake in the high 30s. I reckoned I could simply take some of my proceeds, call a few hard-core investors and mount a hostile takeover at a modest 30-percent premium and either sell the company off in parts or flip it to someone else at 4 euros a share. Besides Kevin's stake, the shareholder structure was wide open. The company had become an undervalued sitting duck ready for slaughter. It would be like taking a penalty with no goalkeeper.

I had plenty of cash and enough devious consorts to ambush and raid the company. I would net about 5 to 8 million euros for about eight months' work. This sounded not only doable but also extremely logical. It took all the wits of my then wife to convince me that taking over VMR, firing her brother and the entire board made little sense in terms of the quality of family harmony and future reunions. She also mentioned that Kevin deserved his chance to fulfill his entrepreneurial dreams. "What's that got to do with profit maximization or anything else?" I wondered.

I do have a high tolerance for conflict when sizable profits are involved. I finally acquiesced but not because a little extra tension in the family would cause me sleepless nights. That was not going to happen. OK, Kevin had been my best friend (until, as I mentioned, he married my brother's ex-wife). So basically I wished him well generally and that counted for something. However, two factors changed my mind. First, the operation was boring. I had been a hostile investor, a raider and greenmailer several times already. Secondly, and more importantly, I would make so much more money focusing on the mother lode of all financial projects: I would build a pure hedge-fund management group.

After all, what was 5 million euros after tax going to buy you these days? A sub-par used jet and maybe a few second-rate landscape Impressionists? How about a real yacht, a majestic 20,000-square-foot Arabic beachfront palace, a proper 8,000-square-foot guest house with a five-acre garden, a helicopter pad and a proper domicile to house family and guests in Mallorca, a smaller guest house to house their guests as well, a major ten-bedroom country estate to shoot and fish and some more master paintings to fill the sad-looking, scarcely decorated colonnade around the inner courtyard? While I could have bought any of these toys as it was, I felt profoundly uncomfortable digging into my investment reserves to do so. It had become quite necessary to embark on another entrepreneurial venture. This time it would have to be large enough to satisfy my insatiable lust for wealth and luxuries.

It was far better to start something new. Positive, creative energy, smartly applied, always has more upside than the nerdy negative energy necessary for dismantling a defenseless, small-time undervalued target. *Ceteris paribus,* it makes sense to focus on big tickets.

After about a year of dilly-dallying, my health had improved dramatically. The most recent MRI showed far fewer lesions in my brain and the burly one on my neck had almost disappeared. It looked like I would not need the anticipated wheel chair any time soon. Switching to cigars had freed up my lungs, the numbness in my left arm was gone and the markets were surely awaiting my glorious return. I had beaten multiple sclerosis. I was healthy and hungry. My brain needed to go back to work. Nothing could stop me now except myself of course. It would take six months to set up all the necessary structures. Then I would be back on the battlefield and busting balls.

Even if someone in Mallorca had tattooed "You are in heaven" on my forehead, I wasn't in a position to see it. Charged up and healthy and dumb as ever, I was starving for monetary challenges, takeover thrills and short sale combat opportunities. Nothing could have stopped me, not even myself. It was comeback time and I was exhilarated.

*

If you are seriously into money, why would you ever want to be anything but a hedge fund manager? Mutual funds charge 1 percent or so of the money they manage. Not only do hedge funds charge 2 percent, they get to keep 20 percent of the profit and hold 0 percent of the risk. That meant if you ran a mutual fund with $100 million under management that had earned 30 percent, you would make a little over $1 million in revenues. The same hedge fund would make you $8 million. The amount of work involved was about twice as much, so adjusted for the extra hassle, the return on effort was 400 percent higher.

By 2002, I had about a dozen years of proprietary trading and hedge-fund experience under my belt and as a consequence was less likely to blow up than before. The European Value Fund at VMR had been the best performing European hedge fund in 1994. Unfortunately for me, the market wanted large caps and growth stocks in 1995 and the fund dropped 25 percent, making it one of the worst performers. I wanted to be right rather than cut losses and preserve capital in those dark days and therefore lost in a big way. That year we learned a lot about limiting losses and letting profits ride. We also learned that too much size and rapid inflows were not conducive to superior returns and small-cap trading strategies.

In the following five years both VMR hedge funds scored sensational volatility adjusted returns, but many investors had already deserted us. Those who remained not only recovered all their losses within sixteen months but also were laughing all the way to the bank. Few did. Meanwhile the long-only business- and capital market operations performed gloriously at VMR as long as the market went up. However, these businesses are notoriously cyclical and need to be avoided at all costs when markets head south.

Given the superior math, my new firm was going to be strictly about hedge funds, a less cyclical and vastly more profitable activity. Who needed the other low margin, cyclical rubble? If you wanted to become filthy rich quickly, you needed to be a hedge fund manager, a major weapons dealer, an Internet genius, a drug baron or a Peruvian Forex dealer.

Like VMR, Absolute Capital Management Holdings started in my billiard room. Our first employee was DR, who had trained in investment banking and research at VMR. When he joined me, he knew very little about valuations and nothing about activist investing. DR was a strange cat. He had been a member of the Houston Youth Symphony and a budding violin virtuoso. He had a poor self-image coupled with an exaggerated sense of self-worth. He almost never got laid because he preferred to insult women rather than charm them. Maybe he preferred boys. While others are trying to sort out their emotions, I am thinking about risk reward ratios and probabilities while trying to calculate the smartest possible path of action. Hiring was no exception. In retrospect, the following interview procedure appears peculiar. At the time, it seemed perfectly sound.

I asked DR and another potential senior employee, Guillermo Hernandez, to jump off a 30-foot cliff in Mallorca into relatively shallow water to prove they had the *cojones* to work with me. I did a backflip to show them how easy it was. The interview process would take less than five minutes and I would not have to waste for month time probing their deeper psyche and motivations while studying their inflated credentials. All I needed to know was whether Guillermo, my potential head trader, would not take undue and stupid risks. He would have to handle billions in trading volume each year and would need to judge risk all the time. I couldn't have him do crazy things like jump off some precipice into the Mediterranean, possibly shattering his head, feet or spine in the process. *Gracias Dios*, Guillermo refused to jump and I hired him.

DR was already working with me but I was not sure he could handle intense pressure. I was undecided whether he should become an equity partner. He would have to jump to show that he was prepared to take risks and endure stress, because he needed to perform heavy-duty competitive verification, take major decisions and cover for me when I was travelling. He jumped, but got serious bruises and walked like John Wayne for two weeks. "Perfect outcome," I concluded. Both guys made the right decision. The interview was over. They were both in and would receive equity in the firm. They became millionaires and they would both learn that "no life is complete without a touch of madness" (Paulo Coelho).

I was on a Necko mission. We would triumph. We would make our competitors look silly while achieving sensational returns and growing our funds under management exponentially. Less than 100 percent effort and perfect results would result in instant flagellation and humiliation. DR responded and, like Susan a decade earlier, did everything from fund accounting, office management, programming and analysis. He sucked at trading but he was an above-average analyst and was comfortable with competitive verification due to his background as a senior investigative journalist. He made a few million dollars with me in three years but cashed out before the IPO. Had he waited one year longer, he would have been sitting on a double-digit million-dollar cash pile.

I had plunked $5 million of my own money into the fund and raised another $5 million in seed money from a German/Swiss family office that would become my junior venture partner. Morgan Stanley was again our prime broker, Fortis was our administrator and Ernst and Young was our auditor. Ullrich Angersbach was my managing partner in Switzerland. He was an intensely private man but one of the most perseverant, hard-working Germans I have ever known, and an invaluable asset.

For the first three years, we worked until 2 a.m. and resumed at 8 a.m. Sundays we only worked for half a day (nine hours). Ullrich's contributions were invaluable, but after three years at this pace, his marriage was falling apart. He halved his hours to fifty a week. On the surface, he was the prototypical German: organized, disciplined, reliable and reserved with a limited sense of humor. Then, after knowing him for a decade, he told me his grandmother had died in a concentration camp.

I was very well known in European finance as a sort of maverick who used state-of-the-art valuation systems and in-depth industry contacts to generate outstanding performance. I was one of the few seasoned and competent short sellers, greenmailers and activist investors with a long and public track record in Europe at the time. However, I was also considered highly controversial by some investors.

Many of the funds I had managed or co-managed in the past had received national and international investment awards, but I was considered volatile and reckless by some potential clients, particularly those who focused on the fact that the VMR European Value Fund had gone from being a star performer one year to shedding a quarter of its value the next in a perfectly benign upward trending market.

In the first year of operations, the Absolute Return Europe Fund returned 29 percent, easily beating all other European hedge funds during the crash year of 2002. The market was down heavily (peak to trough decline of 37 percent in Europe) and the average hedge fund was basically flat or losing money, while the average mutual fund was bleeding heavily. We had scored the top position among hundreds of competitors by educating the market about the two most liberal accounting candidates in the DAX 100 Index: MLP and WCM. Of course, we had substantial short positions in both stocks. The former would decline by 90 percent peak to trough, while the latter would enter bankruptcy, generating an almost infinite return on capital invested. My strategy to stand out in the face of severe market adversity had worked like a dream. The irony of WCM and MLP was that when we began our short raid, there was not a single sell recommendation among the fifty analysts covering these stocks—in fact, the majority was actively recommending buying. This was Bremer Vulkan all over again. Analysts are sheep, and are useless unless they dig deep and wide (competitive verification) or master cash flow, balance sheet and industry dynamics. They rarely do. Economists are often worse and produce too much consensus trash.

Unlike at VMR, our hedge fund performance did not collapse in year two. As assets grew, the office in my Mallorca mansion no longer sufficed. I built a two-story 2,400-square-foot office/residence hall on my property in less than four months. The ground floor accommodated up to twelve professionals while the first floor accommodated employees. We even had a cook, so employees did not have to leave the premises for lunch. Everything was designed to assure the highest degree of effectiveness, efficiency and productivity.

Performance was solid across the board in years three, four and five. We started launching new funds and money was flowing in at breakneck speed. By 2006 we were on the top of the world, scoring both Best European Hedge Fund Group and Best European Hedge Fund gongs awarded by Hedge Fund Review. We bought a well positioned and profitable developing market hedge fund group (Argo Capital Management Ltd.) headquartered in London with offices in Latin America, Cyprus and Asia and a sizable property fund. We were managing over $3 billion and were expected to generate cash flow of $80 million. My share in ACMH was worth about $250 million. The shares had appreciated sevenfold since the initial public offering, and assets under management had increased three hundredfold since inception five years earlier. We had offices in London, Palma, Zug, Rio, Sao Paulo, the Caribbean and the Far East. We were an unparalleled success story. Many of our traders and managers were becoming millionaires. Everybody should have been happy.

Nobody was.

*

In 2004 JR had joined the group to streamline operations, taxation, expansion and marketing. He professionalized ACMH and set the right levers in place for rapid organic growth and sound organizational structures. I no longer ran around the office with shopping bags stuffed with 500-euro notes to pay bonuses.

I had met JR in the late 1990s when I was raiding Farlake PLC, a London-based, stock-exchange-listed fund-management company. Farlake was dirt cheap at six times earnings. JR had an executive position and we had just purchased a 29-percent stake. Our aim was to "merge" the much smaller Farlake into VMR via a public share or cash offer. Farlake's directors were upset because we basically ambushed the company. Had we been trying to please everyone, following corporate etiquette, we would have never scored the stake at such a low price.

Once emotions had settled down, Kevin and I met JR. He is an undersized but very feisty Irishman, and a mean competitor. He is a scratch golfer and was a fierce rugby player at university. He was easily as mercantile and determined as I was. The only difference is that he has less charisma and never understood that you needed world-class talent to achieve world-class results. JR had always surrounded himself with loyal but mediocre yes men, a trait that would come to haunt us later. He was constantly worried about costs and short-term profits rather than quality and long-term sustainability. He should also have shaved his bogus Clark Gable moustache. It made him look too much like a Parisian waiter. Moreover, unlike my former partner, Kevin Devine, JR was no moral anchor. His value system was easily as confused and corroded as mine.

At that meeting, JR managed what nobody had ever done before. He convinced us to abandon our hostile-takeover efforts and support his ambitious growth plans proactively. The math made sense to Kevin and me, so we gave it a try. We could always swallow him at a later date if he did not perform. JR was true to his word and we supported him at every twist and turn. After two years we sold to a larger competitor. We had realized a 400-percent increase on our sizable equity investment and JR walked away with millions. We stayed in touch over the years.

When JR joined, we abandoned the office on my estate. I understood his logic. Stodgy Europeans considered Mallorca a flaky location for an investment management operation. They could not reconcile sunny weather, blue skies and seas with professional investing. I could not care less. My reasoning was: as long we performed far better than our competitors, the money would find us even on the moon. JR was much more into appearances and formality. I disliked the ten-minute commute in one of my convertible cars or my Vespa scooter. I liked walking down the sumptuous balcony stairways with my dogs, passing baroque statues, bronzes and multiple fountains, man-made caves, the tennis court, various terraces with pear and lemon trees, the ponds, past the orange groves, our coatis, sheep, goats and parrots and into the office. Now that was a civilized commute. The idea of getting up and driving by myself through traffic, parking in a tight common garage and then taking a public elevator to an urban office was far less idyllic and quite frankly a brutal and disheartening experience.

Well, I managed to suffer at a high level. Our penthouse office had the best view over the Palma bay bar none. My speed boat was anchored only a two minute walk away allowing me an occasional 100 kilometer per hour adrenalin spin during lunch and after work. While I missed the occasional meal with Susan at the mansion, the Club de Mar yacht club offered an oversized swimming pool and solid Mediterranean cuisine to satisfy my palate. There was little time to party.

In reality, the workload was barely manageable and the pace was excruciatingly demanding as our business was growing by several hundred percent per year. There was very little time to clown around. One hundred hour weeks were the rule. I was managing funds, hiring, marketing, conceptualizing and constantly launching new funds and looking at acquisition targets. I travelled well over a hundred days a year, stopped taking vacations altogether and saw Susan and the children only rarely, occasionally on weekends and late at night. I was turning into Necko.

When ACMH was experiencing this rapid but uncontrolled growth, JR became not only ACMH's CEO but also its second largest shareholder. While I could take the company to market far faster and more effectively than him, I wanted nothing to do with administration, organization, tax optimization, international expansion and reporting structures. I found these topics unbearably monotonous, tedious and intellectually undemanding. "Been there, done that, no need to repeat" was my conclusion. A straight path never leads anywhere except to the predictable, and predictability is the definition of boring. Therefore, I welcomed JR to his new role.

JR's first IPO plan was a total rip-off attempt. I had several dozen IPOs under my belt before hitting forty. In the right climate, I could have listed an open door on the stock market. JR was taking way too long, advisors were changing and we were running up over a million euros in expenses. JR brought in his London pseudo-Establishment boys, did a few Irish jigs and tried to hustle me out of over half of my equity holding. I had built the company, owned the vast majority and was going to end up with 20 percent after the IPO. JR had not of course been there in the first three years of critical growth, yet was going to own as much as me; his London pre-IPO investor buddies would own another 20 percent. That meant I would give away at least 50 million euros and lose control of the company to people I barely knew and did not like.

Luckily, I had arranged a fallback provision. A very clever Israeli dealmaker and close friend, Jacob, was on the sidelines in case JR tried to pull off one of his Fast Eddie moves. Jacob, a former Mossad operative in Moscow and a New York barrister, would outbid and outmaneuver JR at every turn during the negotiations. In the end, Jacob was able to limit JR to a much smaller percentage than he had bargained for initially. We dinged JR's useless London cronies from the deal. Who needed these deadbeats? Some of the names looked nice on paper, but they would provide nothing that would help us execute our aggressive plans. (In return for his invaluable assistance, I helped Jacob score a 35-million-euro payoff on his next greenmail. JR was not too happy, but in the end he walked away with about 30 million euros. Not so bad for less than three years' work.)

During his first eighteen months at ACMH, JR did a swell job in tax optimization, operations, shareholder relations and corporate development. He was also a solid marketer and fundraiser. JR was a bona fide success and well respected by the staff. According to media reports, he was also becoming one of Ireland's richest men. JR's overall plan had always been to develop the company, maximize short-term profits and sell ACMH to a competitor or cash out his stake in the stock market. However, his actions were becoming increasingly counterproductive and irrational.

Something snapped somewhere. JR started screwing Ida, the wife of one of our most gifted traders, C. Maybe JR had taken Andy Warhol's advice too literally: employees make the best dates—you don't have to pick them up and they're tax-deductible. Husband and wife both worked at ACMH and everybody knew about the affair, severely undermining JR's credibility inside the firm. Nobody told me, but I noticed the decline in productivity and team spirit. I asked C. to join me at my Mallorca mansion. He would benefit from the 24/7 facilities and services: pool, whirlpool, tennis, billiard, media room, chef, cleaners and a choice of four houses and fourteen bedrooms to hang his hat. The flipside was, C. was exposed to my nocturnal hours (I rarely went to bed before four in the morning), my ranting about my disintegrating family and a highly probable, major market meltdown. The perverse irony of the

JR/Ida affair was that JR and D. went into attack mode on C. Tired of being mobbed and cuckolded, C. resigned. In his infinite wisdom, JR also started to emasculate not just me but also my most critical supporters. My personal assistant, Daniela, was banned from headquarters and would have to work from my home office hugely undermining my productivity. Our head trader Guillermo picked a heavy dispute with JR over the "*affaire Heatherington,*" lost and went on to greener shores. Ullrich Angersbach, possibly our most important asset for years, had been isolated and shoved into a relatively banal operations position, months ago. He could have been the perfect chief financial officer or head of global marketing. He was board material albeit somewhat pedantic, greedy and risk averse. Everyone who was loyal or helpful to me was either fired or mobbed.

Why? JR knew that the company was intensely dependent on my rainmaking abilities. He actually believed that by making me weaker the company would become more diversified and resilient. He believed others would step in and fill the performance void. He was dead wrong. He still had not understood how the hedge fund industry worked. The industry is populated by razor-sharp commercial minds and not by lemming commercial bankers. Successful hedge fund managers are at the very top of the capital-markets IQ pyramid. That is why they make such obscene amounts of money. If you undermine and destroy these producers, you will be less dependent on them but your investment returns will go down the drain and your profits will evaporate. You simply cannot operate a space shuttle with common field hands. JR's master plan was to move me into marketing, fire my few remaining supporters and have his yes men make all the money. The basic problem with that plan was that the other managers were absolutely unable to achieve the returns I had made for two decades, especially in down markets.

As the funds kept growing and performance pressure increased, all JR could do was hire untalented dimwits incapable of original thought and jammed up with useless consensus opinions. They may have even looked decent on paper, but they were ill suited for the hard-core, contrarian hedge fund industry. Underperformers I had fired for unacceptable results were rehired by JR.

He was maximizing short-term profits and personal loyalty at the expense of long-term economic viability and performance. Worse, he made a classic mistake: by making strong men weaker, weaker men do not necessarily become stronger.

Another major mistake was JR's compensation model. JR paid our top producers significantly lower compensation than our competitors did. He was either dense or greedy enough to believe we could continue to pay world-class traders half of their market value, retain them and continue performing. I interviewed about a dozen budding superstars. None of them joined our firm because the pay was not close to what our competitors offered. This was going on while our assets under management and the number of funds were doubling or tripling. We desperately needed more expensive superstars rather than more poorly paid nitwits. Even our more intelligent board members bought into JR's myths. Meanwhile, I was complaining openly about the lack of able new blood to manage the growing funds. Disaster was beginning to loom.

When ACMH acquired Argo Capital Management for cash and shares, JR went even further and guaranteed our new partners we would never pay more than 20 percent of the overall performance fees generated by the funds to our traders as incentive compensation. The industry standard was 40 to 50 percent, more than twice as much. Even Argo traders were paid by industry standards. This was not only ridiculous but also utterly unrealistic. No one had asked me about this harebrained concession. I neither was on the board of directors nor involved in the negotiations.

The obvious question, which needs to be answered, is why was I not on the board of directors? Why was I, the founder and by far the largest shareholder and a very hands-on and experienced entrepreneur, so far removed from critical decisions? I had been the CEO and chairman of the board at VMR, and I had been on several dozen private and public company boards over the previous two decades. It was only logical, given my history and credentials, to be on the board of directors of ACMH.

However, there were several reasons I preferred not to be on the board. Being on the board of directors of a public company is overrated. It is time-consuming, often incredibly bureaucratic and usually constitutes serious liability risks. I had no interest in being the CEO and the chairman. The idea bored me to death. I had done this already. Why should I possibly want to do it again? Our investors wanted me to concentrate on the funds, not on administration and corporate developments. Moreover, I was considered somewhat of a rogue given the legal issues relating to market manipulation in two specific cases (Sixt and WCM). It was also considered good corporate governance to minimize potential conflicts of interests, such as compensation, option and bonus plans, between the largest single shareholder (also a senior employee) and the other smaller stakeholders. Lastly, JR did not want me to interfere with his running the ACMH Dog and Pony show while he was securing generous salaries, bonuses and option plans for himself and his cronies. As a consequence, it made little sense overall for me to be on the board of directors of ACMH. Unfortunately, my absence from this board also led to at least one fatal mistake, which could easily have been avoided.

JR's 2007 midyear-bonus guidelines were insulting. We were about to experience the exodus of our top managers. The badly needed rainmakers and superstars would never come on board.

Based on exactly the same compensation formula as all other senior traders and analysts, my midyear compensation was over 8 million euros. The only way we could compensate the other traders by industry standards was for me to forsake my bonus in its entirety. My fixed salary was 120,000 euros per year, so I cared about receiving the bonus I was entitled to. I had already transferred more than half of my bonus entitlement to the other managers the previous year. In 2007, well over half of group-performance income was directly related to the funds or the positions I was managing. JR was fully aware of this impasse and was conspicuously absent from all performance and compensation reviews, which before he had always conducted by himself or with D. He had boxed himself and the company into a corner and was making me sweat out his mistakes.

JR and the board of directors had made a very simple bet: if it came down to the wire, Florian would forsake his entire bonus to keep the team intact. Their reasoning was I was getting richer via dividend payments and share sales. That should be enough for me. And the board would not need to revise the idiotic contractual guarantees they had given the Argo shareholders. Finally, they assumed there was no way I would walk away from a $200 million equity stake.

They did not do their math right. The stake had already been reduced by more than half as I had gifted about $50 million to the funds and about the same to my ex-wife. I was no longer the dominant shareholder I used to be. Why should the guy who makes over half the profits forsake his bonus completely, while the board members and senior management were paying themselves record bonuses? Well, they were wrong and they had made a stupid bet based on fallacious assumptions. Working with multidimensional probability scenarios was not JR's strong suit.

I wanted no part of his harebrained plan to move me into marketing and let his inept yes men manage the funds. The pathetic investment results of the ACMH hedge funds after my departure and the liquidation of all of my positions proved the stupidity of his ill-fated, low-cost corporate strategy. The returns sucked across all funds.

JR and I were the reasons for ACMH's success but also for its failure. The high energy levels can at first produce tremendous results but ultimately the destructive tendencies will catch up. How could anyone expect a liaison between a functional psychopath and a functional schizophrenic to succeed over the long term? How could we not run into trouble given our lack of ethics and demonic value system?

So I had kissed my entire compensation goodbye; I was still very rich, but this went deeper. Was I going to reward management incompetence and frail deal structures with my money? No. Would I work for 10,000 euros per month? Forget about it. Did I want to continue working with these clowns? Fat chance. Did I enjoy my job enough to stick around? I hated my job. Did I really give a big crap about my reputation? No. Did I have an inkling of professional pride left in my corrupt, mercantile frame? Surprisingly, yes. This was much more fundamental than being simply about money. This was about respect. This was about taking your core asset, a human being after all, for granted, undermining him at every turn while pimping off him at the same time. I was too busy pulling knives out of my back to run the funds effectively. My professional life had become a senseless, unrewarding game. I was out of there.

I did not receive one expression of gratitude from the traders, analysts or management for this voluntary 8-million-euro wealth transfer. Everybody had been paid in full. Everyone knew that this was only possible because I had moved my compensation from my wallet into theirs. Not one other ACMH executive had contributed a dime to retain talent, and many of them were significant ACMH shareholders as well. If you do not understand why I was upset at the time, you need to pursue a career in child trafficking or serial killing. You will fit in nicely.

I even got calls from some of the bozos complaining that their compensation was unfair and needed to be adjusted upwards. "From what?" I asked myself. Could they not grasp that I had just taken my entire bonus and stuffed it into their pockets? Did they expect me to get a personal loan to compensate them for their paltry performance contribution? Most of them would never see such fat bonuses ever again. Most would be extremely lucky to retain their jobs, let alone prosper in the industry. Most had confused skill with luck and timing. They thought they were actually gifted at what they were doing. In reality, they had just caught a lucky tailwind for a few years. They had simply been in the right place at the right time.

There were a few exceptions. I liked Sascha who had worked for Señor Rico and his Swiss assistant, our two Italian traders, and two Krauts, Frank and Stephan. They were at least competent. Let's see how long the remaining self-titled superstars would last without me: a month, a quarter, maximum one year? The markets were on the verge of collapse and nobody as usual saw the writing on the wall. Nobody at ACMH was capable of making dough in a down market. The party was over, and once again I left just before drunkards began fighting over the few remaining, tired-looking workhorses at the bar. I could not express my thoughts at that time any better than Goethe: "Nothing is more terrible than to see ignorance in action."

Of course, I accept much of the credit for the company's rise and much of the blame for its decline. My insatiable greed and unscrupulous ambition, my distorted value system contributed to ACMH's ascent and demise. Success has many fathers and defeat has none. In this specific case, I am solely responsible for the firm's collapse. This is ridiculous.

Investors knew full well who was the glue that held the firm together and who was the driver that produced the profits. They saw right through JR's bullshit. The share price collapsed by 88 percent within hours of my resignation, and the company never recovered.

However, all that darkness was all in the future. Some of the stories in the following chapters touch on the extreme variety of investing during the ACMH years, both negative and, surprisingly, positive.

8. Diagnosis Positive

It is not from the benevolence of the butcher, the brewer, or the baker that we expect our dinner, but from their regard to their own interest.
Adam Smith

A few years before the great financial crisis of 2008/2009, German politicians and the media began to equate leveraged-buyout fund managers and some hedge fund managers, including myself, to locusts (*Heuschrecken in German*). They would descend on helpless companies and graze on them until all of their substance had disappeared. Besides destroying major companies, we were all making too much money and a disgrace to society. We became the enemy number one of Chancellor Angela Merkel, who saw these investment professionals as the greatest risk to the world's financial stability. Major German newspapers even published photographs of these animals. I had descended from the "Gentleman Share-Price Exterminator" to a mindless, destructive insect.

By 2009 it was painfully obvious even to the most mindless politicians that ultra-liberal lending practices, free-spending governments, dubious rating agencies, sleazy and irresponsible investment bankers, unscrupulous lenders, state-owned banks who bought subprime mortgages, central bankers who allowed the markets to be flooded with low-cost funds for far too long, and misdirected individuals who kept buying homes they could not afford, were the root of the financial demise and the most severe recession since the Great Depression. Hedge fund managers and buyout managers played no meaningful roles in the financial collapse. Angela Merkel was dead wrong.

When I first arrived on the European investment scene in the late 1980s, there were virtually no activist shareholders. Europeans were decades behind

Americans in terms of capital market development. Greenmailing, raiding, asset stripping and short selling were in their infancy. Given zero competition, zero legislation and plenty of fat targets, this type of market was ripe for the plucking from 1985 until about 2005.

Greenmailing and raiding are the purest forms of Darwinist, capitalist mercantilism, a multidimensional chess game requiring significant skills, vast connections and substantial resources. Greenmail is a form of legal, financial blackmail. It involves buying substantial stakes in a target company often with covert or public allies to affect either a complete takeover or at least substantial corporate, financial, or management changes. Frequently so-called friendly white knights emerge to help management while it is under pressure from a hostile aggressor. I have only been a white knight once, and guess what, it was a complete farce. Being a white knight is rather uneventful, overrated and simply less profitable than being the primary aggressor. On more than twenty other occasions over two decades, I had been the dark knight of European finance.

The professional greenmailer is a serious threat to entrenched managements as he is considering all options, from asset stripping, complete takeover, divestitures, spin-offs, board and management changes, special cash dividends, re-engineering, share buybacks and even payoffs to maximize his financial gain. Greenmailers like squeezing inept managements into a corner from which they cannot exit, either handing over the company or paying a heavy ransom to get them off their back. This all sounds rather violent and vicious but once you get used to it, it is just another routine financial operation, sort of like a wire transfer. More often than not, the greenmailer will put an end to poor cost management, excessive compensation and management incompetence. If he cannot execute the necessary changes, his shares are often purchased at a premium or placed with friends of management at a higher price. If you do your homework well, it is almost impossible to lose money.

A more benign and civilized version of the greenmailer/raider is the activist shareholder, normally also a much nicer person than the greenmailer. Activist shareholders are more about making noise to effect change. Their equity stakes are typically much smaller. They often help streamline and build companies in a constructive way. They also violate securities laws far less often.

If you want to taste everything in life—which has always seemed to me to be the whole point of being alive—then that means books *and* sports, uppers *and* downers, boys *and* girls, black *and* white. Logically that also of course means right *and* wrong, good *and* bad. The media likes to pretend there is very little inherently of value in capital markets, but fortunately I know that the number of ethical investments I have made is far greater than my sinful ventures. Very little in life is reducible to black and white conclusions, because truth and reality often reside in grey areas. Positive and negative outcomes often start from the same place—sunshine will help you if you have MS or osteoporosis, but too much of it will give you skin cancer.

So on balance, what do hedge funds, short sellers and proprietary traders add to the advancement of society?

Not that much, is the short answer. Anyone in our profession with one honest bone in their body will admit this. Some like George Soros have become major philanthropists over time, but they were often extremely opportunistic during their moneymaking years. Others like me have become minor benefactors. All in all, the group is a rather heartless and often anti-intellectual, cynical bunch. Yes, we generally improve liquidity and market efficiency. We usually arbitrage the unhealthy fat from the steaks. Outrageous and shameless stock promotions and chronic overvaluations are often limited by short selling. Successful proprietary traders do only one thing: they consistently earn money while employing lower than average risk. Most of us do think more about taking than giving.

Hedge funds rarely fund young growth companies, which improve thousands of lives, create employment and opportunities. I have always been aware of the social shortcomings of my profession, and during my career I have funded numerous health-care- and other similarly positive companies, sometimes by design, sometimes by accident. I have funded and advised dozens of young growth companies, helped them develop and listed them on a stock exchange. They all generate employment.

My critics claim I destroyed many companies, which is too simplistic and frankly inaccurate. I identified overvalued, frequently fraudulent, heavily indebted companies that were destroying themselves. They had only themselves to blame. At worst, I was the predictor of disaster, at times the first messenger of death.

A short seller simply cannot destroy a strong, profitable company. It is akin to biting through kryptonite. It is foolish and shatters one's teeth. Short sellers look for weakness. We prefer diseased, disintegrating patients disguised as omnipotent, healthy and highly-rated magnates like Enron, like WCM, like Bremer Vulkan, like the US dollar and present-day American government debt. Warren Buffett, no less, approves of shorting because it corrects overvaluations. Where there is weakness, corruption, fraud, incompetence and other elements coupled with lofty valuations will attract the short seller. Corporate raiding and activist investing is the exact opposite of short selling. The companies in question are undervalued for all sorts of reasons. Let us not forget that corporate raiding began in the States because billions were being wasted by companies—often on excessive perks for the board—were discovered and quite rightly viewed as morally and financially unacceptable fat in a market that demanded leanness and agility.

If it were all just about the money, I would have limited myself either to dynamic value investing, computerized pair trading or proprietary day trading. Computer and high frequency trading is incredibly mundane and lacks purpose and emotional gratification. Pure value investing is extremely methodical, too passive and too boring for me. Valuation range pair trading is very mechanical and too nerdy for me. I have never been a one-dimensional financier and investor. I have played all the instruments in the capital markets orchestra. And believe me, if you spend your entire time as a short seller you will turn into a deeply twisted and pessimistic misanthrope, clapping when you hear that some CEO has had a heart attack. The psychological and emotional implications of that, even for someone like me who is relatively unemotional, are not appealing. Additionally, if all you do is asset stripping, takeovers or leveraged buyouts, the financial rewards may be high but the emotional returns are low.

Without a doubt, the most emotionally rewarding financial activity is venture capital and actively helping smaller companies become successful larger ones. If these companies do something useful, the emotional rewards are even higher. These activities are extremely risky. Typically, more companies fail or underperform than prosper. However, over the long term, the financial and emotional returns far outweigh the risks.

JDate, still the world's largest Jewish Internet dating site, has led to thousands of marriages every year for over a decade. The company was worth $1 million when we invested. The peak valuation was over $300 million. I provided emergency funding to a nearly insolvent but important vaccine maker, ID Biomedical Systems, at a $17 million valuation. The company survived and prospered and was acquired for $1.7 billion by Glaxo. I funded and advised NuRx Pharmaceuticals and Mologen. NuRx develops retinoid for the prevention of lung and breast cancer. NuRx has a world-class patent library and scintillating upside but was mismanaged and has been a near total write-off. Mologen's activities are concentrated on creating new immunological drugs and therapies to combat cancer and on developing state-of-the-art vaccines for the prevention and the treatment of serious infectious diseases in humans as well as animals. The company has not yet brought a product to market, but the shares have performed reasonably well.

For my own moral gratification, I have always searched for the grail, which is companies which improve the maximum number of lives while allowing me to make the most handsome return on my capital. That company might well be Clinuvel, an Australian late-stage biotechnology firm whose impact on skin cancer and Vitiligo could be revolutionary.

My fascination with human skin began at Harvard. During the probation I was under in my freshman year for having violated at least six important university rules, one of the more serious requirements imposed on me we was not to score less than a C in any of my third semester courses. The contract I had with the professional basketball team in Germany involved commuting between Boston and Frankfurt at least twice a month, and the schedule frequently conflicted with midterm and final examinations.

At the time, I was taking a demanding class in physics and astronomy taught by one of the most famous astrophysicists of our day, Professor Eric Chaisson, bestselling author and educator. My German team had just made the semifinals of the German Basketball Cup competition and I was scheduled to play on exactly the same day as the astrophysics midterm examination. Not only was I contractually obliged to show up, the owner of the club had offered us a special financial incentive if we defeated the reigning German champions, Saturn Köln.

My mother had recently been confined to a mental institution after attempting to commit suicide, and had specifically requested my presence. Professor Chaisson accepted my tall tale, and my examination was rescheduled for the following Wednesday morning, about ten hours after I would get back from Frankfurt. I could study on the flight over and back, surely enough time to wing it. It did not work out that way. Somehow I blanked out completely on the Wednesday itself, thinking it was in fact scheduled for the following day. Chaisson's teaching assistant waited for me for two hours in the examination room, but I never showed up.

On Friday I begged Professor Chaisson to give me another shot. He was a nice man, but he told me, "Florian, you need to take your studies and your scheduling seriously. In real life, you rarely get a second chance. And you are asking me for a third chance here. I am sorry but I will give you a zero for your midterm. You will have to do rather well in your final examination and paper to pass this class." That was a hell of an understatement.

Mastering the subject matter was not exactly a cakewalk for me. My last physics class had been in eighth grade, I knew less than zero about astronomy and I was neither a science nor a pre-med major. The midterm examination counted for

34 percent of the final grade, and the final paper and examination each counted for 33 percent. The best grade I could theoretically achieve, assuming perfection in the form of straight As on both the final paper and in the final examination, was 66 percent, giving a C. That would save me from expulsion; but it was an impossible task. Eager-beaver pre-medical students were taking this class, getting all the top marks. I was in a very deep jam. I would have to take huge risks and come up with something ingenious to impress Professor Chaisson.

I had recently been thinking a lot about bio-racial issues, physiognomy and behavioral patterns, having always been curious about the subjects. I asked myself silly questions such as: why is my skin white? Are Germans really descended from Indians? Do blacks really jump higher because of different muscle structure? Are white people really more buoyant and therefore able to swim better? Is the brain size and brain structure of different racial groups exactly the same? Is a racial mix (such as my then girlfriend Lynne and me) genetically advantageous for the children, or is nurture the more critical factor in determining their prospects? What causes people to have light eyes? And so on. Since my teens, I have been a depository of generally useless multidisciplinary facts and oddities. Twinning some of these with the demands of the astrophysics elements of the course would be a challenge, but my analytical foray into skin types and colors in relation to solar factors, erosion of the ozone layer and its effect on radiation levels sounded promising.

"What if the sun rays are gaining in strength, as Professor Chaisson claims?" I wondered. "Would this not affect all of our lives? Would white people get more skin cancer? Would skin cancer threaten white communities living in Australia and South Africa and in the American South? How would Darwin interpret this trend in terms of natural selection for or against certain skin and racial types? Would the increasing demographic preponderance of darker-skinned people, and the increasing mixing of the races, negate the overall skin cancer effect by offering more UV protection on an absolute population basis? Would the reduction of CFCs arrest the depletion of the ozone layer in a meaningful way, making my analysis redundant? If the sunrays were getting stronger, would not sea levels rise and turn certain semi-arid zones into deserts? Would not plant life and insect migration dramatically change our future lives? What was the rate of change? Would there be any impact during our lifetime? How does one measure this?"

The subject was beginning to interest me. I was already wildly speculating in equities at the time so if I got some kick-ass insights maybe it would boost my investment returns. Maybe firms offering luxury sun and skin protection products like L'Oreal and Beiersdorf (Nivea) would experience much higher long-term sales and profits than currently projected. I looked for pure plays, public companies providing medicines and treatments in the skin-cancer area, but found none.

I knuckled down to study solar eruptions, Vitiligo (an acquired de-pigmentation disorder), skin cancers and Langerhans cell functions. For the next ten days, I lived in several Harvard libraries. My friend Marco Bodor helped fill in a lot of medical gaps in my knowledge and corrected numerous faulty assumptions and conclusions. Lynne brought me sandwiches. My paper discussed the warming of the earth, the rising ocean levels and significantly higher radiation levels. It concluded that skin cancer would increase far faster than presently assumed by the scientific community, and that, *ceteris paribus*, having darker skin would be a distinct advantage.

This was 1979. Nobody had even heard of global warming and rising ocean levels. I called it "warming of the earth." The paper reasoned that darker people indeed had a far superior skin type for the coming centuries but their demographic position in semi-arid zones, especially the Sahel Zone and Northern Africa, would lead to life-threatening disruptions and a battle for ever scarcer water sources. While several hundred million white people would get skin cancer, less than 200,000 per annum would lose their lives from the most malignant forms (the actual number of deaths resulting from skin cancer is closer to 100,000). My personal economic conclusion was sun protection would become a major issue. A company that developed effective sun protection for the highest risk skin-cancer candidates (Fitzgerald 1 and Fitzgerald 2 types) would make an absolute fortune.

I had strayed into anthropology, biology and climate studies, but luckily for me, Professor Chaisson was a multidisciplinarian and called my research paper "profoundly thought-provoking." He asked for my permission to show it to his colleagues in various departments. I was very flattered, aced the final as well, and was allowed to stay at Harvard.

Clinuvel (initially called Epitan) was the exact company I was looking to invest in when I wrote my astrophysics paper for Professor Chaisson. When I began investing in it, the principal compound melanotide was promising. It had no discernible side effects and scientific studies were encouraging. The chief scientific officer, Dr Hank Agersborg, was impressive, and his track record of discovering new treatments and bringing them to market was spotless.

The company, however, was a case study of management incompetence. Over a decade after discovering the compound that would darken skin, no meaningful progress had been made to achieve medical approval or commercial viability. Back then, the company focused on cosmetic applications. Epitan was hoping to patent Melanotan, a medication that would enable a lot of white people to get a healthy tan without burning themselves in the process. The company was bleeding cash and constantly on the verge of insolvency.

Funding, cost management, clinical and regulatory strategy were all in complete disarray. In order to get Melanotan approved by a credible regulatory authority would require a complete makeover; away from sun blisters and towards bona fide medical conditions. We acquired 20 percent of the company and brought other supportive shareholders with us. Our influence was substantial enough to inject a competent, no-nonsense CEO, Dr Philippe Wolgen, and change the board of directors and senior management. We also raised AUS $60 million to complete mission critical medical studies and assured the company had sufficient funds to achieve commercial viability. While we turned around and promoted Epitan/Clinuvel, the shares appreciated 600 percent.

One in five Americans (60 million) will contract skin cancer during their lifetime. No cancer type is more prevalent. The incidence of skin cancer in the rest of the world is even larger. Thousands die each year. Another 50 million people suffer from Vitiligo. Millions suffer from severe sun allergies and other diseases related to sun exposure.

Clinuvel has developed a compound that increases melanin content in skin. Melanin shields the skin from hostile UV rays. It is administered via a minimally invasive subcutaneous injection. The injectable item is no larger than a rice corn, which will induce a perfectly even, protective and lasting tan even on the whitest, most freckled individual. The tanning/protection effect lasts eight to twelve weeks. The product, Scenesse, has been approved for treating EPP (also known as the vampire disease) for people suffering from extreme light insensitivity disorders and is already fully reimbursable in Italy.

When I resigned from ACMH, Clinuvel lost its principal backer and promoter and the share price declined by 80 percent. Yet the company has gone from strength to strength operationally, is very well managed by its chief executive officer, has an outstanding scientific team, a capable board of directors and is in solid financial shape. Much to his credit, Philippe Wolgen, the company's CEO, has focused on the pressing medical rather than the cosmetic applications. This, of course, does not rule out an associated company, a subsidiary or venture partner exploits the cosmetic potential at a later stage.

It is now generating sales and should be very profitable in the coming years. Its product enjoys vast patent protection and there is no competition in sight. As a consequence, it has become a formidable, extremely compelling value investment. Nomura Securities, one of the largest financial institutions in the world, estimates 370 percent potential upside in Clinuvel's share price. The company is selling at a minimum discount of 75 percent to its intrinsic value, and I have not even begun to talk about cosmetic applications. It could be the next Botox. I believe the long-term upside is much higher.

I am vain and rich. Scenesse would give me the perfect tan without aging my skin. It protects me against the sun and I will be much less likely to get skin cancer as a consequence. As soon as I can buy it, I'll get it. Many others will reach the same conclusion. Some will buy the shares as well.

Without my involvement, Clinuvel would have gone bankrupt. I would be exhilarated if Clinuvel saved thousands of lives and dramatically improved the daily existence of millions. I am certain it is already the most emotionally rewarding investment I have ever made.

The second most rewarding investment category is "turnaround" investing, and within this category, my involvement with Borussia Dortmund (BVB) became one of my more interesting and famous activist investments. Regardless of what was said at the time, it was not a rapacious raid on a defenseless healthy company. It was a terminally sick business, and survived primarily due to high-risk equity capital injections and debt restructurings. My behavior was atypical for an alleged destructive locust. How could a locust possibly save rather than destroy a company?

BVB is one of the world's major soccer clubs. No other club in Europe averaged more spectators per game (80,000), not even Real Madrid, Manchester United, Bayern Munich or AC Milan. There are about three million Germans who consider themselves BVB fans. It has won eight German championships, the European Champion's League and World Soccer Club titles. It is not just a club; it is an institution with tremendous history and pride.

In 2004, I bought a 9.9-percent stake in BVB, at an attractive discount to market price, from Norman Rentrop, a major publisher and seasoned value investor who I first knew when he was client while I was at Jonathan & White. Ignoring my own rules for once, we had only done perfunctory research and had no idea what sort of mess we had got ourselves into. We had not talked to BVB's sponsors, their lenders, their former executives or their competitors. Why would we? This was a perfectly manageable stake scored at a great price. Our involvement had already sent the share price up 30 percent, producing a hefty paper return. We were going to make some positive noise and dump our shares in the market with a quick and dirty profit. "Why bother with time-consuming and costly competitive verification?" I thought at the time. We were in touch with two oligarchs only too tempted to buy into a major European football club. We had practically presold the stake before we bought it.

You absolutely need to do your research before entering a position, not afterwards. Do not try to wing it. Upon closer inspection, we found out that BVB was at best insolvent and at worst bankrupt, not cash and asset rich as the balance sheet suggested. The company was bleeding millions on a monthly basis and would be unable to service its debt. There were almost 40 million euros of off-balance-sheet debt not disclosed in the financial statements, and over 100 million of disclosed debt that needed to be refinanced. Senior management was running a very liberal cost management. They had even pledged their trademark ("BVB") and several players as collateral for an emergency loan. Much of this information was not public knowledge at the time of our investment. We had bought ourselves a Bremer Vulkan and I was likely to lose a considerable fortune and be crucified by the media.

The bad news ultimately leaked out into the financial press, and the hopeless position of BVB became all too apparent. The share price teetered. For once, the entire financial and media community were in complete agreement on two things: BVB was going bust and Homm had finally lost his marbles. BVB would be my demise.

We had two options: dump our position and incur heavy losses, or make the impossible happen and save the most financially distressed professional German soccer club. Because we were having a poor month and could not afford another heavy loss in our highly ranked Germany fund, we decided to rescue BVB. Only a certified lunatic would attempt such a hopeless turnaround. We pumped a large pile of capital into BVB via a capital increase and became far and away the largest shareholder, holding just under 30 percent of all outstanding shares. By then we had done our homework and were ready to put our plan to work.

The demands we placed on company and management in return for our money were brutal and diabolic. President Niebaum should guarantee us two board seats. I made sure the CEO personally signed this guarantee knowing full well only the annual general meeting could approve and elect supervisory board members. We had infused our own consulting team to chop operating costs and we were going to fire the entire executive management board and half the supervisory board as soon as practicable. We would win and we would not take any prisoners along the way.

The annual general meeting took place in front of 2,000 aggravated shareholders and over 100 reporters and photographers. I vilified management for cooking the books, utter incompetence and lining their pockets. Executive salaries were halved almost immediately, and within months we had installed a virtually new president, supervisory board, CEO, CFO, head of merchandising and so forth. Things were looking up. Heads rolled daily. To further raise the level of urgency, I told the financial press we should change the name of the club from BVB to something like "The First Dortmund Soccer Club." This would reduce debt by 20 million euros at a stroke, given that management had pledged the brand name for the emergency loan. My recommendation resulted in public protests in Dortmund and led to several death threats.

I had never seriously intended to go through with that. Neither the executive or supervisory board would have agreed to such a radical move, but I suggested it to ensure that everyone knew nothing was sacred when it came to cutting costs. I publically attacked the coach, actually a great guy, and offered a lower paid alternative. My latest hit lists of further casualties would be published within 24 hours after talking with Jörg Weiler, an influential sports journalist who covered BVB for *Bild Zeitung*, Germany's largest daily newspaper.

Because BVB's professional soccer license might not have been renewed, selling some of their better players to raise cash and reduce debt became a necessity. I was concerned that losing several stars meant the team could face relegation from the Bundesliga, which would be a financial and reputational disaster. The constant cost cutting and aggression was taking a toll on performance. As well as losing some of his best players, the coach Bert van Marwijk, who would lead the Dutch national team to second place in the 2010 World Cup, also could not get any of the players he wanted. My image as a hatchet man was generating insecurity in management and amongst player ranks. "Who's next on Homm's list?" was a justified question.

However, there is a limit to cost cutting. Due to the restructuring, BVB had no funds to incentivize superior performance, and at some point incentives need to be provided and the working climate needs to be stabilized, otherwise one enters nightmare territory. Jörg Weiler, who has a wicked sense of humor, came up with the idea of offering the players and the coaches 1 million euros if they qualified for the Champion's League. No rehabilitator would ever sponsor such an insane idea, but I did my math.

We had invested about 35 million euros into the club. If BVB qualified for the Champion's League, the share price would double. ACMH would earn 7 million in performance fees. That would translate into about 4 million in net earnings. If ACMH decided to pay out 80 percent of its net income in dividends, I would earn 1.2 million euros in cash versus paying BVB 1 million.

Assuming a price/earnings ratio of ten, the extra earnings from BVB could easily lift the ACMH share price by 40 million. At the time, my ACMH stake was worth about 200 million euros. Because I owned 35 percent of the shares, the value of my holding in ACMH would increase by 14 million euros. If I had to pay out 1 million to the players, all I had to do was sell 0.5 percent of my holdings. The net value of my ACMH shares would increase by 13 million euros, or 6 percent. This equated to a 1,300-percent return on investment for me.

Jörg's idea was fabulous and I accepted. The reward scheme was well received by the fans, coaches and players and I was dying to pay it. Of course, Jörg did not know why I agreed to his provocative idea. He probably thought I was just another rich vain guy who cared more about his public image than his pocket book.

I officially joined the club, talked with hard-core BVB fan club members and watched part of a game from the *Südtribüne*, where 20,000 of the most rumbustious fans had their home, instead of the VIP section. I even went to two more games.

The financial restructuring was proceeding well, however we needed to convince thirty-eight extremely concerned creditors to agree to our medium-term restructuring plan. The final and decisive creditor meeting was coming up. At this point new management had taken over, costs structures were dramatically improved and BVB was only steps away from selling its stadium naming rights to a major corporation.

The jockeying behind the scenes was intense. If even one of the creditors refused to buy into the financial restructuring, we would have to pour even more money into this black hole without certainty of BVB's survival, let alone a return on our investment. We had provided a standby commitment letter to plug any holes created by opposing creditors. However, even our resources had limits as our investors were questioning my logic of investing into that "stupid German soccer club." In the days leading up to the creditors' meeting, I used both carrots and baseball bats (figuratively speaking) behind closed doors to optimize the outcome.

The creditors bought into the financial restructuring plan and we got a much-needed reprieve. The worst was now behind us. The media was beginning to grasp that the unthinkable was becoming reality. Homm and his partners in management and the supervisory board had saved Borussia Dortmund. BVB's professional license from the omnipotent German Soccer Federation was renewed, and our prime broker Morgan Stanley organized an 80-million-euro refinancing, secured by the stadium. The stadium naming rights brought in substantial annual revenue, and better than expected player transfer revenue was beginning to repair the sickly balance sheet. Peripheral assets had been sold, operating costs had been slashed by more than 60 percent and cozy links had been reduced to zero. During the heat of the crisis, debt was bought at big discounts to face value and restructured at much lower interest costs, enhancing profitability. Within twelve months, BVB went from a 40-million-euro loss to a 6-million-euro profit.

At the height of the crisis, I had publically stated the BVB share price would at least double and that the club would be a major force in the Bundesliga and international soccer within three to four years. I only got sarcastic laughs from the assorted financial analysts and reporters. Three years later, in 2010, BVB played in the UEFA Cup after finishing fifth in the Bundesliga. The club was basically debt free and asset rich and generating positive cash flow. When Dortmund played Bayern Munich in March 2011, the game was broadcast in 191 countries. BVB became Germany's national soccer champion for the seventh time two months later. (They topped even that, in the following year, winning the national soccer championship and the DFB Cup as well.) The shares are up 300 percent. The impossible mission had become a resounding restructuring success, almost on schedule. The professional pessimists had been proven wrong.

I like the Dortmunders, especially the BVB fans. They are very direct, unpretentious, constantly in your face and know how to celebrate and live with adversity. Even Dr Niebaum, who had brought Borussia Dortmund to the top of World Club Soccer League tables, conceded defeat like a gentleman. Despite the fact that I had dethroned him and attacked him viciously in public, we maintained a constructive and professional working relationship during the management transition period.

The management's removal and subsequent turnaround was orchestrated by a hedge fund manager, a former socialist minister and a leading journalist and was executed by a *Mittelstand* entrepreneur. I was the hatchet man. Morgan Stanley, our prime broker, organized the balance sheet restructuring. That task was managed with the help of one of my former senior VMR investment bankers, who had joined Morgan Stanley. Altogether, this was probably the most diverse and heterogeneous group I had ever worked with in a turnaround situation.

President Rauball, CEO Watzke, Coach Jürgen Klopp and player personnel Director Michael Zorc have done a fabulous job. Throughout Borussia's heartwrenching ups and downs, I have become a committed BVB fan. I stay on top of BVB's results every week, eagerly awaiting their Bundesliga and European cup. I even attended one home game in 2011, with a fake beard and yellow black BVB cap, in the *Südtribüne (cheapest tickets, standing room only and the best fans)*. Today BVB won its second German championship in a row, after beating Bayern Munich and its archrival Schalke 04 in the two previous games. I am celebrating their 8th national championship with a few German expatriates who think I am an Australian rugby coach named Alan Jones. After many bottles of beer, countless Jägermeister and tears of joy they are raving "Auch du, lieber Alan, bist jetzt ein Dortmunder. Lass uns noch einen trinken. Leucht auf, Borussia. Prosit!" Overall, we lost money on BVB, but I have never experienced a more demanding, entertaining and emotionally rewarding turnaround. The soccer God has been merciful and kind to Borussia.

During my investment career, I was involved in more than seventy activist investments. My hostile ventures, however, attracted far more attention even though I was much more involved in growing and restructuring companies than short selling or asset stripping them. I was involved in about a dozen companies that were part of major stock market indices also known as large caps. The remaining were smaller and medium-size companies where the competition was minimal and the fruits were hanging much lower and easier to grab.

However, I am not certain that the final results were any better than if I had executed a first rate long/short value strategy over the same time span. Value investing is out of favor when investors are chasing page impressions rather than profits, but who needs to be in those markets anyway? The answer is: virtually all equity mutual funds anywhere in the world! These funds are measured against indices and if everybody buys crap and that crap keeps going up, almost all the mutual funds pile in as well in order to avoid underperforming some ludicrous market index. Consider managing the process and your money by yourself.

Value investing makes incontrovertible sense; but greenmailing, raiding, short selling, asset stripping and building companies is certainly more entertaining and more hands-on. Moreover, it is much more suited to my deranged, psychotic personality.

9. Negative Equity

The art of living is more like wrestling than dancing.
Marcus Aurelius

I am more fearless and calculating than most, but if you think you can go around ripping companies to pieces, indulging in greenmail, openly attacking corporations in which you have massive short positions and firing senior management teams without receiving some serious blows in return, you are insanely naive and need to commit yourself to a mental hospital for immediate treatment.

I've had to take a lot of heavy blows although I didn't deserve most of them. WCM used their extensive property portfolio for years to speculate on the stock market. As long as the market was on the rise, or remaining constant, there was nothing to fear. In a bear market, WCM was very much at risk. The market fell and fell. At a certain point, the bankers and investors became more and more nervous, because the DAX had fallen more than half in the downturn, and WCM, with investments like Commerzbank, suffered much greater losses. Eventually, WCM reached its lending limit, the bankers wanted their money and the WCM stock price imploded unceremoniously.

I pointed out these obvious and well-researched risks publically and was faced with a potential five-year prison sentence. The district attorney charged me for using a clandestine research organization on one side while cashing in on my short sales via the hedge fund organization on the other. He naively called this "market manipulation and a heavy case of insider trading." My research organization, United Zurich Finance, was fully transparent showing me as a full director with a photograph on their website and corporate brochure. ACMH was even more transparent. Anybody who could pull up a website or use a search engine would know in seconds that Florian Homm was involved in both companies. Research and asset management were two different organizations for legal, regulatory and tax reasons. The connections were a matter of public record and knowledge. Yet the public prosecutor, under pressure from the Establishment, engaged me in a two-year witch hunt to prove our research was clandestine and we engaged in large-scale covert market manipulation. Nothing could be further from the truth.

WCM was a major player in Germany, especially in Frankfurt, where they were headquartered. They had enough power to sick the local district attorney on me. After an intensive legal investigation, the district attorney asked me to contribute 20,000 euros each for the youth league and an animal shelter, a far cry from a three-to-five-year prison sentence the prosecution had initially considered. I settled because I did not want to spend another two years in court proceedings. ACMH also did not want me to spend so much time away from the trading desk and offered to cover my legal bills.

The Establishment hates guys like me breathing down their necks and causing trouble. So, as usual, they went after me and not the real crooks. The journalists loved ripping into me as well. Those who heeded my advice and sold early enough saved millions. Those suffering from normalcy bias and trusting higher authority in the face of compelling negatives lost a fortune. How could I possibly be the bad guy in the media? I have never spent a dime in advertising over my entire career. Our investment results were excellent, therefore attracting enough attention. By attacking me, journalists would not fear losing a major advertising account. I had no lobby and refused to buy positive press. As a consequence, I have always been an easy target for journalists, especially those who were influenced by my enemies.

I have had private detectives following my every move for a year of my professional life. My life has been threatened on several occasions and according to the media and reliable sources the Russian mafia, the Hell's Angels and Serbo-Croatian extortionists were looking for me. Over the years, I had become fairly immune to threats. My standard response was, "Take a ticket, and move to the end of the very long line." Threats are part of the business, and they say you are judged by your enemies. Ever since elementary school, I have had more than most.

However, in 2003 I received a very credible threat aimed not directly at me but at my family. I was involved in several short raids at the time when I received a call on my unlisted home phone number. I would love to disclose the name of the company involved but have signed a lengthy nondisclosure and privacy agreement. The conversation went as follows:

Gangster: *Is this Mr. Homm?*

FH: *How the fuck did you get this number and who are you?*

Gangster: *This should not concern you. What should concern you is that we would like you to cease challenging company X.*

FH: *Listen asshole, get off the phone, pick a ticket and get in line. Talk to my lawyers and have a shitty day.*

Gangster: *We really like those new Nike shoes your son is wearing at school. Your daughter also had a really nice haircut yesterday. We took some nice photos of both of them. You want to see them?*

FH: *...No... What do you want?*

Gangster: *We want you to go away and stop messing with our company. We have at least thirty people working in our group with serious criminal records including manslaughter. Do you want to meet them? Probably not, right? But you know what, they would like to meet your children?*

FH: *I know who you're working for, you scumbag.* [I only had three hostile projects at the time and two were rather harmless.]. *I'll think about it. OK?*

Gangster: *Don't think too long.*

FH: *Go fuck your dog.*

Clearly, I had run into a determined opponent here, not some meek corporate grey mouse. These were professionals, not barking dogs. Was the deal worth the hassle? Did I have to prove something, be right, win some Mickey Mouse financial battle and risk the life of my family? Hell no.

The guys behind the threats also wanted 4 million euros in damages from me. That was laughable. My lawyers showed them our "extensive competitive verification research," outlining dubious deals, probable tax evasion, probable fraud, dealing with a notorious gangster, and terror connections in the Middle East and major potential fraud cases in Europe. These guys had teamed up with a Middle Eastern businessman in several joint ventures who was believed to be the financial brain and financier behind 9/11 and was pursued for the largest-ever fraud in German history.

The information had come from first-rate primary sources and was well documented, company filings in Lebanon and covert informers. I had spent several days in Beirut to get written proof, which supported my allegations. Giorgio had also found gold in several European and offshore jurisdictions. After reviewing our research and assessing the potential reputational and financial damage, we settled the silly affair rationally. The 4 million in damages were scrapped and both parties would no longer comment about each other publically from then on. I covered my short position with a meaningless profit. I deeply regret not buying the stock. It appreciated sevenfold within the next two years as the company's management and owners engineered a first-rate turnaround.

Two years earlier, former pre-IPO investors were threatening my family back home in Germany but I used normal police channels to diffuse that threat. It did not leave a nice aftertaste. Just recently, a rogue financier had almost defrauded me personally of 6 million euros and the funds by significantly more.

He failed. I put a serious legal squeeze on this guy and undermined his fraudulent moves at every step. I dumped all the shares in his company in one day driving the share price down by 40 percent. After he ran out of gullible victims and was facing both prison and bankruptcy, he ended his bogus life and committed suicide with a hole in one. *Der Spiegel* called his death "Homm's collateral damage," but I had not put out a contract on this creep. The guy took his own life. Nobody forced him. But, what if he had decided that I was the bad guy and then turned his gun on me? Once again, I did not like the smell of the *affaire*. After the last, far more serious round of threats and intimidations, I was either going to hire some full-time enforcers, which meant high fixed costs, or get connected. I got connected, and appropriately did it with the Greek goddess of wild animals and hunting, Artemis, looking down at me.

At approximately 60,000 square feet, Artemis in Berlin is Europe's biggest wellness bordello. We were equal partners with the founder and manager, Hakki Simsek, who is of German-Kurdish origin. Artemis hosts a cinema, Turkish bath and sauna, state-of-the-art weight room, an exercise area, a roof garden, barbeque area, a restaurant, a Roman-style swimming pool, impressive VIP suites, a few dozen chambers to conduct private business and about twenty apartments for the independent contractors (ICs) who prefer to live on the premises. There are several licensed masseurs and table dancers as well. Artemis is basically a facilities management company. Caligula would have approved.

Customers paid an 80-euro entrance fee. Even the women had to pay to provide their services at Artemis. We were facility managers, not pimps. The ICs who choose to reside on the premises also paid decent but not exaggerated rents. The bar, VIP rooms and restaurant were additional revenue sources. The independent contractors had to get monthly medical examinations, which were kept on file along with passport copies. The ICs paid their taxes and had to prove that they were in Germany legally and fully authorized to conduct their business.

Working morale and productivity at Artemis were both high during my involvement and Hakki was a disciplined, hardworking and fair managing partner. He was liked and respected but ruled with an iron fist. Staff, customers and independent contractors were treated respectfully. Due to intense controls and a permanent goon squad, shrinkage was very low and Artemis operated with a remarkable profit margin.

Pimps and drug dealers were not allowed on the premises and drug consumption of any form was strictly prohibited. Each guest was limited to a maximum of three drinks, limiting violent outbreaks considerably. There were about six frightening fellows to resolve potential conflicts. More than 100 independent contractors worked at Artemis on a given night servicing between 300 to 400 customers.

I had met Hakki via some switched-on property professionals in Berlin. He wanted to meet me for a refinancing as his establishment had experienced a 2-million-euro overrun during construction. He also wanted to expand on a European scale and would require some additional equity funding to realize his plans. The business was wickedly profitable and growing at 30 percent per annum. Even more attractively, all the investment for a second club would be recouped within eighteen months, a minimum 66-percent return on investment. We became equal partners via a private holding company. The investment made perfect sense. I was finally solidly connected to the right people (Kurds) and we were making perverse returns.

The timing could not have been better. Less than a year after our investment, Hakki's support proved invaluable. I had purchased a 10,000-square foot nightclub in the best possible seafront location on the golden party mile of Palma de Mallorca, the Paseo Maritimo. This represented the final stage of the toy market for me. My partner in the club was Paul Bauer, the founder of Wirecard, a major billing-software specialist. Paul was a dynamic and clever IT entrepreneur. He was also, however, somewhat naive about the potential pitfalls of owning a major nightclub in an affluent European metropolis. I had some history in the area because in an earlier life I had restructured a major table-dancing club near Euston in central London and another one in Birmingham, the former 69 Club. Both were sold to John Gray of Spearmint Rhino, making me considerably less naive than Paul.

He was overseeing operations and development, while I was a passive owner. As the club was getting increasingly popular and profitable, Paul received a visit from several well-known and physically intimidating Moroccan underworld figures. Their business proposition was to overhaul our lighting system and provide security for the outrageous sum of 200,000 euros and a monthly maintenance fee of 15,000 euros.

Paul, very much a classic high-tech entrepreneur and not a street rat like me, was completely terrified. For once in his life, he was facing a conundrum that he could not resolve. I told him to relax and asked some shady detectives to collect detailed profiles including photographs, home addresses, telephone numbers, names of business associates and relatives. I then discussed the challenge in detail with Hakki. Paul, who was seriously unsettled by this time, was sent to Berlin to meet Hakki in order to calm down.

I really cannot go into what transpired in the following two days. 64 hours after my conference call with Hakki, our Moroccan friends were summoned to the club for a personal meeting with me. They assured me that their business proposal had been poorly presented and possibly misunderstood by Paul, and that they were very sorry for any complications they had caused. Keeping a completely straight face I assured them that such things happen occasionally and that I appreciate their explanation.

They then asked me if they would still be welcome at the club. I told them that they would be welcome indeed, but that I would appreciate it if they could conduct their more sensitive business on their own premises. I told them I was a great fan of MM as I participate in chess tournaments there and have always enjoyed the hospitality of the Arab people. Upon parting, their CEO kissed the back of my hand with sincere devotion.

During the coming year, our new Moroccan friends spent over 100,000 euros at the club, easily becoming our best customers. In the Mallorca underworld and in one major German newspaper I was christened the "Godfather of Mallorca." They had obviously confused me with my friends in Berlin.

Hakki was more than just my business partner. He is a very tough man but in many ways a kind man. He has been to my house for dinner and I have met his very likable companion. He is more solid, more reliable with more backbone and integrity than 99 percent of all the financiers I have worked with. Unfortunately, I can no longer partner with him. I would have loved to list the company, fund its expansion and promote it as Europe's fastest growing, most profitable and innovative facilities management company. However, I didn't like that pimps were trying to hawk their goods in bulk.

*

I often look at failures and tragedies in the same way as successes—in a detached, analytical manner. Even under intense stress, my mind rarely loses its analytical focus. My vital organs are very stress-resistant. The only times I do not calculate odds is when I am sleeping, stoned, jumping off cliffs or making love. I struggle with certain basic feelings like guilt, regret, pain, fear, remorse and anxiety. I view most of what happens to me as a learning experience. This was true even when I got shot in 2006—although I should have learned a better and different lesson from that experience, and done so quicker.

With over 200 homicides per 100,000 citizens, Caracas is far and away the murder capital of the world. Caracas is three to five times more dangerous than Rio de Janeiro, Johannesburg, Detroit, East Saint Louis or Medellin. Assuming a life expectancy of 80 years, the probability of being murdered in Caracas is about 16 percent and the probability of being shot or stabbed is almost 80 percent. Violent crime has increased 400 percent during Hugo Chavez's reign. Chavez, the champion of redistribution, is the worst micro manager in Latin America. The city has some of the most agreeable weather and is located in a fertile plateau. Extreme wealth contrasts with abject poverty, but not more than in many developing nations. Caracas' GDP per capita is approximately six times higher than Nicaragua's, yet the homicide rate is twenty times higher.

The common perception that violent crime is based on poverty is totally false. Many of the poorest countries also have the lowest crime rates. There is absolutely no correlation between poverty and violent crimes. In Venezuela, violent crimes are purely the result of decades of mismanagement, systemic corruption and misdirected priorities. Venezuela's prison facilities are such that only ten percent of its violent repeat offenders can be incarcerated. There are simply not enough available prison cells. Government and police officials have lined their pockets for decades. Chavez has done nothing to stop violent crime as it weakens his capitalist opponents.

Almost half of all violent crimes in Caracas are committed by the police force. You can order a murder for $10. The Venezuelan government stopped reporting homicide data in 2007, as the numbers were simply too shocking. The country has become the home of 100,000 hard-core Colombian gangsters, who acquired Venezuelan citizenship for as little as $5,000 apiece. Yet Venezuela's sizable oil-based export earnings are more than sufficient to resolve the problem. As long as nobody at the top cares, the situation will get worse.

When I was shot in Caracas in November 2006, I lost part of my lung, my entire spleen, and a bullet lodged in my twelfth vertebrae a few millimeters from my spinal nerve. My friend's knee was shattered by the impact of a .38 caliber bullet. When we arrived at the hospital, they took my pulse three times. I was minutes away from bleeding to death, yet they kept taking my fucking pulse. They had never seen such a normal heart rate after a traumatic shooting incident.

It took me a few years to admit that the robbery may have been a camouflaged assassination attempt as some commentators have suggested. After all, my doctors confirmed that a bullet of that caliber, shot from a few feet, almost always results in certain death. My fellow passenger was "only" shot in his knee. The driver was not hurt at all. The hit was highly organized and supported by the Federal Police. The planning and execution were excellent.

I am not excessively courageous or risk loving. Brain scans show that my frontal lobe is simply not fully developed and I have a different mental, emotional and physical constitution to others. My sensitivity to pain is much lower than average. My pulse is in the bottom 1 percent of the adult population. I am almost clinically dead all of the time. Adrenalin rushes barely affect me. I tried to tell this to the medical staff in Spanish, but they ignored me and kept taking my pulse. Meanwhile I was bleeding to death.

I saw both hell and death in Caracas. A customs official at the airport had informed someone in the police department that two rich gringos were on their way to the city with a limousine, and both were wearing Rolex watches. Shortly before reaching the city center, a police motorcycle with two riders pulled up next to us and started spraying the window with bullets. I was shot in the chest from about two feet, and my fellow passenger was shot in the leg. My partner was relieved of his Rolex as I was slumping on the floor of the limousine bleeding intensely and faking death. I had stashed my cash in my shoes as a precautionary measure. A police car was stopped in traffic not ten yards ahead of us. This very murky incident reminds of my family's horrendous incident in 1948, which some claim was not an accident but an assassination. The Venezuelan cops ignored the incident completely and did not even get out of their car to help as the police motorcycle wound its way from the crime scene.

I got up after the thugs had left. Blood was pouring profusely from my chest at an alarming rate. Within seconds, my white shirt and suit were completely sodden. "This is seriously fucked up," I say to myself as I called Susan to tell her that our kids may not have a father much longer. That done, I told her she should sell her ACMH shares. I figured the robbery would hit the news in Caracas that evening but would take at least 24 hours to be disseminated in Europe. So, if she sold before the lemmings got the news in Europe, she would get a much better price and would technically not violate insider-trading rules as the news would already be public in Venezuela. Calling my own banker would make little sense since I was probably going to die shortly. There would be no use for the money in my coffin. Moreover, the inheritance tax would be higher than Susan's long-term capital gains tax rate. So, from an after-tax cash-flow perspective she should dump her shares first. I also did tell her I loved her in spite of our separation and that she should give the kids a big hug from me. I am not completely psychotic and devoid of emotions. However, I was very much financially focused at the time. Then I terminated the call and made the best out of a hellish scenario.

Barely breathing because my left lung was bleeding internally and externally, and the wound was gushing out blood like a garden hose due to my shattered spleen, I left the limousine. By pure chance I noticed an ambulance stuck in traffic only forty yards away. I had to bitch slap and scream at my fellow passenger to get a reaction out of him. He was traumatized because his left knee seemed completely mangled. We dragged ourselves to the ambulance and I pounded on the door with my remaining strength. The driver came out with a cocked gun to see what was going on. I told him we had been shot. I had used the fat wad of $100 bills from my shoes to stem the flow of blood from my chest. I stuffed ten partially bloodied $100 bills into his shirt pocket and told him to take us to the nearest private hospital pronto, and he responded immediately.

The operation lasted six hours and I lost half my blood. I have a ten-inch scar from my sternum to my belly button. The doctors could not remove the bullet from my spine. It was too embedded, and much too close to my spinal nerve. It is still there. They were most concerned about paralysis and a potentially deadly gall bladder infection. I woke up at three in the morning to the sound of what I thought were firecrackers, but it wasn't New Year's yet. Two gangs were fighting with machine guns and automatic assault rifles, four floors below.

It was less than a week away from the Venezuelan general election and the shooting made front-page news in all the opposition newspapers, highlighting what a war zone Caracas had become under the rule of Chavez. Dozens of reporters and photographers laid siege to the hospital. The Chavez media claimed a teddy bear stuffed with $1 million dollars in cash was found at the site of the incident and they were holding the German millionaire financier for questioning. I was interrogated under the most inhumane circumstances while my life still hung in the balance. Shortly after the operation I was forced to stand for hours while being questioned at the hospital and later at Caracas' police headquarters. Guards with AK-47s were posted in front of my hospital room and at the hospital entrance. There was no way to leave.

The German ambassador was trying to help but was too intimidated to be of any use. The children of the openly critical Austrian ambassador had just been kidnapped, and members of a Chinese delegation had been murdered in recent weeks. The police interrogations were a farce. They weren't questioning me. They were torturing me to extract a quick and dirty cash payment in return for a speedy release. The world had turned upside down. I was the fucking victim, not the perpetrator.

ACMH did absolutely nothing. They sent me a useless lawyer who told me he could not get involved because of "Chavez's rule of terror" against the legal profession. Why had he even come? Obviously, the sleazy lawyer came to collect a few thousand dollars in legal fees from my pathetic partners at ACMH. The teddy bear stuff was propaganda bullshit in the government papers.

Clearly, nobody was going to help me, so I got myself out of that jam. I did not bribe the federal cops but used my blood money to incentivize the hospital personnel to keep a keen watch, and we stuffed a mummy in my bed so it appeared as if I was sleeping. Early on Monday morning the air had cleared with no federal cops in sight. I used my remaining $2,000 to bribe myself past immigration and security at the airport. I made it onto an American Airlines flight bound for Florida and arrived in the early afternoon.

In Miami, seventy-eight hours after the operation, I got a hotel room. Due to our separation, I had not had any physical contact with my ex-wife for months. Now I was more determined than ever to rectify the situation. How could she say no after I had flirted so intensely with death? I convinced her to make an exception. The sex was diabolical as I risked popping my internal and external sutures with every move, yet I felt more alive than ever when I climaxed, achieving the perfect balance between pain and intense pleasure. I finally understood why there are always so many births after wars.

If you have psychopathic tendencies or are a true lateral thinker, you would ask yourself why the chauffeur's window was not shattered, why he was not shot and why he did not have his gun with him on that near fatal Thursday afternoon. That is exactly what I thought on the flight from Caracas to Miami. I had specifically ordered an armed chauffeur and an armed guard and a car with bulletproof windows, knowing full well how dangerous Caracas was. There was no armed guard and the chauffeur did not have his gun on him and the windows were not bulletproof. The only person not shot was the driver. The statistical likelihood that he was in on the deal was much higher than 50 percent.

Once I was safely on American soil, I ordered an in-depth, 24-hour interview to get to the truth. My connections reached even into lowly Caracas. It turned out, without a doubt, the chauffeur was not complicit in the robbery in any way. The interviewers covered all relevant topics and went more than skin deep to uncover the truth. Because he was obviously completely innocent, I paid him a month's salary to compensate him for this stressful examination. I never managed to answer the one remaining lingering question completely in my mind. Why was I shot in the chest and my companion only in his knee? After my operation, the surgeons told me a shot in the chest with such a caliber bullet fired from less than four feet is almost always deadly. The odds of surviving such an assault were less than five percent. I keep asking myself, was this a normal armed robbery that had gone wrong or was I a marked man? I am not sure.

JR and his cheap bastards refused to reimburse me for my emergency travel expenses and medical treatment in Caracas and Miami, which came to more than $20,000. I had failed to obtain corporate medical and Key Man insurance in the past due to my pre-existing multiple sclerosis. "I am going to get these fuckers," I swore to myself. The day of reckoning would come.

I have asked myself why I returned to work after this gruesome episode. The shooting had made me more of a celebrity, a bona fide man of steel. Reading the version of the story in *Bunte Magazin*, I began to realize there must be more to life than accumulating the biggest possible pile of cash. But counter-intuitively—or perhaps intuitively, I don't know which—I did not act on this nascent and unfamiliar realization.

I can see now that this was a moment at the crossroads. Either I saw that there was more to life than the world I lived in at ACMH, and limited time to experience it, or I allowed myself to believe the stuff that was written about me and re-enter the fray as somehow immortal, a view which has psychological consequences of its own. The problem was that I think I was lost, and therefore not only was I unaware of the need to choose a path. I was also unaware that I was even near a crossroads at all.

Clearly, given that I did not walk away from the market at that point, I must have been experiencing some major character slippage in believing my own press. But getting shot is, most people would agree, an extreme event, and one that generates a sense of unreality in one's existence that takes hold to a lesser or greater degree according to the manner in which the individual deals with it. For me, fact and fiction were merging, and it was becoming increasingly unclear which was the stranger of the two. It also did not help that this blending of fact and fiction was repeatedly enforced by later media profiles—both of myself, in which I did not recognize the person in the story, and accounts of certain deals, such as in the beginning of this *Financial Times Deutschland* article on the 3rd of December:

> *"Awfully Nice Investors*
>
> *[…] What has happened since the acquisition by the financial investor at the Stuttgart company, is comparable with a bad guys film, which Hollywood couldn't have done any better. In the main roles: a money hungry upstart, an aggressive hedge fund manager, two thuggish, Austrian financial string-pullers and a worried banker. The supporting roles were also well cast with district attorneys, financial supervisors, and a cheated wife."*

These lines opened an insightful article about our 2007 takeover of M+W Zander, one of Germany's fifty largest companies with over 2 billion euros in sales and 8,000 employees all over the world. OK, my portrayal was anything but flattering—the article called me single-minded, thuggish, mercantile, and the personification of everything the public detests about financiers, but I had heard all that before. Yet the article was remarkably entertaining, well researched and got very close to the truth. The authors had penetrated a wall of silence and despite having zero cooperation from the main players they had managed to unveil the intricacies of the transaction and exposed all of us fairly accurately. In the old days, I would have contacted them immediately and offered them double what they were making as journalists to join me at ACMH.

It began when I chartered a very respectable 100-foot, $7 million motor yacht with four state bedrooms, a chef, a captain and a first mate. The idea was to take the family on a tour of Corsica and Sardinia. Of course, this was not really going to be a family vacation. The business angle was already well organized. I was less certain about the pleasure. At the time, I thought vacations were for wimps.

I had scheduled meetings with a clever yuppie (Martin Gruschka), a German industrialist, an oligarch and a guy called Wennmann, who wanted me in on his fund management company at Cala di Volpe in Sardinia. The Sardinian bay was jammed with super yachts. Most of the boats there were two, three and even four times larger than mine. I felt like a pauper. Brunch at the Hotel Cala di Volpe was easily 500 euros a head, and dropping 5,000 euros at Flavio Briatore's Billionaire Club for some second-rate champagne was a cinch. Tacky first-generation billionaires, plus their entourage of captains, pilots, silicon bimbos, lackeys and other riff-raff, were ruling the joint. The place is a sight to behold: zero class and education, but pure crude capitalism enjoying itself and doing mega deals while sipping vintage Dom Perignon. The joint was buzzing with money and serious operators. I felt very much at home.

In the spring of 2006, I had accumulated a 15-percent greenmail stake in Computec Media, in which Martin Gruschka also held a stake. The company was sold to a high-profile Swiss publisher, Jürg Marquard, for a quick and juicy profit. Now Gruschka had got the inside track to score one of Germany's more dynamic growth companies, the venerable M+W Zander group, one of the world market leaders in the construction of mega factories for chip production and solar panels. It was also one of the German market leaders in the red-hot facilities management and property market. Even better, its owner Jenoptik was faltering, being too diversified, and wanted to raise cash for other purposes.

Gruschka was confident we could secure MWZ at a 50-percent discount to break-up value. I had just liquidated another German high-tech company, Trius, for a 60-percent profit, and our main funds were flush with cash and ready to rumble. Moreover, we had substantial expertise in solar companies, plant engineers and property companies. It would not be hard to find buyers for all the separate units. Therefore, breaking up MWZ and selling the parts would be a cinch and take no more than twelve months. We stood to make several hundred percent on our money and several hundred million euros.

I took my tender over to visit Gruschka at his beachfront villa to hear him out. Of course, Gruschka, whom the *FTD* would later label an arriviste, had no money for a transaction this size. He came to me for several reasons: we managed about $3 billion at the time; we would move far faster than the competing buyout funds and London hedge fund groups; we had in-depth knowledge about the industries in which MWZ operated; and we knew how to play dirty to win.

Gruschka's idea was to front the deal with ACMH, providing most of the money. This made sense. My media profile was horrendous. I had been fined by regulators and prosecutors, was in a messy greenmail battle with the Deutsche Postbank over the takeover of BFG, a largish German bank, had publically attacked the world's largest oil producer Gazprom, and had just liquidated up a German technology company. According to the general media, I was one of the most prominent parasites in Europe. There was a risk that if I appeared on the scene, the sellers would freak and get cold feet. On the other hand, if uncontaminated, smooth-talking Gruschka showed up at the table, negotiations would be more likely to succeed.

So we provided mezzanine-financing convertible into a dominant shareholding in the holding company that controlled all of MWZ's assets. Gruschka's job was to come up with about 40 million euros. He scored the deal at about three times operating profits, an awesome price, but never came up with the money. Indeed, he had taken the shares of the holding company we had paid for as collateral and got a loan from Morgan Stanley to pay some of the money he was obliged to invest into the transaction. Gruschka had used OPM (other people's money), in this case our funds, to meet his obligations. Even then, he was still short 10 million euros.

He had schemed with his associate MM, a dark-skinned little Italian with Sicilian roots, to steal the transaction from right under our feet. Of course, this blatantly violated the spirit of our contracts, but technically, they were now in control of the assets. We were certain we would win any legal confrontation, but by that time money and profits would have been difficult to locate, let alone recover. Their master plan was to make us pure bondholders, pay us annual interest if we were real nice and walk away with a few hundred million euros in profit.

Gruschka had abused my trust and was attempting to steal from our funds. I detested his disrespect and his bogus self-assurance. When I met him and his partner my expletives and threats could have come out of the mouth of a Puerto Rican gang boss, but the two wannabees retained their composure. They thought I was little more than a barking dog. One insider on the deal commented to the *FTD* that "Homm will chase Gruschka to the end of the world if he does not get his money." He was right, but Gruschka and MM did not know this and had no idea who they were dealing with.

We resolved to go to war on multiple fronts. We had notified Morgan Stanley, informing them Gruschka had, in our opinion, fraudulently secured a collateralized loan, engaged combative lawyers to stifle their moves at every turn and initialized criminal investigations by alerting the Stuttgart prosecutors. The heat was on. Within a few weeks the tide was turning. The tipping point was achieved when two of my associates found Gruschka in Acapulco and explained my viewpoint while taking him for a walk on the cliffs. This seemed to work. He was on the phone and apologizing profusely to me. The contracts were redrafted and signed to reflect the new reality. This reality, of course, was not very pretty for the offenders. Instead of making hundreds of millions,

Gruschka and MM would be lucky to walk away with a few million after they had paid back what they owed Morgan Stanley. This time, *we* were going to walk away with hundreds of millions and leave them a few crumbs. We thought we had won.

A few days later, our lawyers checked with the Luxemburg authorities whether the contracts had been filed and the share transfer registered by the Luxemburg courts. Nothing had been done. I was getting suspicious.

Later in the week, I got a call from a former associate, Ronny Pecik, informing me his company Victory had acquired MWZ and he wanted to negotiate the purchase of our convertible loan. Gruschka and MM had sold the company a second time.

Ronny Pecik and Georg Stumpf, a real estate mogul, jointly owned Victory AG. I had known Ronny for almost two decades. He had been our chief contact at Austria's largest bank when we raided or greenmailed Austrian companies like Baumax, the building equipment company. His team, including René Riefler and Robert Schimanko, was outstanding. Ronny and I knew each other as tough guys. However, we fully confided in each other. Ronny was of Croatian descent and his parents had moved to Austria as guest workers. Working long hours and endowed with a sound mathematical mind, he became a successful trader while working for the largest Austrian bank. He made enough money to start his own investment company quite like myself. Ronny had started with less than nothing and had become very wealthy. In that sense his travels were longer and he was more successful in my mind. In many ways, he was just like me: hardworking, obsessive and mercantile. Ronny also had an uncanny ability to endure conflict. He could work three days without sleep or drugs. He was fearless, I suspected he was connected like me and he would be a very tough opponent.

I knew little about Stumpf, but what I could find out suggested a hardnosed and powerful businessman with countless lawsuits and enemies. Indeed, he seemed to have more enemies than me, which was quite an achievement. To make things worse, both these guys were connected with *oligarch no 1*, a major Russian oligarch and one of the hundred richest men in the world. What I knew about *oligarch no 1* was more intimidating. Giorgio's ten-page insider scoop on him was downright scary. I refrain from saying anything negative about him. His life and accomplishments are very public, as are some of his controversies.

There have been consistent rumors the Russian mafia and the Hell's Angels are after me funded by at least one oligarch, who seems to be holding a personal long-term grudge. I don't buy this story. By 2009, these guys were bleeding. These guys would not waste time and money shaking down a former adversary. Some of them even had to sell their football clubs when stock and commodity markets crashed. These oligarchs are looked down upon for their greed, lack of scruples and vulgarity by the self-righteous, know-it-all zealots, who live a risk-free boring existence in the moral high ground. I even caught myself laughing at some of these guys, hanging out at their Datscha's with a dozen whores in private spas larger than those of the most luxurious resorts in Mallorca.

These powerful men, however, were just like me: full of energy, drive and willpower and typically without fear and self-imposed limitations. That is why I counted several of them as my friends. The only real difference was that I came from very old money and they were experiencing the wonders of capitalism for the first time. My grandfather and my great-uncle were oligarchs. All major first-generation fortunes have rogue origins, like the Rockefellers, the Kennedys and the Nobels. Had I been a young enterprising Russian after the collapse of the Soviet empire, I would have been, without doubt, an aspiring oligarch. But I did not see myself as an oligarch. That would imply a huge entourage of underlings, too much gaudiness and mindless spending binges. No, Susan would call me baby-tyke, which stood for baby tycoon, a much more appropriate and endearing label. If I had only two choices, I would rather be an oligarch than a highfalutin moralist.

At the time of the MWZ deal, Ronny, Georg and *oligarch no 1* were buying multi-billion Swiss-franc stakes in major Swiss industrial companies like Oerlikon and

Sulzer. They wanted to build a global technology alternative to General Electric and they did not appear to take prisoners along the way. All in all, one could do smarter things than start World War III against this trio. They would be subject to major criminal charges and civil lawsuits in the years to come.

On a Monday at around 9 p.m., Ronny phoned with the news that he had bought MWZ. I had to come to Vienna right away. I told him my pilot had his day off and I would see him at midday. He told me not to worry, his transatlantic $40 million super jet was waiting for me at General Aviation at Palma airport. I was alarmed. I thought we owned MWZ. What was going on? Obviously, Gruschka had made one of his slippery moves. I had to go to find out more. Upon arrival at Vienna, I was picked up by a driver and a bodyguard in a bombproof Mercedes S Class. I had planned to buy a similar car at the time and asked the driver to tell me about the specifications. He shut me up politely and told me with an obvious Russian accent he was not at liberty to discuss security matters with anybody besides the Victory principals.

Upon arrival at our meeting point I was escorted to Georg Stumpf's penthouse office located on the last floor of the gigantic Stumpf Tower, Vienna's tallest office building. The open plan office with cuisine, bar, mega TV screen and voluminous sofas, easily measuring 7,000 square feet with thirty-feet ceilings and grand windows, offered an unparalleled view over Vienna and reeked of power and new money.

Heavy-hitting businessmen rarely engage in lengthy and polite introductions. They simply do not see the point and get right to the point. Ronny and I seized each other up in about three seconds and shook hands. I had done my last deal with him about a year ago. Georg stuck me as formal and aloof. I expected some underling of *oligarch no 1* or the master himself to show up at any minute, but these were clearly preliminary discussions. I had demanded no lawyers at this meeting. There was no need for the Russians at this point.

Ronny and Georg confirmed that their principal investment vehicle, Victory, had acquired MWZ and wanted to buy our convertible bond at a modest premium to our cost. I told them they were out of their mind. Our legal position was strong, Gruschka and MM had been skunked. About every ten minutes they left the office to confer in private with their lawyers. I had asked their goons to take an indefinite leave of absence and had the palatial office to myself. I had always preferred the minimum number of participants necessary during sensitive discussions. While Ronny and Georg were discussing strategy in another room, I collected all the bits of loose paper around the office for later perusal. I knew from my own experience big-time dealmakers made horrible secretaries. They never picked up after themselves. There were roughly forty sheets scattered around the office full of handwritten notes. I grabbed all of them and stuffed them in my briefcase.

Not surprisingly, we achieved no consensus that evening. Our price expectations were more than 100 million euros apart. I knew Victory wanted MWZ badly. MWZ's solar division fitted perfectly with Oerlikon's, a company they controlled at the time. They wanted MWZ for industrial and dynastic reasons. My objectives were simple: I needed to score the highest possible offer. They were unwilling to pay my price and ready to play hardball. The fronts hardened and communications went dead. I headed back to Palma on Ronny's mega jet.

All communications ceased for several days. Then with a few hours of each other both Victory and ACMH publically announced they had purchased control of the MWZ Group. The media was totally confused, as was the company's management. How could the same asset have two owners? Ronny and Stumpf claimed they were the rightful buyers and Gruschka and MM were the rightful sellers. Gruschka publically supported their story. We claimed we had bought MWZ from Gruschka and MM and were prepared to offer contractual proof.

The documents I clipped from Georg's office showed without a doubt Victory had knowingly bought a legally encumbered asset that had already been sold contractually to us. The papers also showed intricate insider details provided by Gruschka and MM, which they had no right to divulge according to extensive confidentiality agreements. It made little sense to waste these documents on the media. It would make far more sense to keep our powder dry, so we kept quiet and put the ammunition in storage.

From Morgan Stanley we learned Victory had taken over a 30-million-euro bank financing from Gruschka, which showed they were financially committed. We also knew from our penthouse meeting that Gruschka and MM had not received a dime from Victory. We felt we had achieved a more solid legal footing after the Acapulco cliff-top discussions with Gruschka if the matter went to court. Those scraps of paper from Georg's office were especially useful, according to our lawyers. Our prospects of getting a better deal than what Ronny and Georg had offered initially were improving.

Meanwhile MWZ's bankers were panicking. Of the two owners claiming the same asset, one was a disreputable locust and the other was a pair of big-time speculators backed by an oligarch shaking up Europe's corporate landscape. The bankers feared having to write off over 300 million euros in loans. Management was nervous and employees unsure about their jobs. MWZ management had no idea who to believe. The German SEC was alerted because the change of control at MWZ could result in a painful 62-million-euro payoff to minority shareholders in a listed MWZ subsidiary. On the other hand, Victory knew we had no interest in operating MWZ or spending another year carving it up ourselves. Regardless, Ronny knew I could handle a fight and would not fall over and drop dead. Also, Georg and Ronny would not shy away from a protracted nine-figure legal battle. They employed dozens of world-class lawyers. A positive legal outcome could not be predicted with certainty, and I had no desire spending the next three years in court.

During the disputes with Gruschka and during the negotiations with Victory, my relations with MWZ's senior management were excellent. I was informed about every move made by Victory and Gruschka. I had worked in construction when I was thirteen, knew something about engineering and could speak plain German. Georg and Ronny were very gruff and instilled a sense of fear in senior management. Gruschka, with his affected worldly all-knowing airs, became the laughing stock at MWZ. He arrived at the company grounds with a helicopter on several occasions. The first time he landed in his oversized chopper, the employees thought something terrible had happened. They were right.

However, we had counted out Gruschka and MM too early. In spite of ball-crushing setbacks, these guys were not giving up and kept rearing their ugly heads. Gruschka, fearing he would be left in the dust by either Victory or us, had secretly transferred MWZ assets to a Swiss shelf company. They were now asking for a 30-million-euro payoff to go away. Victory and we laughed at that klutzy manoeuver. Georg and Ronny finally understood what Gruschka and MM were: nasty, small fry trying to play in the big leagues. How could these operators sell a company to two separate entities, which they had already transferred to an opaque Swiss limited-liability shell beforehand? These guys had a very interesting take on commonly accepted legal principles.

Gruschka and MM wanted to grab 200 million instead of settling for a surefire 80 million profit, and ended up with nothing. You did not want to mess with Homm, and even less with the unholy trinity of Ronny, Georg and *oligarch no 1*. Victory and ACMH were engaging in genuine contract negotiations and placed Gruschka and MM in the top decile of our respective shit lists. We were breathing down their necks. Not surprisingly, they ended up with nothing but tears, regrets and migraines.

We finally came to terms. I never knew what happened to the founding Zander family, which owned a 27-percent minority stake. They had alternatively negotiated with ACMH, Victory and Gruschka and altered their allegiance a few times too often. They were way too flippant and volatile and as a consequence could not be trusted. Given the nature of the deal and its participants, I assume they got shafted. Georg Stumpf fired MWZ's CEO. I wired him 500,000 euros severance payment from my personal account to compensate him for his unswerving support and loyalty. Georg, Ronny and *oligarch no 1* would spend a lot of time and money fighting civil and criminal prosecutors in Switzerland in the years to come. Georg owns MWZ now. Gruschka and MM are probably still doing shaky deals. MWZ is alive and appears functional.

Of course, our stake in MWZ was worth more than what we sold it for in an orderly market. But this was a profoundly infected transaction on several levels surrounded by dubious social climbers, tycoons, an oligarch, nervous bankers, famous politicians, a cut-throat hedge fund manager, prosecutors, regulators, fickle and litigious minority investors, a possible 62 million liability, endless legal complications and unspoken threats by seriously dangerous people.

Ultimately we sold for less than MWZ was worth. So what? It didn't kill anyone. People die from getting shot, not from making a 100-percent profit in less than eighteen months.

10. Liberia

In my view, the humanity of our world can be measured against the fate of Africa.
Horst Köhler

During the early years of ACMH, I became increasingly aware of my legal vulnerability. In 2001 I had to pay 5 million euros in back taxes. I was avoiding rather than evading taxes, but as usual, I was treading a fine line. They had also found one of my Swiss bank accounts, which held the proceeds from the sale of my French beach home in the Medoc. The French tax authorities had reported me to the German tax authorities. They never charged me with tax evasion because I had neglected to earn any taxable income on the account after the sale. The account was jammed with cash. I had sort of forgotten about it. I was lucky. Tax evasion can easily result in a ten-year prison sentence in Germany.

One of the companies I was raiding was preparing a 4-million-euro lawsuit against me. My moles informed me the Munich district attorney would detain me and place me in custody if I passed through Franz Josef Strauss airport. I had been charged and convicted of share price manipulation (a misdemeanor) by BAFIN, the German securities regulator, and the Frankfurt prosecuting attorney was charging me with insider trading, a criminal offence punishable by a 1-to-5-year prison sentence if convicted and a multimillion-euro fine. My children were the subjects of a very realistic kidnapping scenario. Two mad discontented investors had threatened my mother with severe physical punishment if I did not compensate them for their losses. I had intensive links to Mossad, Israeli arms conglomerate Raffael, and senior government ministers like Shimon Peres. I was being watched from all angles.

The icing on the cake was personally managing funds for a German-Syrian businessman. He was not only heavily embroiled in the largest industrial fraud in German history (the Flow Tex affair, resulting in a 4 billion Deutschmarks loss) but also the academic sponsor for Arabian students at the Technical University of Hamburg. The terrorists Mohammed Atta and Marwan al-Shehhi were enrolled at the university albeit not funded by our client. An AK-47-toting special financial crimes operations unit raided VMR's Luxemburg offices, handcuffing several senior employees and confiscating all documents and computers. We were suspected of terrorist activities and money laundering for Osama Bin Laden & Associates as well as the Flow Tex gang. These guys tried to corner me by threatening my wife with prison for calling herself a securities analyst rather than a banking analyst on some irrelevant job description. That was as pathetic as it was laughable. I was 200 percent innocent, but my ears and eyes were wide open. I sensed my own vulnerability.

Besides the obvious threats, there were numerous collateral risks: rogue clients, fraudulent trustees, disgruntled investors and malicious partners and employees. My choices were simple. I could retire, spin a smaller wheel, or hedge my risks. Given that I was making too much money and having too much fun to quit, I decided to master the challenge of achieving immunity from prosecution.

I had co-sponsored with Gold-Zack the Grand Master Tennis Tournament in Aschaffenburg, Germany, and in Mallorca. I loved watching the tennis greats like Yannick Noah, Boris Becker, Mats Wilander, John McEnroe and others. During the Mallorca tournament, I was introduced to an alleged German diplomat, Thorsten Schütze, domiciled in Monte Carlo and Puerto Andratx in Mallorca. Thorsten chartered one of my planes on occasions. We would meet mostly socially. He was a rather secretive and circumspect figure.

Eventually he introduced me to Sir Thomas Bowden. Sir Thomas (aka convicted career criminal Albert K.) promised the world to me. Initially he worked towards an ambassador-at-large assignment for Argentina. This effort failed miserably. Then he tried to make me a World Health Organization delegate for Lithuania in Geneva. When I discovered his key contact was an executive secretary at the Lithuanian Embassy in Madrid, I became rather skeptical. Proper diplomatic appointments are complicated legal affairs requiring serious protocol and extensive formalities.

We travelled to Liberia shortly after the end of the civil war, but nothing valid resulted from this effort. I finally decided to expose Albert and his crony Thorsten to the media and the authorities after they tried to convince me some UNESCO stationery and plastic nametags constituted a political appointment. Bowden had blown my retainer on fancy cars and fast women, although some of the money was returned. He was apprehended by Interpol several years later and has served time. He has offended some very serious people and would do well to keep a low profile. He ratted out all his contacts, providers, intermediaries and clients to negotiate a shorter prison sentence. He tried to implicate me as well but had no proof of any wrongdoing. I had wasted over a year with this debauched career criminal. On the other hand, I had learned what it took to become an accredited diplomat officially. I concluded there would be no more shortcuts and no sleazy intermediaries. I would do it myself and I would do it right.

I liked the idea of becoming a diplomat. In high school, I wanted to join the German Foreign Service, but by my early twenties I had realized most diplomats were basically glorified bureaucrats with lots of privileges, little power and poor monetary compensation. The prospect of doing something constructive in the developing world was a secondary consideration, sort of like working at Walpole Maximum Security Prison. I would be able to mix thrills with doing something useful. I was certainly qualified to become a diplomat. I knew a lot about economics, finance and the Third World. I was versed in political science and spoke several languages.

15,000 freed American slaves, who settled there between 1821 and 1822, colonized Liberia. President Monroe (after whom the capital Monrovia is named) and the American Colonization Society funded them. The colonists adopted the American constitution and implemented the Southern Plantation system, enslaving much of the indigenous population. Forced labor, basically a euphemism for slavery, in Liberia was only abolished in 1936.

I decided to work for Liberia because my input would have the greatest effect there. I had been on friendly terms with Dr Richard Tolbert, the son of Liberia's former President William Tolbert, while working in New York. Richard's father and twenty-seven others were executed by the notorious Samuel Doe in 1980, sparking the first major episode of violence that would result in three civil wars spanning fourteen years, killing approximately 300,000 people—10 percent of the population. When I chose Liberia as my diplomatic homeland, one year after the end of its civil war, the country had hit rock bottom, was intensely unstable and dangerous. Liberia hosted the largest contingent of United Nations soldiers anywhere in the world at the time.

It was the perfect choice: an exciting, disreputable bloody mess with serious long-term upside and the chance to gain diplomatic immunity at the highest level. There was no downside. In 2003, I introduced myself to Liberia's ambassador to France and presented my qualifications. It took a year to become appointed as cultural attaché and slightly longer to be accepted by the French Foreign Ministry and accredited at UNESCO. Even better, no money needed to change hands. All they wanted was hard work and measurable results. I more than fulfilled their expectations. After the election of President Johnson Sirleaf in 2005, the ranks were purged of all sham diplomats. I remained, survived and prospered.

I have been to many conflict zones and impoverished regions during my life, yet I was unprepared for Liberia. 80 percent of Monrovia's buildings were destroyed. The entire metropolis was without electricity with the exception of a few emergency generators in the dilapidated government buildings. Large and densely populated neighborhoods had no toilets and sanitation whatsoever. Prostitutes were offering their services for 25 cents. Malaria and other diseases were everywhere, and heavy drug use was rampant. At night, the entire city of over one million inhabitants was pitch-black. I met a former tribal warlord, a member of parliament, who devoured his enemies to make himself invincible. Other warlords killed innocent children, tore out their hearts and ate them, and drank their blood before entering battle. Walpole was a country club compared to Monrovia. My visits to Liberia are humbling and make me feel grateful for the privileged life I have led. Liberians without five cents in their pocket joking and laughing cleansed me of my heightened sense of self-importance for days.

I have gradually discovered the emotional return on giving or doing positive deeds. Indeed, electronic measurements prove that "giving" results in a degree of emotional satisfaction five times greater than receiving or taking. Humor and self-irony also pay handsome dividends. People who laugh a lot live seven years longer on average. The apostle of greed and fortune working for one of the most destitute and hopeless places on earth seemed kind of funny to me at the time. While people think you are either a diamond smuggler or arms dealer when you tell them you worked for Liberia, my attachment to the country and its people has produced fabulous emotional returns.

Charity and diplomacy became synonymous for me as I have been representing the country since 2003 without a cent of compensation. Accepting pay for the work would be like robbing a welfare recipient. On average, Liberians earn $40 a month—that is if you are one of the 15 percent with a job. 80 percent of the population lives below the poverty line, meaning they subsist on less than $1.25 per day. Liberia is the fourth poorest country on earth, with a GDP per capita of $500. This equates to just over 1 percent of American GDP per capita. Before Samuel Doe's 1980 military coup, Liberia had been growing for years. It not only had the largest shipping registry in the world, it was also one of the most important centers for company formations. Liberia was a net food exporter and an important regional leader in mining, timber, fishing and agriculture. It used to be called Little America.

The United Methodist University is the leading private institution of higher learning in the country. I had funded a chair for Entrepreneurial Studies and had offered a $6,000 prize for the three best papers on entrepreneurial development in Liberia. Over one hundred reports were submitted and I reviewed the top twenty. The three winners had all produced Harvard-Business-School-quality treatises. The standard of the work blew my mind, given the minimal resources these students had at their disposal and the fact that they grew up in a war-ravaged country.

To date I have funded Liberia's National Basketball Stadium, named after my ex-wife and me. I largely financed the construction of the Liberia Renaissance Educational Complex, far and away the most outstanding state of the art public school in the country. Many of my clients and contacts contributed as well. I have worked for years to strengthen Liberia's efforts at UNESCO with two other generous individuals, and have in large part funded the renovation of the Liberian Embassy in Paris. I have also contributed to political parties, universities, religious organizations, and so forth. My total contributions are in the low seven figures, but I have been told I am the largest private donor to Liberia. The Liberian UNESCO effort has risen over $3 million in grants and services since it was established during my tenure. It is performing better than ever due to capable professionals in Paris and Monrovia.

Additionally there is the Liberia Renaissance Educational Complex, which is the brainchild of Professor Dennis Harper, my former math teacher and basketball coach at Frankfurt International School in Germany. Dennis had contacted me at ACMH and presented an intriguing concept for launching a number of elitist, tuition-based private high schools in West Africa. He had taught in Liberia and had been the coach of Liberia's national basketball team before the civil war. We had many common acquaintances there, so we decided to do this project together. I would raise the funds and Dennis would manage the project. The idea was to commence in Liberia and then export the concept to other more affluent West African nations. I personally funded Dennis' research and agreed to fund one pilot school personally.

It took about six months before we had major fallout. Dennis is a fine academic, great educator and charitable man, but he is not a shrewd business magnate and doesn't know about such practical business matters as cost control, budgets, fund raising, competitive contract bidding, personnel recruitment, organizational structures and corruption. He was too nice, too averse to conflict and too naive to handle this project. He had bought land that was too far away from the capital from his cronies, hired an incompetent principal from America, and built a defective fence for an outrageous amount of money. I had no choice. I had to ask my high school math teacher, friend and coach to resign. The project was about the business of education first and foremost. It was not about niceties and social conventions. For me, it was simply another necessary restructuring, no different from Clinuvel or Borussia Dortmund.

Upon his resignation and with the advent of a new and capable board of directors, we immediately changed the focus from tuition to free admission based on merit and need. There were other schools available for the wealthy. We wanted to sponsor bright children who deserved a chance and whose parents could not afford a superior education. A usual, the *Spiegel Magazin* suspected deviant financial motives for my involvement in Liberia. But even the resourceful investigative journalist Beat Balzli could not find proof of any wrongdoing. My record in Liberia is clean.

We replaced the American headmaster and selected an experienced and cost-effective Liberian builder to construct the premises. The school was completed almost on schedule and on budget (no easy task in West Africa) and was inaugurated by Liberia's President Elect, Lady Ellen Johnson Sirleaf. The LREC is positively impacting the lives of hundreds of destitute Liberian children, who are receiving a First World education in a Third World country. I express my most sincere gratitude to President Johnson Sirleaf, Ambassador McKinley, the board of directors, Marcel and Olivia. This venture would not have succeeded without them. The LREC needs to be handed over to the Liberians by 2013. The Liberia Renaissance Foundation will supply critical equipment for several years thereafter, but ultimately Liberia has to assume its own future. The school needs to be run by Liberians for Liberians. They have capable leaders and managers and are smart enough to take control.

When I first visited the country, its capital had no electricity and no sewer system. There was one two-star hotel. Dengue fever and malaria were rampant and Monrovia was a very unsafe place. During the last three years, however, Liberia has been growing at a tremendous pace. President Sirleaf is doing an outstanding job. She is the most determined woman I have ever met. She stands for everything that is estimable about Liberia and intelligent development in Africa. I am blessed to know her. Meanwhile much of Monrovia is back on the grid, construction activity is booming and the country will be entering its third year of ten-percent-plus economic growth. I am glad I have made a small but noticeable contribution to Liberia's renaissance, although it continues to be in some ways an insane place. Perhaps that is precisely the reason I am drawn to it.

Part V
The Cloud Forest

11. On the Run

I feel like a fugitive from the law of averages.
Bill Mauldin

Fall 2007: Cartagena de Indias, Colombia

I had procured a new identity, incentivized airport security to be less diligent than usual, and made it safely from Spain to Colombia with my cash intact. The great thing about moving anything into Colombia is that it is a breeze. Most people try to move things *out* of Colombia, not in.

I started reading Garcia Marquez novels in Paris, which launched my early interest in Colombia. I had worked and visited Colombia many times since the early eighties. During college, Rodrigo (aka Rod-Man), the son of famous Colombian author Gabriel Garcia Marquez, was my friend. Rodrigo was outwardly mellow but inwardly intense. I liked him because he was sincere, genuine and never conceited. He is almost as tall as me, strong and surprisingly agile for his big frame. I met his old man briefly at Harvard. He struck me as deep, brilliant and somehow withdrawn. I thought to myself he was obviously not born with a smile on his face. I only realized this fully when I learned, reading his captivating memoirs *Living to tell the Tale,* that he almost chocked at birth and was revived with rum. However, brief the encounter and surrounded by several eager admirers, Garcia Marquez had a philanthropic, all-knowing twinkle in his eyes, a bit like "the most interesting man in the world" in the Dos Equis beer commercials. As usual, I lost touch with Rod after college and predictably he attended none of the Harvard reunions. Rod became a successful photographer, director and filmmaker in spite of the overwhelming fame and literary omnipresence of his father. Surprisingly Rodrigo, according to all accounts, has managed to remain compassionate, likable, curious and critical of social injustices.

Because of Rod's old man's terrific novels and my vivid imagination, Colombia was always a magic and ferocious place for me. I completed several Spanish courses at Harvard to manage the language. I always imagined I would live in Colombia one day. During the eighties and most of the nineties, there were only two ways to travel the country as a foreigner: either as an impoverished back packer or as a well-armed and protected operator. Visiting clients throughout Colombia, while working in New York, constituted heavy risks. These were easily on par with the challenges of conducting business in Peru during the heyday of the Shining Path. My money laundering activities took me to Bogota, where security could be arranged, goons and armored cars were readily available. While traveling to Medellin, Cali, the godforsaken pacific coast and the Valle del Cauca, I became a tourist without means and relevance. Barranquilla, Santa Marta and the Sierra Nevada where completely controlled by the guerillas and traveling there constituted incalculable risks for gringos. Luckily, my clients would meet me in beautiful Cartagena, which remained quite safe throughout the conflicts.

Colombia remains the mother of all contrasts. It has produced historical figures like Bolivar and epic literary minds like Garcia Marquez but also narcotics industrialist Pablo Escobar and the infamous cocaine queen, former Miss Colombia, Angie San Clemente. It is larger than Spain, France and Portugal combined. It has deserts and imposing mountain ranges, Amazonian forests and highly productive farmland at various altitudes. It is the only Latin American country with a Pacific and Atlantic coast. It has been the largest cocaine exporter but also the third largest coffee and the largest flower exporter worldwide. Colombia is rich in minerals such as copper and nickel and has large deposits of silver and gold. Colombians are vastly friendlier than any other people in Europe or North America. They detect bull-shitters quickly and have an edgy in your face way about them. Colombia boasts more plant and animal life per unit area than any other nation on earth. There are over 2,000 species of birds and over 3,000 types of orchids.

The country has been at war with its occupiers, neighbors or with itself for 170 out of the last 200 years. Of course, this has affected the national psyche. Over four million inhabitants have been displaced due to civil, guerilla and narco wars, second only to Sudan with 4.5 million displaced. US intervention has been a positive. I have talked to dozens of Colombians in regions with major cocaine and ganja production. They all say they have less money than before but value the relative tranquility more than the extra cash flow. Many refuse to travel to the United States because they are treated like scumbags upon entering. Others are upset because the US severely punishes weed producers in Colombia while marijuana is readily and legally available as a medical treatment in many states in America. Regardless, the war on drugs has weakened the guerillas and reduced violent crimes, especially kidnapping and murder. On the other hand, the Colombian military got a bit carried away. They murdered about five thousand completely innocent civilians, dressed them in rebel uniforms, to collect bounty fees, promotions and earn extra vacation days. Of course, drug production is still monumental in Colombia. An ounce of quality weed can be sourced under five dollars versus three hundred dollars and a gram of almost pure cocaine rarely costs three bucks versus one hundred in Frankfurt. I reckon the share of the drug trade in the county's economic product has declined from 37 percent to about 23 percent over the last fifteen years. Nonetheless, Colombia was not for the faint of heart when I arrived, even after significant relative improvements since president Uribe assumed power in 2002. Even today, Colombia remains schizophrenic. Love, hatred, humanity and brutality are all children of the same family constantly quarreling for supremacy.

Nobody would suspect me of going there. Colombia is largely controlled by the United States where I am a persona non grata legally. Only insiders knew large swaths of Medellin, Bogota and Cartagena were by now perfectly safe especially compared with the most murderous nations on earth to the north: Honduras, El Salvador and Guatemala. Nobody, not even my ex-wife, knew I was still connected in Colombia. Surely only a psychopath would live in Latin America's nerve center of homicidal activity after having been shot less than a year earlier not very far away in Caracas, Venezuela. Nonetheless, I had to keep a low profile. My photo circulated around the world, at least in those places where people read English-language financial newspapers or watched Bloomberg or CNN. I needed to make sure the gringos and Europeans vacationing there did not recognize me.

My abrupt departure followed by the ACMH share-price collapse would certainly lead to full London and Frankfurt Stock Exchange investigations into possible improprieties. Mobsters, gangsters and detectives were on my trail. I had considered plastic surgery along with my new alias. The thought was ridiculous. I was confident I could beat all legal challenges if I had to confront them. I had done that before on several occasions. My defense would be formidable and implicate and sink numerous other ships in the process.

On the other hand, spending one third of my remaining high-quality life in court while exposing myself and my dwindling fortune to intense risk, seemed like a suboptimal course of action. "Do I want to be right and squander ten of my best remaining years proving it through the lengthy judicial process—and risk getting shot or incarcerated—or do I want to live a good life right now, while I am still relatively young?" I asked myself. The answer was obvious.

Cartagena was colonized by the Spaniards in 1533, and competes with Havana as the best example of Spanish colonial architecture in the Caribbean. It is a jewel. It contains the very impressive San Felipe Fortress, a gorgeous cathedral, a magnificent walled city and numerous monasteries, mansions and squares. The beach is similar to Miami's, the women are uncomplicated, gorgeous, and know how to enjoy themselves. Cartagena's surrounding countryside is very scenic and diverse. Not far away, the Sierra Nevada mountain range boasts the highest coastal elevation anywhere in the world. The city is actually a remarkably safe place because of its very alert and helpful tourist police. It also has several larger banks with solid capabilities to conduct discreet private banking. Best of all, the locals couldn't care less about global capital market developments.

Giorgio had prearranged a four-week lease on a colonial palace with six bedrooms, a swimming pool, a splendid courtyard, covered walkways with arches and a spacious rooftop terrace with a large Jacuzzi and outstanding views. Staying at a hotel or going to restaurants was not an option. The hotel would want a photocopy of my fake passport. The risk of being recognized, with the financial media blasting my photo around the world, was simply too great. All the better newsstands were selling the *Financial Times*, the *Wall Street Journal,* even German newspapers. Giorgio made sure we had a full-time chef who did not speak a word of English and two Indio maids who kept the place immaculate. I had to lie low and stay outside of the radar for at least two weeks before I could enjoy the city. I kept myself busy swimming, reading and watching old classics on the Movie Channel.

Yet I've never been a fugitive in the legal sense of the word. From 2006 to early 2012, I was officially registered in Paris and was listed as a member on the UNESCO website. As a result, I was accessible via the embassy and Liberian UNESCO delegation. Furthermore, I could also be contacted through my lawyers, whose details were printed in my press release of September 2007. There was and is no arrest warrant outstanding for me anywhere on the planet. I was not and am not running away from the law. The London and Frankfurt stock exchanges' investigations found no wrongdoing. I've heard that a Racketeering and Criminal Organization Charge (RICO) filed against me has been dismissed. There are some manageable legal problems on the continent. But a fugitive may also be fleeing from perceived threats to his liberty, life and wealth. Indeed, a fugitive may be running away from responsibilities, conflicts and even themselves.

During my career, I had stepped on countless toes. Moreover, I suspected that some of ACMH's 3,000 clients might engage in legal action or sick bad people on me. The probability that at least some of our very wealthy clients had made their fortune on the dark side and would seek retribution was high.

I had managed to upset Gazprom, the world's largest energy company and the crown jewel of the Russian economy and the Russian government. I had attacked the company openly at the Deutsche Bank Hedge Fund conference in Moscow as one of the chief speakers. Then I gave an interview to the *Moscow Times* deriding Gazprom's shoddy shareholder practices. The story made it into *the New York Times.* A major and highly credible German publication, *Wirtschaftswoche*, suggested the Russian mob was trying to shake me down. I had dinged *oligarch no 2*, a major arms dealer with alleged KGB contacts, refusing to buy his asset management operations in Moscow in 2007 after intensive discussions. And I had not only messed with *oligarch no 1's* Austrian cronies but also had co-organized heavy short raids on *oligarch no 1's* major European holdings, Oerlikon and Sulzer, shortly before my departure.

I had been involved in a major, ugly battle with Erich Sixt, the owner of the Sixt car-rental and used-car empire. My contacts to a Syrian-German businessman were known to the intelligence community, as were my meetings with Simon Peres and my contacts to Rafael, the Israeli arms conglomerate.

I was unsure how Hakki Simsek, the German-Kurdish owner of Artemis, would react when he learned I would no longer fund his ambitious expansion plans. I had disciplined Moroccan gangsters in Mallorca and suspected one especially vindictive client had ordered a hit on me.

There are enemies and there are enemies. Some of mine were of the worst kind imaginable. Without a doubt, my life could be at risk. These were only the enemies I knew. I heard rumors from unreliable sources that a major FBI and SEC task force had been formed to charge and incarcerate me. I viewed my departure from public and private life more as a necessary, self-imposed exile. I never fully disappeared since I have been in regular contact with several former friends. I testified in public court proceedings as a witness. I continued my work as a diplomat and I met with several people from my past. I was even in regular contact with former ACMH associates and other business contacts. I chose to lead a private life, safeguard my funds and protect myself. I shrank my network from 10,000 to less than ten individuals.

The primary reason for going so deep under cover, though, was because I needed distance and isolation to make sense of my life. I wanted to determine who I would see, when, where and under what circumstances. I no longer wanted to be accessible to anybody including journalists, former colleagues, and business partners, even family. I wanted to shed all responsibilities and determine every single hour of my existence.

My great game plan based on Necko's life, which I formulated in my teens, had not worked out. I had been an overachiever in sports, learning and wealth creation, but the disease of accumulation meant I was striving for a sense of completeness or satisfaction that I could never attain. My dream to build a dynamic, self-sustaining highly profitable asset management group, which could prosper without me, had failed miserably. Nevertheless, I had been fully prepared to make all the mistakes on the path to financial grandness, even though I sensed along the way it was not going to make me happy. I may even have known this—and I *still* did it. *That* is where the mania, the tragedy lies.

I looked at the financial crisis and could not help but see my own crash mirrored in that collapse. Capitalism was feeding on itself, spinning out of control and all its destructive tendencies on show. The capitalist system is choking on its own excesses, corrupted by the major industrial, media, military and financial forces. Politicians played along seeking to maximize their power and incentives manipulating and rigging economic data and fudging financial statements like Enron. It is all about the shift away from a value system, the dislocation wrought by over-reach in the absence of any self- or external restraints. The umpires have been bought and thoroughly corrupted. The game is rigged for those who have the funds and power to manipulate. My disease stems from the fact that my personal value system disintegrated gradually, then collapsed and disappeared. I barely had a value system growing up to begin with. My youthful values were throttled by bourgeois ambition and materialism. Only after crashing, did I discover which values are lasting and truly gratifying.

If the US hadn't gone off the gold standard—i.e. its value system—it would not now be the biggest debtor in the world. The value system before the Great Depression was similarly out of control, and lo and behold, it imploded. Whether we are talking about a government or an individual, the dangerous obsession with wealth and unrestrained capitalism without governance always, always leads to excesses, followed by severe financial setbacks and then repression. "How can we achieve growth, happiness, health and prosperity for the electorate at large and not just for the elite few?", and "Are we leaving our nations a better place with a brighter future for our children and grandchildren?" should be our foremost concern.

My mother tells me that I am paying the price for the life I chose, and of course, she is right. Half a decade in seclusion and without family and friends hurts. There are heavy bounties offered for my head in Europe and Panama and all sorts of scumbags are chasing me around the globe.

My shell had got progressively thicker as I sought to absorb bigger and harder punches, to the extent that the shell itself began to dominate and crowd out the inner core and became the reality. I had moved palpably away from my own better self. I had been shot, and my life had become increasingly senseless after separating from my soul mate, Susan. My working life was nothing but a mounting wall of frustration and I was spending all my waking hours with vicious, backstabbing parasites. I knew that would not change if I stayed, and nor would the endless grinding against weakness, mediocrity and incompetence in so many of the staff, nor the constant need to dodge tidal waves of volcanic aggravation. Additionally there was increasing evidence of my own debauchery, and physical and mental degeneration. All my anchors had gone. The mission had failed, and I came face to face with utter disillusionment.

Bang.

Goodbye, market.

*

Beyond knowing that a complete break with my past was unavoidable, I had no answers at the time as to what to do differently. I would need to experiment and dig deep to find solutions, and required minimum interference and noise during this process. I had forgotten how to laugh. I was taking myself way too seriously. I wanted to have fun and go fly-fishing in Slovenia, ride a Riva on Lake Garda, read Garcia Marquez novels in a Cartagena colonial mansion, go to the Louvre for six hours, dive Belize, run on the beach in the Medoc, walk the Great Wall of China, reside nobly in maharajah palaces, sample great burgundies and hike through the Tuscan countryside for hours without receiving 300 telephone calls per day. And I wanted to do this on my own. I was disgusted with myself and disappointed many of those around me. I had no energy left for anyone else, not even my family.

Of course, there were real threats to my wealth, liberty and health as well. I suspected ACMH would blame me for its likely demise rather than assume responsibility for their shortcomings. Given the litigious nature of our industry, I was concerned their lies would result in lawsuits, regulatory, civil and maybe even criminal action. I believed my ex-wife would chase me around the globe using private detectives, after her substantial shareholdings in ACMH were reduced to a mere pittance after my departure.

Possibly the single most important reason for leaving was my somber assessment of market prospects. Every single reliable indicator I trusted signaled market meltdown. I knew ACMH had failed to attract or retain first-rate talent. ACMH needed proven moneymakers in bull and bear markets with a long track record able to think completely out of the box like Kyle Bass of Hayden Capital, who made fortunes from shorting the US real estate and banking sectors in 2008 and 2009. We needed large and radical contrarian idea generators based on superior knowledge not on broker trash talk. My short ideas on the US prime mortgage sector were not followed through by our head of research, a solid but unimaginative analyst, a few months before my departure. I even interviewed about half a dozen gifted traders in 2007. None of them accepted JR's ridiculous compensation package. These guys wanted $200 million under management and retain fifty percent of the performance fee. JR offered less than half. Consequently, we landed none of the badly needed stars that would take ACMH to the next level. Most of our long-short managers were nothing more than glorified long-only mutual fund managers. Management was naive and totally clueless about short selling. They had never made money in a down market. I had scored my best returns in market mayhem but Antonio Porsia and Sascha Wassmer were not enough to safeguard and perform with billions in our portfolios. You simply cannot expect amateur footballers to win the European champions league. Of course, holding twenty percent of the assets in less liquid securities in 2007 was largely my mistake. I deserve part of the blame. At least 80 percent of our managers would never master a serious correction, let alone a major stock market debacle. I had no interest being part of this agonizing death with both of my hands tied behind my back by ignorant board members and executives. It would be far better if ACMH would liquidate the portfolios and return the funds to the investors as quickly as possible. Where was my upside? I had won more major international investment awards than any other German fund manager and I was solvent. There was nothing left to accomplish.

I shirked my familial responsibilities because I was burned out and self-centered facing serious threats while burning the candle at both ends professionally. I had given my ex-wife sole guardianship of my children in early 2006, abandoning all rights of ever seeing them again without her explicit approval. Nor was I in any shape to contribute in a meaningful way to their upbringing. Susan had lost all faith in me and was already dating other guys. I had spilled so much bad blood and destroyed the little credibility I had as a father and husband. For the first time in my life, I felt genuine regret, maybe even guilt. They had moved to Florida more than a year before. I was forever condemned without appeal to the fogginess and loneliness of money. I had also defaulted ethically and morally. Nothing was holding me in Mallorca.

I was certainly not going to move to the US, the epicenter of incarceration, litigation, military aggression, obesity, debt addiction and big brother, any time soon just to be closer to my children and drop another $20 million in Susan's coffers. It was better to go underground and make a fresh start. Regardless, the fact remains I ran from my fatherly duties. I was a coward and had chosen the path of least resistance.

I was certainly not going to be target practice for hit men, litigators, extortionists, law enforcement officers and rogue customers. I had lost over two thirds of my shares in the divorce and my share grant to the funds. Since I had no faith in ACMH's survival with or without me, my time would be far better spent optimizing my personal portfolio returns. I instructed my trustee Diego to accumulate nothing but Swiss francs, gold and highly rated long-term government and corporate bonds. Had I still been at ACMH this would have been my recommendation to all fund managers. Under no circumstances was he to buy or own any shares, equity or hedge funds.

After my departure until May 2008, my reasoning was very muddy. I could not differentiate between real and imaginary threats, often teetering on the precipice of early stage paranoia. I wore sunglasses and a Borsalino at night, grew a beard and behaved weirdly. I looked a lot more like a capo of the Palermo mafia than a German financier. Doing bong hits almost daily with Giorgio didn't exactly defog my brain. I hired a bodyguard, Ernesto, a ruthless and nasty character. He had been a sergeant for the Los Pepes in the 1980s and early 1990s. The Los Pepes squadrons are credited with murdering and executing hundreds of family members, associates and friends of Pablo Escobar. Ernesto was one mean dude. He liked *putas*, showing off his gaudy watch and toying around with his Ruger.

I sensed it would be best to let the dust settle and collect intelligence before showing my mug in any of my former haunts. Without the slightest doubt, detectives and goons were on my trail. The protection specialists working for me had uncovered incontrovertible proof. People were trying to shake me down in a number of places. Fortunately, my enemies were far away from my new base, looking for me in Alicante, Zurich, Prague, Rome, Monrovia, Paris and Vienna.

Without any meaningful friends and challenging conversations, I was also becoming profoundly superficial. A binge on toys, antique and replica furniture and a Bogota apartment kept me mildly distracted, but after a year I had not managed to find a satisfactory companion.

Then I met Patricia through my Jewish-Colombian real estate broker. She became the chief lawyer handling my property interests. She also chaired several of my holding companies. She was in her mid-thirties and already a full partner in a prominent law firm. She was assigned to the law firm's wealthiest investors and very involved in listed and private investments in South and North America.

Patricia was twelve years younger than me and easily looked another five years younger when I met her. I immediately noted her statistical and visual appeal as a potential longer-term partner. Her Spanish was refined and she spoke fluent Italian, German and English. Her Argentinian family had moved to Bogota from Buenos Aires during the Junta persecutions and never returned. Her older brother was shot on a speedboat in the Bahamas swapping dollars for a ton of cocaine by Colombian gangsters.

Her father Sandor, a retired left-leaning philosophy professor, had been targeted by the Junta and received political asylum in Colombia. Her mother had died of cancer when Patricia was a teenager. Sandor had never remarried. Patricia was his only surviving child and his only remaining love.

She was a delight to look at, understated and friendly, well mannered and only spoke when she had something to say. Patricia was gorgeous, a ten by my reckoning because she was neither a poser nor unpleasantly vain. Her father had instilled a deep sense of social responsibility in her. While her male university classmates were hanging out at the Bogota country club drinking mojitos and the girls were getting boob jobs, she was teaching and feeding disadvantaged children in Ciudad Bolivar, a neighborhood I would not visit by myself on the safest day of the year: Christmas day. At her law firm, she took on more pro bono cases than any other partner. She was a major fund-raiser for one of Colombia's most effective charities providing school lunches for thousands of underprivileged children.

She told me she never married because she never fell sufficiently in love with anyone, certainly not enough to compromise her independence. She did not want children. She already had 6,000 she was nourishing five days out of seven. Having children of her own would mean thousands would go without regular meals. Her IQ was measured at 153 during university and she was both intensely curious and a shrewd observer.

Her father was absurdly affluent for a university professor—the family Chapinero mansion was worth at least $5 million, even in a nervous property market.

Patricia was earning about $90,000 per year before bonuses, a very handy sum for someone living at home with her father. She spent $2,000 per month on her fabulous and timeless wardrobe, preferably Chanel, and split the remainder between savings and charity. Dad paid for cars, food, utilities and maids. Her considerable annual bonus was wiped out by trips to the most exquisite locations around the world with her father.

When Patricia was not feeding destitute children or representing the rich and infamous, she traded her online security portfolio via E-Trade and Fidelity Online. She was also managing her father's accounts, which must have been considerable because her real-time Bloomberg connection alone was costing them at least $2,000 per month.

I moved very slowly on Patricia. There was plenty of time and opportunity and no need to panic. I had learned she had split up with a long-term boyfriend who wanted kids and a homemaker. Wealthy customers and senior partners were constantly making moves on her. They were routinely dismissed with a smile and kiss on the cheek.

My strategy was not to invade her private space too quickly but to bring her out of her all-business shell. I needed to get her to talk about her dreams, her views, her father, her life, her hobbies and travels and hoped I could trigger an emotional response. I needed to attract her curiosity by being evasive and mysterious about myself. I needed to look attractive and fit but not pampered.

I studied the Ciudad Bolivar in a thirty-year-old Chevy with my bodyguard Ernesto and a local guide on a safe Sunday morning. While flying to Chile, I asked her to translate passages of Dante that I did not understand. All the authors I read during our travels were left-leaning or Colombian like Garcia Marquez. I wanted Patricia to see I was interested in her country and yet cosmopolitan enough to make insightful comments about countries she should visit.

My alias was an intriguing recluse from a disadvantaged background who had made a modest fortune selling contraband cigarettes for the National Liberation Front of Corsica (FLNC). Knowing full well her dad had rebelled against the Junta and granddad had fought with the Republicans during the Spanish Civil War, I thought the rebel capitalist character might work. Later on, after the FLNC lost its effectiveness through internal disagreements and violent altercations with other Corsican rebel groups and French anti-terrorist units, I moved to Asia where I set up distribution networks for Western tobacco manufacturers. I sold my business for a considerable sum and wanted to live in South America to get to know its people and customs better.

Most of the images that formed the picture I was painting were close to the truth if not based on reality. When I told her my dad had abandoned me twenty-five years ago, that I had been shot and my sister had died after a painful bout with MS-induced pneumonia, she gave me a soft kiss on my cheek. She told me about her difficult childhood in Argentina moving from place to place just a few steps ahead of the Junta's secret police, her mother's fatal struggle with PML (progressive multifocal leukoencephalopathy) and her dad's support for at least one left-wing Colombian rebel group in her teens. My act was becoming reality; we discovered a lot of common ground and became a couple. I very much liked Patricia but could never love her completely.

Because I was a client of her firm, she insisted our relationship be completely clandestine but she would tell her dad. I easily agreed. I had no interest in making friends or socializing.

We travelled to India together spending seven wonderful days in a cabin on the Royal Rajasthan on Wheels, but our relationship as lovers lasted less than a year. The relationship had to end. I was aching to tell her who I really was but I was unwilling to risk exposure. The downside of revealing me to her was far greater than the upside. Moreover, Patricia wanted to go to Corsica with me to meet some of my former comrades and visit my old haunts. The first part was easy. I knew Corsica well. The second part was impossible. Some of my friends in Paris were Corsican gangsters but my contacts to FLNC rebels were at best superficial. We were not going to go to Corsica anytime soon.

One dreadful Sunday when I was entering Patricia's home office, a stapler hit me full force on my forehead. Patricia flew towards me and started hammering me with her laptop. Luckily, I raised my arms just in time to avoid a serious blow to my face. She was screaming, ranting and raving like a mad woman. I managed to hold her from behind, smothering her flailing arms as she was kicking my shins and feet with her stiletto shoes. Meanwhile she was shouting at me, "You fucking liar, impostor, capitalist pig. Disgusting hedge fund manager! How could you? How could you lie to me for this long? Scumbag, pile of shit…you suck. You're an asshole. I will hurt you. I will destroy you. That bullet in your back is bullshit too. The only bullet you will ever see is the one my dad's friends will blow into your head. Wait till I am finished with you. Let me go, fascist pig. I bet you even lied about your MS."

She had never sworn in my presence before. She carried on for at least three minutes while I was holding her, and her screams turned into convulsions, sobs and then tears. I finally let her and she sank into a plush leather armchair pointing to a pile of old *Bloomberg* magazines, one of which featured me on the front cover.

She did not kick me out but locked the door and asked me for an explanation. We spoke for almost ten hours as I told her everything. I apologized sincerely and shed real tears. She was a strong woman who confronted her challenges the moment they showed up on the horizon, let alone in her face. She questioned me then threw tornado-like tantrums and beat my chest. After she settled down, she asked more questions and bitched me out again. "You lied to fuck me. Are you proud of yourself, Machiavelli?" But the velocity of her attacks was receding gradually. Sometime close to midnight, she was sitting on my lap and we were kissing like teenagers on a first date. Patricia was more vulnerable and tempting than ever as she led me to her bedroom and told me, "You could have trusted me Florian. You know this is the last time." I touched her cheeks with both of my hands and kissed a solitary tear away. "I know, believe me I know," I whispered in her ear.

Patricia ultimately realized I was not a total impostor. She grasped my fear of exposure. Her distrust abated, but it was over. She knew I adored her, maybe even loved her, but she had always sensed I was holding back. So was she. She was married to her work, her children and her father. Intuitively she never trusted me completely. I could see a small hint of doubt as I was recounting some of my taller tales or withholding potentially damaging information.

Moreover, I had already given my soul to Susan. I could not give it twice. While Patricia and I had a formidable relationship, it was never all-encompassing. She decided not to expose me but asked me to contribute $200,000 to her foundation instead, enough money to provide decent meals for 1,000 schoolchildren for a year. I gladly complied. She knew I had given ten times more to Liberian children.

Her father's comment to her on seeing us break up was simply "*C'est la vie, ma cherie*" and gave her a long hug. To me he said, "I understand what you did but you hurt my daughter and I should punish you. But I believe you genuinely like her. Try to be good to each other and make the best out of it." Patricia eventually forgave me, but as a friend and not as a lover. This highly principled angel was not going to relapse, ever. I honored her decision. I had no choice. Maybe we would be friends, I hoped. After years of hanging with lowlife broads, I knew Patricia had reawakened a sense of purpose and direction.

We became best friends. She called me BB for Bad Boy and I called her MT for Mother Teresa. When I could get away with it, I called her CC, which stood for Chanel Communist. We would see each other regularly and she took a sincere interest in my challenges. We would take long walks, fly fish or go horseback riding on weekends. I would accompany her to the Ciudad Bolivar several times a month. There was no risk, as Colombia's Mother Teresa was loved and known to all. She was dating again. This time it was a French doctor, Bernard, a great, genuine guy who had worked for *Medicins sans Frontieres* for years. Sandor, Patricia, Bernard and I spent New Year's together in Cartagena. Sandor and I played chess while Bernard and Patricia frolicked rather loudly in the bedroom above us. "*C'est la vie, mon cherie*" I thought to myself.

During the spring of 2011, after the birth of her son, Patricia decided I had to be a father to my children, even if the risks I was facing were still daunting. "If you don't, I'll call Bloomberg myself or make you give the rest of your money to my foundation," she said only half joking. "All children need a father. They need you. Love them and show it. You can help them. You have changed. You're a lost soul, but you're not a total selfish asshole any more. They may hate you at first but they will like you eventually. I like you even after what you have done to me. Bernard hates all bankers but he thinks you're almost tolerable."

"Thank you very much," I told her.

"Go back and get your big love as well while you're at it. Don't look at me like a cocker spaniel, you coward! So what if she rejects you? Are you going to screw dimwits for the rest of your life? So what if they lock you up or take your money? You barely exist, let alone live. Stop spending like an idiot and start giving. Start taking risks again. Start with your family. Give yourself to your children and your soul mate. You don't even deserve them. But you must try. And by the way, good luck."

She was probably right. I just did not want to admit it. I had been thinking along similar lines for the last months but always ended up discarding such thoughts as pure flights of fancy.

*

When Patricia dumped me, I had discovered perpetual tourism as the perfect escape valve. I had bought *1000 Places to See Before You Die*, the mother of all sightseeing bucket lists. I was marking the places I had already visited and ranked all the others on a spreadsheet on various criteria.

I had strange knowledge gaps in several obvious places like China, India, New Zealand and Sri Lanka, but less obvious ones in Portugal, Umbria, the Caribbean and Eastern Europe. In less than eighteen months, I would knock off over 130 world-class locations to fill my emotional vacuum and bring my total to 342 places.

Patricia was spending most of her free time with Bernard, but when I was in Cartagena I enjoyed being with her dad, who seemed to become a surrogate father for me. He trounced my ego by embarrassing me at chess and asked me deeply personal, probing questions. He would join me on trips within South America but never for more than a week at a time. He loved being close to Patricia and her French fiancé. Within a year he had become my mentor and closest-ever friend.

For the life of me, I could never understand how a socialist philosophy professor without any family wealth could live a multimillionaire lifestyle. As I can be rather direct, I would ask him point blank about the source of his fortune and he would always respond in the same way, "Clever investments. You especially should appreciate that." One evening in Cuzco eating guinea pigs after visiting the city's exquisite monasteries, Sandor engaged me in a series of bizarre questions.

"Bad Boy, tell me what do you call someone who is consulted by a married couple when they have trouble?"

"A marriage counselor of course."

"What do you think an accomplished marriage counselor earns?"

"Maybe $100,000 a year?" I guessed.

“I don’t know either. I have never hired one but that number sounds realistic. Let me ask you another question. What do you call someone who settles industrial disputes?”

“Well there are two types, a mediator or an arbitrator, depending on the agreements involved. If a satisfactory outcome is achieved they could earn a few percent of the transaction sum involved.”

“Assume two companies in a country have decided to divide up a market. One company works in the left half of the country and the other works in the right half. Each party promises not to compete with the other on price. Occasionally there are disputes because some very aggressive salesmen may work where they don’t belong and money is lost and everybody gets upset. Who would fix that problem?”

“Sandor, in a well-functioning economy such disputes rarely exist because what you are describing would be considered price fixing. Most developed countries have a cartel office, which fines such companies.”

“Now, assume there was no such office but a private entity resolving such disputes. Rather than paying fines to that office, the parties agreed on a mediator or arbitrator to determine a solution whereby one company pays another for damages. Now assume both parties agree to the proposed solution; would that not be better than engaging in a ruinous price war?”

I was starting to grasp where Sandor was heading, but just to be sure I didn’t let him off the hook yet and played stupid. “Well in that case, and assuming there is no cartel office or consumer protection agency, a smart arbitrator would certainly be worth his weight in gold.”

“That is right BB, such a person deserves to be paid well, would you not agree? And let us make another assumption. Assuming one company is struggling and the larger one wishes to take it over, the entity which helps one company buy another is entitled to a percentage of the transaction, is it not?”

"Of course it is," I replied. "This is mergers and acquisitions and I have done many such transactions. I have earned as much as 5 percent on smaller transactions and 2 percent on very large ones." Before he could carry on I said, "I finally figured out what you did to make your fortune. You were a successful marriage counselor and matchmaker for very rich Colombians. Am I right?"

"Exacto. During my golden years, I settled many marriage disputes and made many happy matches. I was very much respected and I was paid in cash most of the time but sometimes in kind—coffee beans, cattle, other stuff. And when I made enough I retired in the north of Bogota in this lovely area and focused all my attention on Patricia and the university."

"So you got out before there were too many divorces and fights and too few agreements?"

"That is exactly what I did. I got out a few years before 1994."

"Does Patricia know you did this?"

"Patricia has always been incredibly perceptive, even at 18. She never liked all those unhappy people around me. She is the one who asked me to quit."

*

My trustee and associate of ten years, Diego, destroyed most of my personal fortune in 2009. I have a sound numerical memory, having been trained that way for decades, and I knew in conversations over time that the sums no longer added up. I asked for accounts, summaries, details of which vehicles the investments were now moving in, and so on, and they never came. He actually used the words "Trust me." Whenever you hear those words, jump off the nearest building.

Ultimately the confession came. He had gone against my explicit instructions and rather than buy or retain ultra-defensive, high-quality investments like gold and Swiss francs, he had placed 80 percent of my funds in worthless promissory notes and Madoff. Madoff! Irony can sometimes be brutally vengeful. Was this poetic justice in action?

The gold I had bought he had somehow managed to sell at a loss. His company had earned a paltry sum in kickbacks and commissions, but he thought he was doing the right thing and knew more about markets and timing than me. He had catapulted himself from modest beginnings to a position of reasonable wealth. Somewhere along the line, he had lost his orientation. He dumped his Swiss wife and married a much younger Eastern European import. He was hanging out with tycoons and thought he was part of the club. He wasn't. He was one of the army of thousands of trustees, private bankers and family officers who administer significant fortunes and who get out of their depth all too easily, whether from simple incompetence or because they suffer from character slippage and delusions after having been the smallest bit successful.

The saddest part was that an in-depth interview with Giorgio's friends revealed he was partially telling the truth. He had squandered the funds of many of his other clients as well. His company was teetering on the brink of insolvency, he was alienated from his family and had already spent several months in involuntary confinement. He had been embroiled in a messy tax dispute and was using aliases for several of his clients, including yours truly. My legal remedies seemed less than ideal, given that lawsuits only make sense if there is lots of money around to satisfy the plaintiff's case. We settled our differences and I was staring at a $30-million write-off, which was more than 70 percent of my wealth.

To aggravate matters, the accounts of some of his Soviet bloc customers had been frozen for using aliases and buying passports, and when eventually the authorities discovered my accounts and my identity in the aftermath of exploring this issue, they went on a witch hunt. When asked why I was running accounts on an alias, I replied quite reasonably it seemed to me that it was preferable to me that my wife did not know about the money, given that the love factor between us was not as strong as it used to be.

Another reason I went so deep with my money was because I know very well how rogue the state apparatus can get. When I was playing professional basketball in Germany in my early twenties, I was at Frankfurt airport once when I opened the door of my VW and must have scratched the car next to mine very lightly—I didn't even notice it at the time, and the damage would have cost 30 Deutschmarks, maximum, to repair. Germany was full of deputy sheriffs, and one of them took my license plate and reported it to the police. Some prosecutor then deemed me to have committed the offence of "fleeing from the scene of a crime," which in turn led me to being placed on an Interpol list, and much later I was arrested when crossing the border into Austria. Ten years on and the big trial in Berlin took place, at which of course nobody could remember anything.

Nevertheless, these things stay with you, and the deeper the cover, the further away from the Kafkaesque state apparatus I could get, the happier I would be—especially if it meant avoiding any sort of legal processes in the States, where witch hunts and politically motivated vendettas will always ensure the impossibility of a fair hearing.

As it happened, my long-standing fears about how such processes can quickly spin out of control proved to be very well founded. In another vengefully ironic sequence of events, my efforts to protect myself instead initiated a further fall from grace. After Diego had been exposed, Giorgio was arrested on a European Arrest Warrant when he tried to leave Italy, and I faced thirty hours of questioning by federal prosecutors, who thought I had embezzled or defrauded ACMH funds of $500 million. Their sources were Internet articles based on systematic lies and misrepresentations by my enemies. They had little else to go on since I had never addressed any of the allegations. These guys thought they had discovered Robert Vesco junior. They had also established a large task force to prove my guilt and lock me up. They thought I was using not only Giorgio and Diego but also dozens of mules and dark-side operators to launder half a billion dollars.

I was facing a multi-year investigation covering half a dozen jurisdictions. Many of my official bank accounts were frozen as well as those held by my alias. They froze dozens of accounts of innocent investors in Switzerland, including my mother's. They were going all out to nail me. I had to sell my entire property and investment portfolio at fire-sale prices to prevent further damage. I was not yet poor but my resources were now less than ten percent of what I had upon resigning from ACMH, and I needed to watch my nickels and dimes. And once again, I was facing severe penalties and possibly time behind bars. My lawyers were eating into my cash reserves and my entire cover was blown. I was so screwed it was almost funny.

I was not a fugitive but the subject of an international money-laundering investigation. The prospects were painful fines, which would reduce my fortune to a pittance, jail, or costly and time-consuming trials. My options were rather limited. Reuniting with my children and travelling to the US was out of the question. Squeezing Diego was not going to yield further returns. The man was a shambles, financially and emotionally. The authorities had even frozen the modest $500,000 settlement we had extracted from him.

I had never abused my alias to get loans or embezzle funds. I was a first-time offender. My likely penalty was probation combined with a stiff fine if the money-laundering charges did not stick. I had never bribed foreign officials and ultimately that charge was dropped. My wealth, however, had largely evaporated and it kept bleeding. I needed to economize for the first time in two decades. It was also becoming increasingly likely I had to make a public statement setting the ACMH record straight once and for all. At least that way the misinformed prosecutors may stop thinking they had cornered Madoff's European doppelganger.

It amuses me how those chasing me but mostly my money believe they will capture great fortunes. All that effort for nothing! Think about it. Divorce, share grants, market declines, rogue trustee(s), frozen funds, fire sales, documentation and administration costs, distressed asset sales. I swear this is true and I'm prepared to take a lie detector test on this topic at any time. Anyone capable of using Excel and willing to do some competitive verification will come to the same conclusion: Homm's alleged fortune has evaporated to a pittance, not even two percent of his peak balance sheet valuation and hardly worth chasing. The upside of this unfortunate scenario is that my enemies, who are incapable of higher math, will continue to search for this non-existent Golden Fleece like mad alchemists while expending tremendous emotion and energy. My personal gain is that my far more modest life style has instilled a sense of modesty and even humility. I appreciate the gift of life and its occasional plentitude much more than ever before. I am endlessly more grateful. This may be hard to believe, but think the impossible.

At that juncture, however, I thought I only had three choices to restore my net worth. I could become a full-time criminal and work for an international organization. This option had significant appeal as one allegedly retired operator had offered me a job overseeing his $1 billion portfolio. He was not concerned with the allegations against me and offered a lovely asset and identity protection package to sweeten the deal. My annual operating budget was a whopping $5 million. He suggested I consider plastic surgery to feel safer and be less recognizable. The deal would enable me to recover my lost fortune in three to five years, but it also meant never seeing my mother again or ever reuniting with my children. The break would be absolute and forever.

The second alternative was to start a professional white-collar operation specializing in cigarette smuggling or VAT fraud. I could hardly reenter the investment world and begin managing money or doing deals. Who would trust me? Nobody would give me a dime. The cigarette or VAT scams would easily generate $30 million within two years, scoring a minimum of 1,000-percent annual return on investment. As with the first option, this path also meant I would never be able to become a father in any meaningful way. The risk of exposing my partners and me was too high.

My final option was the least comfortable because it meant economizing dramatically and changing my lifestyle, hoping my remaining funds generated enough return to retain my lawyers and afford a modest lifestyle. It would also entail confronting the allegations against me, making myself available to investigating prosecutors and police. Ultimately, it meant exposing what had really happened at ACMH and possibly embroiling friends in a royal civil and potentially criminal mess. I could no longer fund the Liberian Renaissance Foundation to assure its continuity. Liberia's UNESCO office was likely to be shut down for lack of operating funds.

I could do some research for people who trusted my analytical judgment and pick up a few extra bucks once in a while. Option 3 was horrifying from an economical and lifestyle viewpoint. It also required lots of courage to confront my ex and my children. But it was the only way to address the two biggest failures of my life: abandoning my children and short selling my soul mate. I was tempted emotionally but my wallet was screaming bloody murder.

Would I join the dark side, live well, safely and comfortably, or would I seek forgiveness and become a father and risk bankruptcy, maybe incarceration and exposing my friend Michael Kloter, the only person on the ACMH board I liked? Any profoundly rational and analytical person would pick the first option hands down. Family and fatherhood were often overrated. Divorce rates were topping 60 percent. Most married couples had little to say to each other. There were probably ten million other suitable women for me in the market. Kids surrounded by a wise and loving mother did not need an impoverished, self-involved, disreputable and confused father. Bringing my problems into a clean, orderly and untainted household was out of the question. If the reunion worked and I then had to go on the run, they would suffer again. Maybe a stray bullet meant for me would hit one of them. Susan had plenty of admirers and was dating actively. How could I possibly move to the States? They put people in prison for twenty years for miniscule offences, which in Europe were treated as misdemeanors. It made perfect sense to disappear once and for all.

While I was contemplating this conundrum, Sandor with the help of my private bankers foiled a kidnapping attempt orchestrated by my bodyguard Ernesto and his lawyer slut Colombian partner. He had defrauded one of my smaller bank accounts using copies of my alias documents to fund the operation. He was only several days from kidnapping me with a few of his former Los Pepes buddies. We found the stash he had stolen from me in his closet.

Their plan was to get the cash from my safe, pilfer my Colombian bank accounts and then dump my body somewhere outside of Cartagena. Sandor's friends interviewed Ernesto and his *Licenciada* girlfriend.

It was time to relocate, preferably to North Africa or Antalya to meet with my investigators and European connections to devise a game plan. I swore to myself never to reside in Central or Latin America again. The crime rates were simply too high and a free-spending gringo like me was a target few criminals could ignore for long.

As usual, when I faced a major crisis, I felt the need to go on a trip. The professor had a great suggestion: "Let's hike to the Lost City in the Sierra Nevada de Santa Marta." We would discuss real options and risks. I knew I was facing a major decision. There could be no hybrid solutions. Once I made my choice there was no turning back. I desperately needed Sandor to guide me.

12. Fact and Fiction

History is a pack of lies about events that never happened,
told by people who weren't there.
George Santayana

The last time I checked Google there were 4.3 million page impressions when you entered my name. I would have bet a fortune people would have lost all interest in my fate several years after my exit from the world of finance. However, this does not appear to be the case.

Many of these web entries are fiction. The lies about me are big. They are blatant and they have been repeated so often almost everybody—including regulators, journalists and prosecutors—believe them. The hatchet job on me is all over the media. I have never responded to these allegations.

I ran from confronting ACMH's lies at the time because to do so would have entailed exposing Michael Kloter, a dear friend, and Andreas Rialas, a sincere and decent guy, to substantial litigation risks. These lies have tended to be treated as fact by the media in the absence of any refutation or countervailing voice. And because this treatment of lies has had legal ramifications, I feel compelled to expose these ludicrous allegations for what they are.

I feel strongly about addressing the pivotal accusations not because I cannot live with a disastrous reputation but because of an inherent sense of fairness and objectivity, which never quite left me. Other people I have known have also been unjustly crucified by the media or by their former employers. I even hired some of them and worked with many others. These character assassinations and truth perversions insult my intelligence and offend my sense of right and wrong. I try to form my own opinion. I judge people by their actions, their overall achievements and most of all on how they interact with me. I have worked with controversial people, radical concepts and challenging projects my entire life. It goes along with being a pioneer. And I plan to do a lot more pioneering in this life.

On a practical level, I aim to spend the last third of my professional life developing and growing my new health care concept, Maximum Impact Medicine, into an international charity powerhouse. My sordid, one-sided reputation and media portrayal will seriously hamper my ability to raise funds and build critical relationships. Enough is enough. I am the wretched underdog. Everybody has thrown rocks at me for years and it hurts. It's time to show some teeth and bite back.

I lambasted Necko earlier for denying awareness of the Holocaust while he was a major military supplier and forced-labor employer during Nazi rule in his autobiography. I also questioned his payment ethics relating to the controversial purchase of Billy Joel's grandfather's textile empire in 1938. I have neither walked in Necko's shoes nor faced his demons. After the war, Necko spent time in prison and was questioned for his role in Nazi Germany. Years later, he was rehabilitated. Besides being very vain and image-conscious, Necko may have been reluctant to address these delicate topics not only for reputational reasons but also because he feared financial and penal repercussions. My earlier armchair criticism, from a safe and comfortable distance, was too easy and superficial.

Let's start with the obvious. I will never win the Mother Teresa or CNN Heroes award. I am too big, too brash, too controversial and simply not that altruistic. My investment career spans almost thirty years. Two maximum three years are under heavy legal scrutiny. In my defense, I could claim I did everything totally legally at least ninety percent of the time. But I will not. Let us get this right from the start, I am not a career fraudster like Bernard Madoff who sat in his office for a quarter of a century doing nothing all day but inventing returns and fabricating bogus investments. I have had my dark days, but for the most part, I have been a totally legit and very successful investor and entrepreneur.

Let me begin with the most ridiculous negative portrayals before I address the more serious allegations. Surf on the Internet yourself. Wherever one looks my media image is fantastically one-sided. It seems even Charles Manson evokes more understanding and Christian sympathy. These hatchet jobs make everybody feel so virtuous and self-righteous. One Internet feature depicts me as "WANTED" for major fraud and running an international crime cartel based in Venezuela and Panama. My vice powerhouse is allegedly based on half a billion dollars I stole from investors. This is simply not possible. I have made some dumb investments but I never stole $500 million. In the best case, I made 20 million on my Hunter partnership.

All in all, I didn't earn a net of 20 million dollars in the controversial HWM engagement but lost 20 million dollars net. This was because circa six months before my departure, I transferred liquid ACMH equity stakes of my own worth over $40 million, at no charge, to a variety of funds.

A front-page article in *Bloomberg Magazine*, a major financial publication, by award-winning journalist Mr. T., portrays me as a pathological liar. The article either states or insinuates I lied about my education, my basketball career and even my birthplace, basically everything. Needless to say these underhanded allegations and insinuations amount to cheap character assassination—utterly subjective and quite frankly unprofessional. Not a word about my charitable work or a long list of professional achievements. Meanwhile the author regurgitates ACMH almost verbatim, reiterating their utterly absurd allegations against me like a credulous simpleton. Normally T. is a rather bright and objective journalist. I stood him up for the interview as I was on my way to Colombia, but that is no reason to crucify me publically by spreading blatant lies.

Barron's, another major financial publication, claimed I had deviously screwed some Brazilian mixed martial arts fighter, Wallid Ismail, out of his "rightful" multimillion dollar stake in one of our venture investments, ProElite. I swear on my life I had never heard of this character before this article was published. I have never met Wallid nor done anything to rip him off. What do these journalists smoke when they invent these tall stories? Does anybody edit or even verify these fairy tales any more before they get published? These fabricated myths are harmful and distort the truth. People, who should know better based on their education and experience, accept them as fact, even experienced prosecutors.

Others claimed I owned a boat, which, like the evil man I am, was called *No Remorse*. Of course I felt remorse, mostly about my own stupidity, hurting and disappointing my soul mate and the children. The name implies you are feeling remorse and are trying to cover it up. I never named the boat anything—it was called *White Star*. To be fair, when I arrived on the island and was retired and had more time than sense, I did have a speedboat called *Flo-Toy*, a portmanteau of "Florian" and "toy," which at least I thought was amusing. Nonethless, the charges against me are not that comical and do not make for pretty reading. It would be cowardly for me not to address them.

We have already established that I am not a saint. Moreover, I have openly admitted my unhealthy and excessive love affair with wealth accumulation for most of my life. My financial career has numerous bright spots but there is plenty of controversy, one civil misdemeanor (Sixt) and one conviction for market manipulation (WCM) resulting in probation. I am investigated for money laundering and using a false identity.

My major detractors claim the following: that from 2004/2005 until 2007 I secretly and illicitly held a fifty percent stake in a US broker dealer called Hunter World Markets (HWM). I then used this dealer to secretly accumulate $500 million in smaller American companies in the ACMH funds. I pumped these shares to inflate portfolio values. Finally my opponents claim I made about $24.9 gross million in profit distributions from HWM and selling shares to the funds.

My employer knew full well I owned fifty percent of HWM. Nothing about my stake was secret. Virtually all my assets were held through offshore corporations. My Hunter stake was the only asset of any substance I owned directly and openly. The information was a matter of public knowledge fully disclosed to and publically available from FINRA, the securities industry regulator. The US regulator had to approve my ownership in the first place. The allegation by my former employer that I secretly owned HWM thereby deceiving ACMH, investors and regulators is 100 percent untrue and I can easily prove it.

The portfolio positions were anything but secret. All fund holdings were fully transparent to ACMH compliance and the internal fund auditors, the CEO, the CFO and any board member who cared to review or receive the information either in print or electronically. The information was also available to external bankers, auditors and administrators and on a daily basis. Annual fund reports, numerous stock exchange filings also provided significant detail. Any claims that these holdings were secret or obscured by me is 100 percent fraudulent and I can easily prove it. Yes, I invested heavily in US growth companies. In fact, all other fund managers at ACMH held these less liquid smaller US companies in their portfolios at one point or other as well. There was absolutely nothing illegal about that. We conformed to the investment restrictions spelled out in the investment prospectuses.

The third allegation relating to inflating fund values is more complex. We funded companies at prices that were below their market values. When it came to valuing these positions we would use market prices and not our cost basis, which was accepted and common industry practice. If you invest in a company at $5, which is then valued at a market price of $10 your net asset value obviously increases. Our accountants had all the relevant information at their disposal. They never qualified the fund valuations in spite of regular, intense, in-depth and diligent accounting reviews during my tenure. Both our hedge fund auditors (Ernst & Young) and administrators (Fortis and State Street) were without doubt among the European market leaders and considered the gold standard in the hedge fund industry. Our prime bankers were powerhouses as well: Morgan Stanley, the largest prime banker for hedge funds at the time, and Deutsche Bank, the largest and most profitable German bank in the world. Our bankers constantly reviewed and monitored the validity and completeness of our holdings for margin purposes. After my departure our auditors, administrators and bankers uniformly resigned. I had worked with these organizations for years prior to setting up ACMH. When I resigned, the ACMH board paid a third-tier accounting firm to become the new auditors and restate the numbers, shifting all blame for portfolio declines on to me.

My major error was too many smaller, less liquid early-stage growth company holdings going into the greatest bear market in eight decades. Blame me for making poor investment decisions.

After I resigned, investors had little faith in the board and my colleagues. ACMH shares lost nine tenths of their value. Investors wanted their money back. ACMH was forced to sell millions of shares placing downward pressure on their portfolio holdings. They not only had to sell. Everybody knew that and took advantage of it. They were selling on to a monstrous down market. Moreover, without their most active investor and promoter, me, many of these cash-consuming growth companies would falter on their expansion path and run out of steam. A few survived and seem to be doing all right. ACMH obtained high losses in the funds after my departure. Once again, they tried to shift all the blame resulting from their inept portfolio management on to me. I offered $1 million in ACMH shares to retain top managers. The ACMH board refused my offer and stuck with JR's imbecilic manager compensation formula. Instead of restructuring ACMH, they lost all their top managers within months and continued spreading vicious lies about me. Not only did they have to shut down all ACMH operations, they spent millions of investor funds in lawsuits and private investigations.

The last allegation is the most serious one. HWM sold shares held by myself to the funds. Given price discounts of fifty percent to market price, the fund's performance benefited from these sales at the time of purchase. I also did sell shares at a loss. Yet on average, my purchase price was even lower than the fifty percent discount allowing me to generate profits trading with the funds. I was ACMH's chief investment officer and a major shareholder in HWM at the same time. Of course I was conflicted. I made several stupid investments as well. But it can be useful to hear both sides of a story. My detractors always omit one major detail: I donated approximately $40 million in liquid and unrestricted ACMH shares to three ACMH funds before I left the firm. ACMH could have easily placed these shares with investors. Had they handled my resignation intelligently and managed the company well instead of lying compulsively and running ACMH into the ground with a dwindling talent pool and appalling performance, these shares would still be worth a considerable fortune today.

Regardless of my moral and legal arguments, my behavior can be considered opportunistic and unethical. However, whether my actions constituted criminal or civil fraud is an entirely different matter.

After all, my superiors were fully informed about my HWM stake, the fund holdings and my cross dealing. By never reprimanding me, they condoned my actions. Moreover a disgruntled former employee, let us call him DR, had informed numerous clients, regulators and even major newspapers in Europe and the Americas about my stake in HWM, fund valuations and cross dealing. The ACMH fund prospectuses allowed senior professionals to earn brokerage fees, investment banking income and even capital gains on fund-related transactions. I had never signed any document restricting my personal dealings, and why should I? Few if any of our senior traders and managers did. I was not the ACMH compliance officer, the chief executive, the chief financial officer or the chief legal counsel. Yet all these people were fully informed. The CEO and CFO signed off on many of our HWM transactions. They personally signed and authorized wire transfers from ACMH to HWM. Nobody on the board of directors represented my interests. I could not be expected to regulate myself. It was ACMH's responsibility, not mine, to be transparent and forthright with their investors. I never concealed anything. I did not have personal email or a private cell phone. All my telephone records and emails were available to ACMH all the time. I did not even have my own office. I sat a few linear feet from ten other traders and analysts. People could hear every word I said and observe everything I did, all day long. The only guys with private offices were the CEO, the CFO and the compliance manager. Within ACMH, I was completely transparent and accountable at all times. Does any of this make me a fraudster? I doubt it severely. But I could have exercised restraint and moderation. And I should have been less greedy.

Without exception, our clients were professional, extremely wealthy private or institutional investors, many with in-house lawyers and substantial legal resources. Yet only two clients out of around 3,000 ever sued me. And those two clients were closely related. One of them sued organizations and people as a livelihood. What does that tell you? If I were such a frigging criminal, hundreds of former clients would have gone after me. Interpol, the FBI, the BKA and so forth would have hunted me worldwide within a few weeks of my resignation.

I was consumed by greed and ambition—not so different from thousands of Wall Street creatures who had lost their moral compass, millions of consumers and other debt-addicted junkies, government officials who rigged economic data and nations which lied about their debts and deficits. I was still athletic and slim in 2007 but one lady who I would see every summer for years told me I had aged a decade in just one year. My fuse was very short and I was easily irritated. I had lost my lightness of being, my irreverence and my sense of irony. I remembered standing in front of the monumental mirror in our palatial hallway like an aging Dorian Gray, trying to smile at my reflection. I could not physically do it. All I could manage was to produce a grimace of a man who took himself and his plight way too seriously. I was ugly and had lost the ability to laugh genuinely from the inside out. I used to be amusing. Now I was mostly a self-centered, philandering, primitive jerk, who looked and felt older than Kronos. Where was the boy who used to feed the deer in the mountains?

Yet life is full of complex contradictions. So I looked, felt and behaved like a jerk. Some of the things I was doing were conflicted and unethical. On the other hand, I had never been more generous and more successful in raising funds for charity projects and introducing potential donors and investors to Liberia. I took the kids on a four-day extended weekend trip on the yacht and a very special helicopter ride, I shut off my cell phones and tried my best to be a dedicated and lovable father. I had never done that before in my life. I felt I was coming apart and on the way out. Maybe my conscience was awakening. I wanted my kids to know I cared about them and that they were important to me. I was Doctor Jekyll and Mister Hyde.

My nature has always been restless, manic and obsessive. After the age of 17, I committed myself to material excellence. I suffer from AWD (Acute Wisdom Deficiency) and may even be FSS positive (Fatal Stupidity Syndrome). Nothing succeeds like excess but nothing self-destructs like excess either. I was at best marginally sane praying to false gods in 2006 and 2007. Getting shot should have defogged my brain but did not.

My greed had gone overboard as my relationship with Susan disintegrated. Susan had always been my external self-restraint mechanism. I seem utterly incapable of self-restraint. But I am learning. In early 2006, she talked me out of buying a 25,000-square-foot $20-million mansion with sixty acres, its own mountain, ponds, and mind-blowing views over Palma Bay. Another time I offered to buy her any villa or yacht anywhere on this planet for her birthday, and had brought real estate and boating brochures for her to peruse. She just shoved them aside, asked for a lovely dinner with the cell phones off and my undivided attention for three hours. Susan never mutated into a high-society charity bimbo, always retaining her class. While the VIP glamour and celebrity scene entertained her, she never became a slave to wealth and power. She loved fine arts and enjoyed luxury, but she always remained true to herself and her priorities: family, children and the pets. Without her, my moral anchor was too small to withstand the allure of fast toys, fancy clubs and even faster women. She had witnessed my style drift over the years and there was little she could do about it. I was doomed.

When we separated and she moved to Florida with the kids, I lost it. My success in life was reduced to my wealth, my toys, my nightclub and my Russian paramour. I was mostly sad and lonely, not having much fun and increasingly uninspired at work. I did not even like myself. Giorgio, my friend, advisor and mule, nicknamed me the Zombie. A business partner called me a hamster locked in his diamond-studded hamster wheel. I was on auto control, like a robot, mechanically motioning through a small glittery world of luxury objects and plastic dolls as long as my battery had enough juice. Blame me for being greedy, stupid and conflicted. I blame myself.

My defense is multifaceted. Don't get me wrong. I am not claiming innocence by reason of insanity, but it would obviously be a viable strategy given my mental constitution. Allow me to blame my parents. I was the victim of my amoral upbringing in a shallow, unloving, materialistic environment. My overpowering German-Jewish mercantile genetics led me astray. I was the illegitimate son of Ronald Reagan and Margaret Thatcher, and my older brothers were Ivan Boesky, Michael Milken and Gordon Gekko. They taught me all I know and formed who I became. How can I be blamed? Will somebody please cut me some slack somewhere, or do I have to take full responsibility for my own actions?

Maybe we are all dupes of fate and destiny. Our spasmodic attempts at self-determination only serve to amuse and invite the ridicule of the gods watching us from above. My gradual transformation over more than three decades from a bright but withdrawn kid to star athlete, Harvard scholar, VIP serial entrepreneur and imploding hedge fund manager had been predictable and completely predetermined like a Greek tragedy. I felt and knew I was heading for the abyss during the tragic phase. I could have gotten off the trail several times. The warnings could not have been more obvious. Did I stop? No, I went over the edge like a bumbling, zombie, flesh-eating cow. Luckily, the descent did not kill me.

If I could do this all over again, I would never have expanded ACMH beyond ten highly capable professionals managing no more than $500 million. I would have taken six weeks' vacation a year with my kids and wife, been content with an annual $3-to-4-million paycheck, satisfied investors, enjoyed manageable portfolios and zero conflicts. This sounds moderately appealing but also a trifle uneventful. But then I would not have helped Liberia and hundreds of children would have gone without food and a First World education. Borussia Dortmund would certainly have gone bankrupt, relegated to the fifth division bumming out millions of hard-core fans instead of winning their seventh German championship. I would never have funded JDate. Tens of thousands of marriages would not have been consummated.

Most importantly, Clinuvel would certainly have train-wrecked without my involvement. Thousands of acute EPP (vampire disease) sufferers would continue to live in misery. There would be far less hope and far more suicides related to the vampire disease.

During my studies at the Harvard Business School, I got to know the wife of a powerful head of state because her son was a member of the same association as I, and we got along rather well together. This remarkable woman suffered from photodermatosis, which influenced the quality of her life in many ways very negatively. Unfortunately, she took her own life. Today I am convinced that this awe-inspiring person would still be alive today if the Clinuvel medication, Scenesse, had been on the market back then.

Because of Scenesse, millions of light-skinned people may soon be able to enjoy an active outdoor life and work style without contracting skin cancer. Millions of Vitiligo sufferers may be cured. So I wrecked my marriage, and my kids thought me a jerk. But I have emerged a better human being. I could be a much better father now if prosecutors and gangsters were not breathing down my neck. Maximum Impact Medicine, my newest charity creation, is well on its way conceptually and structurally. I am vastly optimistic about this revolutionary, highly focused health care concept. I'm qualified to make it succeed, I've got the energy to make it succeed, and I know how to do it. I just need to be allowed to do it.

Self-flagellation and hindsight are vastly overrated. They have rarely reversed past mistakes. Things are often more complex than they appear. Guilt is a dreadful, negative and a terribly incapacitating emotion. Earnest reflection and objective self-analysis make infinitely more sense. Repeating severe errors is not forgivable and reeks of fatuousness. Strangely enough, my horror trip into the entrails of high finance has led to many positive outcomes. What does that tell you? Life can be stranger than fiction? Mine certainly has been. A coin has two sides? Do not judge a book by its cover? Another cliché? I have absolutely no idea.

I am intrigued by the fact that all the journalists, plaintiffs, prosecutors and criminals who are so eager to punish me or lock me away have done far fewer positive things for other people during their allegedly all-important careers than me. There is only one obvious rhetorical question with an equally obvious answer: How can such a villain, the antichrist of finance, do such upright things? Maybe he is not such a complete villain after all? I am getting very close to justifying my sinister existence via self-righteous masturbation, so I will stop after this final point: regardless of all these different moral, legal and analytical perspectives, I am sincerely grateful my legacy has impacted the lives of many others positively.

13. Above the Clouds

There is nothing with which every man is so afraid as getting to know how enormously much he is capable of doing and becoming.
Søren Kierkegaard

Sandor had selected the Sierra Nevada de Santa Marta for very specific reasons. He wanted to drag me away from my comfort zone and introduce me to a clearer way of thinking. He insisted my travels thus far were more of a five star luxury diversion than true hermetic introspection. His recurring theme was for me to detach and take a journey into the heart of darkness, a voyage without comfort and certainty. By assigning me to in-depth self-discovery in a demanding and hostile environment Sandor believed I stood a greater chance of grasping what truly mattered. He was also in love with this natural wonderland, his former operating base, and wanted to show it to me.

The Sierra Nevada de Santa Marta should rank as one of the ten natural wonders of the world. It is located in northern Colombia and constitutes the highest coastal mountain range on our planet, reaching an elevation of almost 19,000 feet (5,750 meters). That is 3,300 feet higher than Mont Blanc. On a clear day, you can bathe in 30-degree water on the coast while observing the towering snowcapped mountains only thirty miles away. There is no way to drive into the Sierra and visit the lost city. Even helicopters are no longer allowed. There are only primitive paths on which quads or motorcycles are useless. Horses and mules are the most the privileged traveler can hope for. There is a risk of contracting malaria, dengue and yellow fever. There are jaguars and pumas weighing more than 100 kilos. During the rainy season, the trek is often described as green hell.

La Ciudad Perdida (LCP) is a major historical and archeological site about a three-day hike from the coastal resort town of Santa Marta. About 1,300 years old and founded by the Tayrona civilization, it was only rediscovered in 1972, when a group of local grave robbers found a series of stone steps rising up the mountainside and followed them to the abandoned city. Gold figurines and ceramic pots began showing up in the local black market until the authorities declared LCP a protected national historical site.

LCP is at least six centuries older than Machu Picchu and its population was three to five times larger. The trek to LCP is far more excruciating and entertaining than the popular Inca trail. The tourist density is infinitely smaller. Few tourists thrive on encounters with paramilitaries, guerillas or narcos. LCP was probably abandoned during the Spanish invasion. It features terraces carved into the mountainside, large walls, tiled roads and several circular plazas. A few homes have been rebuilt. The views do not match those from Machu Picchu, but the near complete absence of tourists and souvenir shacks, the dense subtropical vegetation, the eerie silence of the cloud forest easily make up for it. Most of it has not been reclaimed from the jungle. There are 169 terraces over a four-kilometer radius, substantial walls and stone carvings.

The general area has a rather messy recent history. It has been the battleground between the National Army, right-wing paramilitary groups, left-wing guerillas and narco traffickers. Both right- and left-wing groups are aiming to control the local coke production. The paramilitaries have the edge for now, given their proximity to the military, the peasant farmers and the ruling party. They are not really military units. They are just fascist drug dealers who used to work for the police or the Colombian army. Eight years ago, the National Liberation Army, one of the left-wing guerilla groups, kidnapped eight tourists. They were released several months later. Others have been killed. These days the Colombian army patrols the area more diligently. There are several hundred professional soldiers monitoring the area. The six-day hike is 52 kilometers and is only suited for people with above average fitness and endurance. It starts at Mamey, a forlorn hamlet a miserable two-hour drive from Santa Marta. The shortest daytrip is three hours and the longest is seven. If you are fugitive, do not take this trek. Military and passport controls are frequent and can be intense. Fortunately, based on a tenfold increase in the cost of our voyage, Sandor had ensured we would not have to deal with any unwelcome military interrogations.

The climate and topography in the higher elevations is highly conducive to the cultivation of coca leaf. Because it is a natural park, the Americans cannot fumigate the coca plantations, making it a valuable agricultural domain. The indigenous cultures have cultivated coca for more than 1,000 years. Chewing the leaves gives the Kogi people plenty of extra energy to pick fruits, work their fields and make babies. They create a powder from sea shells, which they mix with coca powder. The stuff may keep you awake but tastes nasty and releases far less dopamine than processed cocaine. We had been offered near 100-percent pure cocaine in Santa Marta but declined the offer. Sandor had always been a consummate professional, never mixing business with pleasure, and I was not going to relapse with hundreds of hard-core military goons around. Moreover, my mind frame would be too euphoric and I was likely to reach impure, purely emotional and utterly tainted conclusions.

We were sweating waterfalls from the onset of our trip and by the third day, I counted 100 mosquito bites. It was raining cats and dogs. We visited a local cocaine factory. The owner/operator, a charming and engaging fellow, encouraged me to take photos with him. I had to laugh, the rogue financier and the cocaine producer together, but refused. Sandor gave him a one hundred dollar tip to seal his lips. His mini-factory was closed down recently. Our little travel unit was quite a sight by itself: the white-haired, sinewy seventy-year-old professor, the German giant, our dwarfish Indio guide Pablo, our AK-47-toting goon and two emaciated, overworked mules. It seemed like we crossed at least a dozen rivers and streams. At one point we were river wading on slippery rocks for an interminable half-hour. We took baths every day in the rivers or in pools, picked bananas and never seemed to stop chewing coca leaves or drinking the malt.

Occasionally we passed other trekkers, some of who were clearly coked out of their minds and greeted us with vast dopamine-induced enthusiasm. Others had passed the point of a happy high and appeared more like zombies. Sandor was attacked by a wild boar sow, which was protecting her offspring. Our goon wanted to gun it down with his AK-47, but Sandor hit its snout several times with his walking cane and it disappeared into the forest. We saw fist-sized butterflies, frogs, poisonous toads, snakes, toucans and lots of other extraordinary birds. By the third day the less emaciated of the two mules became my personal ski lift. I was holding onto its tail while he pulled me up various slippery slopes. Sandor required no such help and ridiculed me every time I reached for the mule's tail. He was in remarkably good health and fine spirits. While I bitched like hell, he never complained once during the entire journey.

The last ascent was the worst. It was pouring buckets and we had to climb 1,200 slippery irregular stone steps at a wicked incline to reach the Lost City. By the time I reached the zenith, my thighs were shaking. We retired in a favela-type hut, got the only cold beer within three days of hiking and slept like zombies for ten hours. The next day we explored the Lost City.

The professor had given me one question to contemplate at the beginning of each day. I was allowed to talk to him during the day but never about anything personal. At dinner, we would discuss my answers for thirty minutes. At the end of this period, I had another thirty minutes to write down my answers, but never in more than three sentences. I will save you the mad thoughts, trials and tribulations it took to find them.

Day 1: What are you afraid of?

I am afraid of emotional commitment. I am afraid of trusting my feelings. I am afraid of losing my freedom and financial independence (poverty).

Day 2: What have you achieved?

I have lived a selfish and exciting life and I have enabled one company that will save thousands of lives and improve millions. I have also helped children.

Day 3: What is your legacy?

Excess, too much is never enough; intensity, live fast and furious; possibility, you can be and achieve anything you want.

Day 4: Will anybody really profoundly care if you die on this trip?

Five, maximum six people.

Day 5: What would you change if you could?

I would be with my woman, be a father to my children. I want to be free and live without fear. I would like to stay healthy, live, help and travel.

Day 6: What choice will you take?

I will overcome my challenges. I will trust my emotions and feelings. I will leave an overall positive legacy. I will no longer play god with the lives and careers of others.

I was horrible at reading signs. When I was living in paradise, I rushed to get out. When I was shot in Caracas, I should have eased out of the business, instead I doubled my efforts. However, by this time my human capital had been growing as my financial capital had almost disappeared. My choices were confirmed within four weeks after finding the Lost City. A blind man could have read the signs this time.

My potential partner for cigarette smuggling had been framed by vengeful cops for a minor offence he had never committed. And another plan, I prefer not to elucidate, also fell apart. And it turned out the guy who had offered me a job managing $1 billion was not quite as retired as he had intimated. He was nabbed by the DEA and was looking at over a hundred years. He decided to snitch, ratted out several dozen hoodlums and joined the WPP. The former retired Narco czar died several months later during routine surgery.

God was making my choices for me. My son Conrad, named after Joseph Conrad, the writer, had forwarded a little essay he wrote about me via my Spanish lawyer, and Isabella included a small portrait and a poem. I was immensely grateful. The clouds finally lifted. This was the moment I finally knew, without the slightest doubt, where I was heading. This is what my son wrote:

> *Big Fella*
>
> *The giant of a man strides through the Spanish streets during the heat of the afternoon. A cocky stride, chest puffed out like a peacock, hands swinging up and down his body. He occasionally snaps his fingers to no apparent beat other than the one in his head. The sultry 47-year-old winks and smiles coyly at a woman, examining her like a cartel lord at a Miss Bogota pageant. My mom just shakes her head and rolls her eyes, used to it as Dad takes a deep, pensive puff from his Cuban cigar.*
>
> *He slides his long fingers through his silvery blond hair. Florian makes the dull, cemented sidewalks of downtown Palma look like a red carpet event. He owns the street and we follow like court attendants three strides behind him. He flaunts his gauche, ostentatious Rolex, awkwardly raising it as if he was looking at the time, garnering looks from the German tourist crowd. Droplets form on his chest. He undoes the last button on his sheer, tapered Italian silk shirt, revealing a foot-long dark scar. He turns to our guest who is struggling to keep up with his pace. The visitor gives my dad's chest a curious glance. "Oh this little wound? I got it from being shot in Venezuela." Followed by my sister confusedly asking me, "Isn't that one from a shark attack in South Africa?"*
>
> *We walk on in the same harried fashion for a few more blocks, my dad being outrageously generous to the beggars on the streets slipping twenty-euro bills*

to them. He asks our guest how much he has donated to charities, then goes and tells his outlandish amounts. He once gave the pizza delivery boy 1,000 euros because he and his sister lacked the funds to see their mother who was suffering from terminal cancer.

He quickens his pace, speeding ahead, "I can't stand walking at this pace Susan. I'm going to go buy another cigar and meet you at the restaurant," and races off. We find him at the restaurant in a thick cloud of smoke in front of his pint-sized Cuba Libre. "Susan, can you believe these people? The women here are all flirting with me. Can't they see I'm with you?"

14. Maximum Impact Future

Money has never made man happy, nor will it. There is nothing in its nature to produce happiness. The more of it one has, the more one wants.
Benjamin Franklin

While I wholeheartedly agree with Benjamin Franklin, money can provide significant flexibility and independence, especially for wise people with a rock-solid value system. For almost three decades, I believed more money equals more happiness. Dense people like me needed to lose their family and fortune to fathom that there is no correlation whatsoever between money and felicity.

The most difficult thing in the last few years since my departure from the financial world has not been the pressure from Resch and his contracting bodies or the merciless and one-sided media reports, but rather the maliciousness and lack of character in the people whom I once helped and who later stabbed me in the back. Thank God that a few simple people, with much fewer resources than I had, stood by me in my darkest hours. Without exception, my false friends were all very well situated, well-earning, and privileged people. This disappointment chills me to the bone and saddens me deeply. On the other hand, these circumstances were a sign to me to concentrate my charitable efforts on far away from luxurious charity fests, and on those who are powerless and without means: the great host of underprivileged and needy in Africa, Asia and South America.

Having returned from the undead, it makes much more sense to maximize my emotional rather than my financial returns. Furthermore, it appears I am more likely to grow my human capital by giving and sharing rather than by taking and accumulating. I am also having fun again and laugh frequently, occasionally even about myself. The best I can do in the future is not to repeat cardinal errors and focus my energy on actions that make me feel happy, positively challenged and more complete. Maximum Impact Medicine is becoming the part of the plan. Here's the deal.

In the middle of 2011, I turned on CNN late at night. The documentary they were showing was about some Jewish doctors operating on very needy patients somewhere in the heart of Africa's darkness. In his spare time the doctor was voicing his frustration that just a few dollars could save or at least dramatically improve the lives of several people suffering from debilitating trachoma, elephantiasis or worm infection. He would bring a few pills and syringes with him whenever he travelled in Ethiopia and Eritrea on behalf of his medical charity. He and his fellow doctors would spend most of their time operating on children. Some of these operations required several doctors working for several hours. Once he was done and settled into the village the camera filmed him giving a few injections and handing out a few pills to patients suffering terribly from very common infections and diseases such as severe eye infections, swollen limbs and skin disease. I saw this doctor positively altering the lives of five people in less than ten minutes while spending less than $5 on medicine.

I was profoundly impressed. Quite a few former patients he had treated in this manner months ago came up to him to thank him. They told them they were doing well, had jobs or were starting a family. This guy was bumming out. He was frustrated and wondered why there was nobody else running around Ethiopia doing the quick fixes full time like him. These doctors were performing demanding and high-tech and rather costly operations per day to remove a few deformities. I did the mental math. On a great day these guys would operate on four patients at an average cost of about $600. The pills and injections were just a sideshow. Had each of them simply handed out pills and given injections the cost would have been lower but they would have positively altered or saved at least 200 lives. The impact would be fifty times higher and the cost would be much lower. No wonder this doctor was frustrated. Meanwhile a chimpanzee could have injected twenty people and given trachoma medicine to twenty others, producing ten times the health-care benefit than the charitable surgeons from New York.

My lights went on and luckily somebody was at home. The complete lack of logic and the obvious opportunity for improvement was screaming at me from the idiot box. The Liberia Renaissance Foundation was spending about $1,000 per child per year to provide nourishment and a First World education. For $1,000 we could enable 1,000 patients to work and function normally. Until I watched this documentary, I had no idea these treatments were so inexpensive and uncomplicated.

I remembered my extensive travels in Latin America, all over Africa and Southern Asia since the age of thirteen. I had seen countless cases of the very diseases this doctor was treating. Many of these sufferers were unable to work or contribute, but otherwise they were not initially in hopeless shape. They had simply contracted a disease from dirty water or a virus, which prevented them from leading a more productive and rewarding life. Medicine was usually not available in these godforsaken places and the diseases progressed unabated, often resulting in permanent impairment and even death.

Did that mean a million dollars, which we had spent to build the Liberia Educational Complex, could positively change a million lives? Did that mean a charity could advertise that for every dollar they collect, after all expenses, they will save or at least significantly improve one life? I studied the subject matter for several days. The conclusion was mind-blowing: Assuming smart sourcing and logistics and some economies of scale, $1 would *easily* save or improve one life. This was huge. My mind was on fire. To this day, I believe watching this program at two in the morning was not coincidence. The gods had thrown me a gigantic bone in my general vicinity and were placing bets to see if I would be able to find and munch it.

There are approximately a dozen major debilitating, life-threatening diseases which can easily be cured with medicine or prevented by vaccination at a cost of less than $1 per patient. For example: trachoma, the leading cause of preventable blindness, affects over 35 million people, yet is often easily preventable for very little money; diphtheria, an upper respiratory tract illness, which afflicts tens of millions, can be prevented by a vaccine and treated with both antibiotics and antitoxins. These diseases are typically most common in Africa, Southern Asia and Central and Latin America. Let's take Lymphatic Filariasis (LF), also known as elephantiasis. LF results in the abnormal enlargement of body parts causing pain and severe disability. 120 million people are infected and 40 million are disfigured and incapacitated. The disease can be cured by a single dose of two medicines given together. Most westerners think LF is some obscure disease from over a century ago, exemplified in the movie *The Elephant Man*. Yet this disease has been diagnosed in 81 countries.

There are other interesting disease categories known as forgotten or neglected infectious diseases. They are forgotten by the developed world because these diseases are largely restricted to poor developing countries, frequently in Africa. For example, Schistosomiasis or snail fever affects 200 million people in developing countries worldwide, half of them in Africa. While "only" 200,000 people die from it annually, the symptoms can be very debilitating including blood infections, chronic liver damage, chronic kidney failure, seizures and right-sided heart failure. Among human parasitic diseases, Schistosomiasis ranks second only behind malaria in terms of socioeconomic and public-health importance in tropical and subtropical areas. Prevention is best accomplished by eliminating the water-dwelling snails that are the host of the disease. Acrolein, copper sulfate, and niclosamide can be used for this purpose. Schistosomiasis is readily treated using a single oral dose of the drug Praziquantel annually.

The World Health Organization has built an extensive database covering the treatment costs of many diseases in many nations and regions. This program is called WHO Choice. I fully expected it to include the ten most common Neglected Diseases. I was wrong and shocked. WHO Choice was addressing a few of the major neglected diseases, but there was much more emphasis on very costly and complex treatments, with huge sums spent on treating AIDS and mental illness, for example, or for extensive vitamin supplementation. The quality of life and economic impact from curing these neglected diseases offers a vastly more superior cost-benefit profile than addressing the high-profile, high-cost medical conditions presently favored by the Western medical charities. The basic cost of keeping one AIDS patient alive in a developing country could cure several thousand others of equally incapacitating conditions. That is hardly logical. There are cost-effective medical treatments for several "tool kit" diseases. For as little as 79 cents, people can be treated with a four-drug combination to treat multiple infections. Unlike HIV/AIDS, which requires daily treatment for life, some of these diseases can be cured with one dose of medication. This type of disease management is possibly the most cost-effective global health initiative. This is the area where MIM aspires to be one of the most important and innovative medical charities.

These low-hanging rotting fruits hold back economic development and human happiness in almost all of the poorer developing nations. A handful of major charitable organizations and health initiatives like the Gates Foundation and the Clinton Initiative are increasingly tuning into these forgotten ailments. The economic impact of significantly curing and containing these preventable diseases with a few hundred million dollars per year generates billions of dollars a year in productivity gains and economic growth. The ROC (Return on Care) of MIM treatment goes into hundreds of percent.

I am lucky. My background enables me to run MIM. I have supported several charities since my late teens and founded the Liberia Renaissance Foundation. LRF is not only effective. It was also a very lean organization during my stewardship. I have managed a multinational corporation before. I studied developmental economics at Harvard and have invested in developing nations for three decades. I had worked in Africa, lived in and travelled to Third World countries since my teens. Because I had funded numerous medical companies for more than two decades, I have a rudimentary understanding of basic medical science. I know how to work with doctors, pharmacists and researchers. I have completed and structured countless deals and partnerships. When I launched the LRF, I had studied the dynamics of the charity industry on a global scale and applied what I learned in Liberia. I am not a one-dimensional luxury whore. I can adapt to extreme and adverse conditions and I can deal with conflict and resolve challenges.

What blew me out of my socks was the power of the marketing message: Give $1—Save one Life! Save ten Lives for $10. All I have to do is stop smoking and wire my annual savings and we would save thousands of lives. We could incentivize smokers in a global "save lives" campaign by encouraging them to quit and hand over some of the savings. Or we could go to cigarette vendors. The advertisement on the box could read: This box of 20 cigarettes will save one life. That would be a nice contrast to *Smoking Kills*. I would love to see a collection box with huge print in every Burger King and Kentucky Fried Chicken advertising: Have you saved a life today? Donate a dollar and save a life.

Imagine you were a person who only had $10 to give and 100 charities were competing to get those $10 from you. All the causes are honorable. There would be several who would aim to find a cure for cancer, multiple sclerosis, HIV and Alzheimer's. Others would focus on education, clean water, malnutrition, animal cruelty, habitat and wildlife preservation, global peace, infant and maternal mortality, and so forth. You interview each one of these charities and ask them only one straightforward question: Tell me exactly how my $10 will achieve measurable results that make our planet a better place and assure me that at least $9.90 will be used to benefit those in need. Imagine the answers. There is only one answer that stands far and above all others: with one hundred percent certainty, MIM can guarantee that your $10 donation will positively and fundamentally alter or save at least ten lives within a few weeks of receiving your funds. Moreover, we would prove that less than 10 cents are used for overheads and administration.

Can any other charity make two equally compelling and precise claims? Moreover, can any other charity provide the same precise positive emotional return to the donor? Think about it.

I visualize kids in European and American communities hitting up adults for donations fully armed with punchy brochures. I envision hundreds maybe thousands of local MIM chapters worldwide raising millions per year. I have never considered a venture with so much upside and zero downside. Even if I failed completely to attract others, my personal contributions alone would improve many lives. If others copy the idea, who cares? That would mean more positive change. My emotional return would not suffer. I would like to see this happen any which way. But I want this to be big. The only question is how big we can make it.

Of course, many compelling ideas falter because they are poorly executed, while many mediocre ideas succeed because they are well executed. There are similar charities and the concept of cost-effective medicine is well advanced. Nonethless, MIM is a unique and compelling concept. Well executed, it should be a smash hit, an evergreen. First-rate analysis needs to identify accurately which treatments provide the greatest health benefits to the patients and economic benefits to a region and country at the lowest possible unit cost. This sounds easy but requires heavy data mining, programming and regression analysis. The analytical software has to be fully dynamic and easily scalable. Fortunately, useful information is available from the World Health Organization regarding treatment costs by nations and regions for many diseases. Without a doubt, the information is neither optimal nor complete but it is a solid reference point. I know how to design the analysis, but MIM will need gifted programmers to produce the right results.

Sourcing, storage and distribution will be another key success factor. MIM will obviously seek donations of medicines and vaccines from pharmaceutical companies, governments, NGOs and medical associations. However, we will also purchase deeply discounted medicines and vaccines in bulk opportunistically. It will be critical to structure strategic sourcing agreements with pharmaceutical manufacturers as well as organizations that can store, distribute and apply the medicine locally. Marketing and fundraising is the heart of any successful charity. There are numerous promising avenues to maximize inflows both from institutions and from households. We will treat all our donors like superstars. They are all lifesavers. Our donors will receive unparalleled emotional rewards on their investment and excellent PR. We will organize pro bono activities for high school and college students around the world. Promoting the MIM message is a cakewalk.

The organization itself needs to be as lean as possible to assure the highest percentage of revenues is allocated towards treatment. My major corporations were always the leanest and most profitable in their industries. My mission is to build one of the most effective, low-cost sourcing, distribution and allocation structures in the medical charity field. Alternatively, I am considering working with highly efficient charities such as the Brother's Brother Foundation to ensure the medicines reach their ultimate destination in the most cost-effective manner.

Rest assured, MIM will be extremely tight on administrative overheads. Our donors need to know that once we have reached critical scale, less than ten percent of our donations are spent on administration. That certainty will make them much more willing to donate generously. Given my controversial image, transparency, accountability and ethical standards must be the best in the charity world. Every conceivable and potential conflict of interest must be avoided. We need to be more immaculate than the Virgin Mary.

I would like to pull this off. I figure I have 25 productive years ahead of me. I hope that I will not be the subject of an international arrest warrant, have a bullet in my head, be sequestered or rot in a prison somewhere anytime soon. That would make it difficult to develop and promote this charity. Nor can I be involved in multi-year lawsuits, which would keep me away from work for months. Most people would discourage me from even considering the idea given my sordid reputation. On the other hand, I believe I can exploit my notoriety and media presence to promote such a positive cause. I like the idea of rising from the ashes. If I prove less than effective and a better man can be found for the job, I will gladly accept a demotion.

I am looking forward to the travelling. Working in very poor regions cleanses your soul and increases one's gratitude. Moreover, there are many countries I would like to visit. I have never been to Ethiopia, Darfur, Eritrea, Sierra Leone, Sri Lanka, Papua New Guinea and many other nations that could benefit considerably from MIM. I like the idea of travelling officially with a real passport for a change, holding down a real job. I am getting tired making up stories wherever I go. Hanging out with smugglers, assassins, IRA operatives and dark-side kingpins and their administrative support staff is overrated, bears too many collateral risks and is simply getting boring. I'll miss the gangsta bitches. They're a little deranged, but very hot. I am looking forward to a tamer, more civilized circle of associates. I guess I am getting old and conservative. Perhaps I am simply imitating Necko again or my sister Barbara. Barbara became a pillar of conservative values after her long flirt with communism and revolt. When Necko had lost his empire, he could have laid low and relaxed. Instead, he started funding thousands of promising amateur athletes through the *Deutsche Sporthilfe* and left a great legacy. Maybe I can leave an even greater one. Either way, I have turned the corner and for once am heading in the right direction.

For decades, I was praying to false gods and lost my power, wealth and family. Hardcore criminals, bounty hunters and powerful organizations threaten my life and my liberty. During my voyage, I discovered that our modern western version of earthly success guarantees failure. Too much is not healthy and less can be more. I learned giving is more rewarding than receiving. Gratitude and compassion make better travel companions than greed and blind ambition. "Live and learn" has replaced "Too much is never enough" as my favorite maxim.

Conrad's insightful characterization was more rewarding than reaping millions flipping value management shares. Isabella's compassion for those in need, neglected animals and forgotten elders in nursing homes, touches the heart of a cold-blooded hedge fund manager. I am grateful for Susan's love for almost two decades in spite of my distorted gestalt and immensely grateful for her raising our children single-handedly. I apologize with all I have for the grief and ongoing problems I have caused her and my children.

I was the product of materialism and excess, the whacky child of the roaring eighties and nineties. When I was a master of the universe, I ridiculed remorse and guilt as useless emotions. Guilt and remorse are indeed detrimental to success in the world wealth maximization. In the far more relevant human sphere they are vital to our sustainability and development. Guilt can often be self-destructive. However, it can lead to remorse, which often inspires positive behavior and change.

The outrage and disgust I have faced since going private is no different from the collective outrage of the Occupy Wall Street movement against the abuses of the Establishment. There are, however, two major differences between my abuses and those of the status quo. The Establishment crucifies its independent, less-established outliers such as me or other hedge fund managers to detract from the vastly more destructive and material criminal acts of the senior banking and political Establishment.

The second important difference is that I have already reached rock bottom and have shifted towards a more conscientious and gratifying value system. Our society still prays to the demons of consumerism and wealth accumulation, the gods of net worth. Its implosion is still ahead. Financial, economic and social order will crash in 2013, but certainly no later than 2016, or enter a prolonged period of severe civil and financial repression accompanied by increasing social injustice, dislocation and unrest. The combination of an increasingly aging population and national money printing machines running at full speed is a toxic one.

In late 2007 I was diagnosed with severe VD-D, also known as Value Deficiency Disorder, a very common and often fatal medical condition afflicting high-level financial professionals and many members of the Establishment. Medical philosophers such as Deepak Chopra opine VD-D, not obesity, is the single greatest threat facing Western civilization, suspected as the primary cause of gluttony, self-righteousness, intolerance, aggression, denial, hypocrisy and reckless financial behavior.

Heavily afflicted by VD-D I joined Sociopaths Anonymous (SA) in 2008. I can now proudly say, "I am clean!" I have not committed any mean-spirited vile acts for 1,492 days. All my "crimes" since entering treatment have been entirely victimless. I have to break the cycle of patriarchs accustomed to reckless unscrupulous and uncaring behavior. A more conscientious, likable and caring man is gradually emerging from the ashes of defeat.

Humor benefits greatly from grasping absurdity, especially one's own. As usual, the gods are laughing at me. The hullabaloo surrounding me, my furious strife for purpose and my moral makeover amuses them greatly. They will roll the dice that determine my fate. Maybe the toss will be favorable allowing me a new lease on life, the prospect to improve thousands of lives via Maximum Impact Medicine or in some other way and see my children. Maybe the toss will be fatal. I might get a double tap in the head this time or get locked up for eternity. That would do little good for anybody, least of all for me. Therefore, until my enemies lose momentum or interest, I have to remain a shadow walker, a hunted man and missing father. *Que Sera, Sera.* D.O.M.[1]

[1] Deo Optimo Maximo, "to the greatest and best god"

Epilogue—Months Later

My biggest spiritual challenge is to transcend my little, vain, self-obsessive, ego-manic world. I am far from being detached from my oversized id. I do not like the old Florian, but I have to forgive this creep to move on. Fortunately, at some point, we become whom we decide to be. I am no longer the same person who began writing this book. If you had seen the first draft, you would have puked. It was even more self-obsessive. Paraphrasing Paulo Coelho, what I do every day now will redeem the past and impact the future. My mission is to transform my personal tragedy and failure into something useful. I am entering largely unknown territory presently: family, faith and compassion. Thus far, and in spite of rather discomforting external circumstances, this path feels right. I have never been happier, more grateful and more at peace with myself.

However, navigating the world's oceans on my yacht is not without serious challenges. In a YouTube video several older men are in a poorly lit room flashing 1.5 million euros stacked in 500-euro bills. I know what the amount looks and feels like. I had more in my briefcase wandering the streets of Cartagena with my nose dripping with cocaine snot. That makes thirty packages of one hundred 500-euro bills which are about one centimeter high depending on the packaging and age of the bills. The amount comfortably fits into a big shoebox. But these details are beside the point. This is bounty money and meant to be paid to anyone who can locate me and get me to fork over 30 million dollars. One of my best friends, a serious former dark-side heavyweight, calls the whole show amateurish, clumsy and highly suspicious. The video would almost be funny if these goons and the money offered were not for my head but somebody else's. So, I can only smirk but not really laugh when I see it.

I believe this video is about getting the money in any possible manner including torture and then whacking me. If I were to live, these guys know full well they would have to spend the rest of their lives looking over their shoulders. The last guy who tried to extort me, a German crook living in Florida, ended up in a van without windows, hijacked by four Irish goons and urinating in and defecating in his pants while being lectured on his inappropriate business deal. There could be a second dimension, however. Forget about the money. This YouTube episode reminds me of Patrick Flanagan, the protagonist in John Grisham's novel *The Partner,* who is chased by a rogue senior executive and some corporations. This could be about making me go away. These guys are already committing acts that interfere with ongoing investigations and civil lawsuits and constitute several felony charges under US criminal law. They are also infringing on my constitutional civil liberties while committing libel. Their interpretation of the law is more than just liberal. It is criminal. And the media is helping them spread their message. What they do not know is: the money is no longer around. It is gone, annihilated by rogue trustees, fire sales and costly new identities while I was on my discovery mission. They're chasing a phantom.

A newspaper article stated that these guys represent clients whom I have allegedly defrauded. If I do not hand over the money to them, the article says, the goons would hand me over to the FBI and I would have to spend the remainder of my life in the can. There are two fundamental flaws with this train of logic: justice does not want me! If it did, there would be a global arrest warrant outstanding for my apprehension and this would be a matter of public record. The Liberian government would have been informed immediately. The second flaw is that these alleged former clients had years to sue me in court to recoup their funds. That's what normal people do. Why did they wait almost half a decade to hunt me down? Why did only three clients ever sue me when we had hundreds of clients with in-house lawyers or huge legal resources? Why did the manhunt begin when manuscripts of my autobiography were being made available to potential publishers? There are only a few individuals or groups who would act in this manner.

One could very well be the Croatian Bronco, born January 1964 in the former Yugoslav Republic. I once jointly purchased a property with an equal partner from him for about eight hundred thousand dollars. These funds were impaired when authorities began freezing my funds and his. Bronco was pissed off. Bronco is not a joke. According to former friends, he likes to stick guns into people's mouths when he runs out of arguments. Others suggest he was a former longtime associate of an imprisoned Russian arms dealer. Worse, Giorgio, whose business is to know everything all of the time claims Bronco was a Dalmatian drug lord with extensive activities throughout Europe and to a lesser extent the Americas. According to my own detectives, Bronco inspired a convicted felon and serial fraudster, who claims to have joined the good guys (right!) after spending a near decade in the American penal system, to launch a manhunt offering a bounty for my head through a Panama website.

I know Bronco only superficially, but I know he is a businessman at the core. Bronco thinks bottom line. Once his anger abated over the loss, he might have decided to go after me, not only to recoup his property-sale proceeds but also to extract an additional profit and exact some sweet revenge. Why not turn adversity and loss into a winning proposition? Bronco reasons that Homm can hardly involve the authorities to help him. It's open season and I'll get the trophy before others. Bronco, however, is dangerous because he is calculating, quite intelligent and ruthless. Friends and family have been called, harassed and threatened. I wish he understood that my fortune has dwindled to a pittance. Giorgio can confirm this well beyond reasonable doubt. After all, he handled substantial sums for me. I encourage Bronco to fight for his funds in court. He sold his property in good faith and there was absolutely no way he could ever have known the origin of the funds could be suspect, nor could anybody ever prove that his $800,000 were not the result of totally legitimate activities.

The other potential customers of the bounty hunters, who play around with money in the video, could to all intents and purposes be former or current supervisory board members and high-ranking management executives of my former employer ACMH. It is definitely conceivable that the directors and top managers attained 50 million dollars from the sale of ACMH shares and the exercising of stock options—perhaps they even received several more millions in commissions, dividends and bonus payments. Most of them had to have known everything about my alleged shady business activities, the mini-stocks I sold and my participation in the brokerage house in Los Angeles, or at least have suspected it. These former directors had to keep up a front of innocence and shift the entire blame in my direction. Those directors, who knew nothing, could be accused of gross negligence. When the new untainted directors joined the board of ACM and its funds, the old directors had two choices. They could admit their full knowledge or spin a tale of lies. Admitting full knowledge and approval would land them in lawsuits. Their only choice for survival was to implicate me and disavow any knowledge of my activities in order to retain their credibility and their money. No wonder they spun such a web of lies. Not surprisingly, given this mammoth institutional obfuscation and plethora of public lies, I have safeguarded sensitive documents evidencing activities that are far more sinister. I am not a snitch, but if I were to die of unnatural causes, this data will be released.

Only fools and those who know absolutely nothing about banking and fund administration would believe ACMH's public proclamations that they had no idea I held US microcap positions and co-owned a US-based broker dealer without their knowledge, awareness and approval. I am amazed how utterly naive and dimwitted the journalists have been reporting on this story. The allegedly hidden information was either public and/or fully available electronically to dozens of ACMH employees and directors, several external intermediaries 24/7 and even regulators! If I were to testify, some of these folks could have a lot to lose: their reputation, their funds, their relationships, their standing, and possibly their liberty. The more recent ACMH directors have burnt millions suing and tracking me with nothing to show. The ACMH funds performed poorly after my departure and clients lost hundreds of millions. ACMH's lawyers have searched for me before. They hyped their website through search engine optimization to locate me and have harassed family and friends with private detectives and lawyers. Given their behavioral patterns, they could well be behind the most recent global manhunt just like Bronco.

However, the ACMH scenario is different from the Bronco scenario. If the facts and the true course of events were ever to be revealed through my testimony and supporting evidence, heads might roll. Therefore, some people may be very keen to see me underground either figuratively or literally. Therefore, this chase may be as much about money as getting me out of the way. Of course, my list of enemies is long. I could always be wrong but there are some very compelling motives why some people would want to demonize me in the public eye as the sole perpetrator, while assuring at the same time that I stay off the radar screen until all relevant statutes of limitation have expired or until I am well underground. Would I make life miserable for my enemies? Certainly and on several occasions, I have. These days, I would rather move on and focus on a positive agenda, but I cannot ignore these goons, their clients, their tall tales and considerable resources.

This topic saddens me for two reasons and not because my life has become completely whacky and unpredictable. First, that amount of money could dramatically improve the lives of a million people suffering from curable diseases. Why waste it hunting a guy without it? The other reason is because I used to be one of the boys. I was almost as ruthless as those chasing me. I never ordered a hit but I came close on three occasions, twice when my life and the well-being of my family were threatened. Luckily for me, I never entered that door. I am not the grim reaper, nor the Lord who passes final judgment.

I did a lot of things for money, which I find either despicable or hilarious today. I have caused enough grief, direct and collateral damage in my life. It is high time to move on to greener pastures. Until recently, I could never forgive my enemies. But luckily I have progressed. In recent months, I learned that forgiving and praying for your enemies offers amazing spiritual returns. However, I have so many enemies and barely know where to begin. The beauty of forgiveness is that you rid yourself of useless emotional baggage. You also send a message of compassion, peace and love at the same time. Therefore, why, in your right mind, would you not want to forgive your enemies? I have sought out people I have harmed and asked them for forgiveness. I need to forgive my old self as well. I do not like the old Florian. If I met him today, I would call him a lost, misdirected soul. I also realize I am only human. We are designed to make errors. I have made more than most.

For three decades, upon entering Harvard, I had moved progressively further away from matters of real importance to worldly concerns of power and wealth. My futile search for lasting inner tranquility in the material world led me to a former stripper, the dark side, questionable financial practices and dubious business partners, the neglect of my children and profound emptiness. The result was an ever-increasing soullessness, complete confusion and an idiotic fascination with material things.

Today I laugh heartily when I see massive yachts, 20,000-square-foot mansions, personal jets and their self-important owners. The other day I creeped into a luxury resort and used the lavish facilities for free. I no longer need but still appreciate these accouterments on occasion. I have been perfectly comfortable and happy without them. This does not mean I do not enjoy the "good things" in life, but I have moved beyond conspicuous materialism and consumption. I am finally leaving Mammon behind. I still like money. If you don't, you'll never get it or keep it. But money has only two purposes: financial independence and putting it to good uses. Beyond that, the quest for wealth is senseless and causes nothing but complications and trouble. Constantly tracking the evolution of your net worth is worse than senile dementia.

Technically speaking, I was supposed to be smart guy with academic degrees from Harvard, extensive language abilities, diplomatic credentials, authorship, a serial entrepreneur and other such blah. But I had missed the meaning of life, at every important turn for about three decades. Even worse, I could never read or refused to see the signs along the way. I was diagnosed with multiple sclerosis and got shot but still I remained blind, self-obsessed and one-dimensional. To add insult to injury, I was with a saintly woman for two decades who tried to tell me all this. Then I lived in paradise with my family in Mallorca without a care in the world and did not recognize where I was. My ears, eyes and soul were blocked. The message could not get through. I continued on my mindless mission to become a billionaire, and like an aging, rusty, creaking money-printing press, I finally collapsed from excessive wear and tear. Only by imploding, writing this book and discovering faith did my life change.

If my single-minded pursuit of power and wealth does not epitomize foolishness and worse stupidity, what does? This leaves me few options. One is to laugh at myself. I have to. After all, we're only human. I need to continue to live and learn. I am grateful for my experiences and the insights I have gained along the way. My new voyage is about gratitude, generosity, sharing, loving and joy. It is not about me this time but about others. It is really about faith and family, dimensions of life I never fully grasped or cared much about before. This voyage has only started but it is already more rewarding than all my walks on the wild side. The seas are once again turbulent, yet I'm sure I will navigate them safely this time and find a safe harbor. I have found faith and my destiny. I will gain Susan's forgiveness and capture the hearts of my children. I know and feel I have the best mentors and guardians helping me this time. I am a blessed and a very lucky man.

FSC
www.fsc.org
MIX
Papier | Fördert gute Waldnutzung
FSC® C083411

Zeitfracht Medien GmbH
Ferdinand-Jühlke-Straße 7
99095 Erfurt, Deutschland
produktsicherheit@kolibri360.de

Druck:
CPI Druckdienstleistungen GmbH
im Auftrag der
Zeitfracht Medien GmbH
Ein Unternehmen der Zeitfracht - Gruppe
Ferdinand-Jühlke-Str. 7
99095 Erfurt